REMEDIES RECLASSIFIED

Remedies Reclassified

RAFAL ZAKRZEWSKI

OXFORD
UNIVERSITY PRESS

OXFORD
UNIVERSITY PRESS

Great Clarendon Street, Oxford OX2 6DP

Oxford University Press is a department of the University of Oxford.
It furthers the University's objective of excellence in research, scholarship,
and education by publishing worldwide in

Oxford New York

Auckland Cape Town Dar es Salaam Hong Kong Karachi
Kuala Lumpur Madrid Melbourne Mexico City Nairobi
New Delhi Shanghai Taipei Toronto

With offices in

Argentina Austria Brazil Chile Czech Republic France Greece
Guatemala Hungary Italy Japan South Korea Poland Portugal
Singapore Switzerland Thailand Turkey Ukraine Vietnam

Published in the United States
by Oxford University Press Inc., New York

First published 2005

British Library Cataloguing in Publication Data

Data available

Library of Congress Cataloging-in-Publication Data

Zakrzewski, Rafal, 1973–
Remedies reclassified / Rafal Zakrzewski.
p. cm.
Includes bibliographical references.
ISBN 0-19-927875-X (alk. paper)
1. Remedies (Law) I. Title.
K2315. Z35 2005
347'. 077—dc22 2004029055

ISBN 0–19–927875–X

1 3 5 7 9 10 8 6 4 2

Typeset by Newgen Imaging Systems (P) Ltd., Chennai, India
Printed in Great Britain
on acid-free paper by
Biddles Ltd., King's Lynn

To the memory of Professor Peter Birks

Preface

This book is about the law of remedies. It probes its foundations, delimits its boundaries, and sketches an outline of its structure. It does not purport to be a textbook on remedies in the mould that has been forged over the past three decades. Instead it presents a new paradigm by focusing sharply on court orders. In doing so it shows how each kind of court order gives effect to pre-existing legal rights in a civil case. Conversely, it shows how various substantive rights are effectuated in court orders.

I have not attempted to give a full account of the law relating to each remedy, much less the rights which it effectuates; that would be an impossible task for a work of this nature. Instead I have attempted to provide sufficient detail to illustrate the argument presented in the first part of this book by reference to familiar examples of remedies and substantive rights. Although the examples are mostly drawn from English law, all common law jurisdictions share the problems discussed in these pages and the analysis is equally applicable to all such systems.

This book is based on my doctoral thesis which was submitted to the Board of the Faculty of Law of the University of Oxford in 2003.

Sadly my greatest debt of gratitude cannot be repaid. It is owed to the late Professor Peter Birks. It was a great privilege to have attended a few of his lectures and seminars, let alone to have been one of his doctoral students. Without the inspiration and support of Professor Birks this project would not have been undertaken, and without his guidance and generosity of time it would not have been completed.

I would also like to thank my examiners Professor Andrew Burrows and Professor Andrew Tettenborn for their encouragement and helpful comments. I am also grateful to Peter Butler, James Edelman, Steven Elliot, Laurence Emmett, Simon Gardner, and Michael Rush who commented on parts of this work. Of course, the responsibility for any errors contained herein is mine alone.

My doctoral studies would not have been possible without the financial support of the Banking & Financial Services Law Association, the UK Government through the Overseas Research Studentship scheme, Oxford University, Linacre College thorough the Heselton Legal Research Scholarship, Lincoln College, Mallesons Stephen Jaques, and Clifford Chance.

It has been a pleasure to work with John Louth, Gwen Booth, Heidi Young, and the staff at Oxford University Press.

Finally, I thank my partner Kirstyn for her understanding and support.

R.A.Z.
London
September 2004

Contents

Table of Cases

Table of Legislation

1
Introduction

Remedies are fundamental to private law. Every person who turns to the courts for assistance in a civil dispute seeks a legal remedy.[1] But even well before situations become litigious, people retain lawyers, often at great expense, to document their dealings in such a way that, in the event that things turn sour, they will be able to obtain a legal remedy or be immune from one.[2] An understanding of remedies is consequently of great importance to both litigation and transactional lawyers. As Tettenborn writes, 'we must always remember that legal advice is, at bottom, simply advice as to the remedy likely to be available (or unavailable) to the client.'[3] It is not surprising then that books are written and courses taught under the title of 'Remedies'. What is surprising is that the foundations, ambit, and structure of the law of remedies have so far eluded close scrutiny.

Some books on remedies do not discuss, even superficially, what ought to be treated as a legal remedy and why.[4] Yet, as Waddams observed:

> [T]he scope and meaning of this legal subject area is by no means settled... Theoretically, almost every legal question could be posed in terms of remedies, but this would give the word so wide a meaning as to be useless. When reference is made by a writer to the virtues of studying the subject of remedies as a whole, the meaning of the word is evidently being restricted. If the subject has coherence, as is often claimed, there must be a unifying theme. The whole cannot be worth looking at unless the parts have some connection.[5]

The unifying theme must be sought in the concept of a remedy.

The word 'remedy' is constantly on lawyers' lips. Legal remedies are claimed, sought, found, had, requested, elected, chosen, pursued, used, available, refused, allowed, obtained, awarded, dispensed, granted, given, provided, fashioned, and

[1] 'The *remedy* is the goal of litigation': E. D. Re and J. R. Re, *Cases and Materials on Remedies* (4th edn., New York: Foundation Press, 1996), 1.

[2] Goode and Worthington point out that '[a]ny change to the legal remedies available upon breach of a commercial contract will necessarily alter the content of the obligations agreed to by the parties': R. Goode and S. Worthington 'Commercial Law: Confining the Remedial Boundaries' in D. Hayton (ed.) *Law's Futures: British Legal Developments in the 21st Century* (Oxford: Hart, 2000) 283.

[3] A. Tettenborn, 'Remedies: A Neglected Contribution' [1999] *Denning LJ* 41, 41.

[4] For example, B. Andoh and S. Marsh *Civil Remedies* (Aldershot: Dartmouth, 1997).

[5] S. M. Waddams, 'Remedies as a Legal Subject' (1983) 3 *OJLS* 113.

enforced. They are described as common law, equitable, statutory, discretionary, as of right, *in rem, in personam*, proprietary, personal, specific, substitutional, monetary, non-monetary, coercive, non-coercive, enforceable, constitutive, declaratory, judicial, non-judicial, self-help, civil, private, public, or administrative. But, rather disturbingly, as Burrows points out '[t]he concept of a remedy has rarely been subjected to rigorous analysis.'[6]

As a consequence, remedy is used synonymously with a wide range of different terms and, what is probably worse, by way of contrast to an equally long and diverse list. It is used synonymously with action, response, redress, and relief. It is used in contradistinction to wrong, injury, cause of action, liability, substance, institution, and doctrine. Most confusingly, it is used both as a synonym of right and in opposition to it.[7] In short, the concept of a remedy is unstable. It comprises a number of different but insufficiently differentiated legal concepts.

Birks drew attention to the promiscuity of this term and identified a number of different senses in which it is used.[8] These senses will be examined and elaborated in Chapter 2 where the extent of the concept's instability will become apparent. Chapter 3 will then illustrate this point further by showing that writers on remedies are sometimes insensitive to the problem highlighted by Birks. But the exposure of the term's instability raises issues of great importance which Birks did not address. It will be demonstrated that a careful selection and rigorous application of a stable concept has profound implications for the way in which we think about remedies and in particular the way in which we classify them. It will serve to identify where the boundaries of the law of remedies ought to lie, show how the law of remedies could be logically structured and, reveal how remedies function.

A stable core meaning of remedy will be identified in Chapter 4. Remedies will be broadly approximated to court orders. They will be rigorously separated from substantive rights, that is, rights which can be said to exist prior to the making of a court order. More strictly, remedies will be identified as the rights immediately arising from certain judicial commands and statements which aim to redress a pre-suit grievance, usually an actual or threatened infringement of a substantive right.[9] The stable concept will serve to circumscribe the scope of a discrete law of remedies.

[6] A. Burrows, 'Judicial Remedies' in P. B. H. Birks (ed.), *English Private Law Vol. II* (Oxford: Oxford University Press, 2000), 18.01.

[7] In *Re T H Knitwear* [1988] Ch 275, 291 (CA) Caulfield J stated that 'There are certain sets of facts where the right of subrogation is obvious. . .I approve of the distinction between right and remedy in relation to subrogation and say that subrogation is a remedy. . .'.

[8] P. B. H. Birks, 'Three Kinds of Objection to Discretionary Remedialism' (2000) 29 *U Western Australia L Rev* 1; P. B. H. Birks, 'Rights, Wrongs and Remedies' (2000) 20 *OJLS* 1.

[9] Thus excluding rights arising from orders which merely assist in the preparation for a trial (such as orders for discovery or interrogatories) and orders which merely assist in the present or future enforcement of other orders (such as freezing injunctions or contempt orders, attachment of earnings orders, garnishee orders, and charging orders).

In Chapter 5, the received classifications of remedies which are used as the basis for numerous books and courses on remedies will be reviewed and shown to be seriously defective. A new taxonomy built upon insights derived from the critique of the old will then be proposed. It will be based on the relationship of the remedies to the substantive rights that the claimant seeks to have realized. It will be seen that the vast majority of remedies function by replicating such rights; however, it will be observed that a number function in a transformative manner. The development of the new taxonomy will provide a better understanding of the relationship between substantive rights and remedies. It will also provide important insights into the role that judicial discretion plays in the grant of both common law and equitable remedies. These will be developed in Chapter 6.

Thus this work examines both the domain and the taxonomy of the law of remedies. However, this cannot be done adequately in the abstract. A book about the arrangement of remedies which said nothing of their operation would be irritating to the reader and difficult to follow. The taxonomy is brought to life by a description of the operation of various remedies. For this reason, some account of particular remedies is given, but hardly more than an outline, in Chapters 7 to 13. The aim is merely to show what the law of remedies looks like under the discipline of confining the term 'remedy' to a single meaning. This part is not intended to be a detailed treatise on particular remedies or the rights that they effectuate. Nor is it a comprehensive treatment of the entire law of remedies. It is an outline of how such a treatment will look when the ambiguities inherent in the term 'remedy' are eliminated.

This part will systematically compare how each order that may be made by a court in a civil case gives effect to the rights of the parties to the dispute. Conversely, it will show how various types of private law rights are given effect in various remedies. Particular primary and secondary (or remedial) rights, such as rights to damages, will be disentangled from the remedies which effectuate them. However, such substantive rights will be discussed only in so far as it is necessary to show that they are either replicated or transformed in particular remedies.

By the end of the survey of particular remedies, the reader should be rewarded with a better appreciation of the relationship between remedies and the rights that people have before coming to court, the effect of particular remedies on such substantive rights, the functions of various remedies, their relative advantages and disadvantages, and the role of discretion in the grant and refusal of remedies. Previously obfuscated features of and similarities between various remedies will be revealed.

It will become apparent that a work on remedies should provide examples of remedies. This requires the forms which court orders take to be set out. Law students, and many transactional lawyers, speak about injunctions, decrees of specific performance, or orders for an account of profits without ever having seen one. As will become clear, the orders are sometimes the best indication of what the rights of the parties were found to have been in particular cases.

An examination of the forms that court orders take is illuminating. For example, one learns that an order for the recovery of land may operate not against a particular defendant but the world at large, that an order for the execution of a trust is virtually identical to an order for specific performance, or that an order for an account on the basis of wilful default includes a consequential order for payment which is not different from an order for equitable compensation. It is important to be aware of these matters as they clarify our understanding of the substantive law. It is only when we know what the court will order that we can say with any confidence that we know what substantive rights the right-holder actually has.

Providing examples of court orders is not something that current works on remedies do, even when they equate remedies with court orders. Indeed, it will be seen that most treatments of remedies move too far into the field of substantive rights. They discuss the content of rights generated by events such as wrongs or unjust enrichment in great detail. Consequently there is a strong tendency to end up with an overlap between the law of remedies and areas of substantive law. It is a central tenet of this work that the law of remedies must not include parts of the law of substantive rights under a different name. Substantive rights should not be labelled 'remedies' and studied as such. The law relating to court orders is evidently different from the law relating to rights which exist prior to the making of court orders.

Knowledge of remedies requires one to understand not only when particular remedies are available and what they confer on the claimant but also what results they bring if they must be enforced through the intervention of sheriffs or bailiffs. Thus, when describing the functioning of particular remedies, this work will also discuss enforcement to show briefly how they can be carried through to realization. The law of enforcement is not part of the law of remedies just as the law of substantive rights is not. However, a grasp of enforcement mechanisms also provides an understanding of the relative advantages and disadvantages of particular remedies. Furthermore, familiarity with the consequences of granting particular remedies allows one to better appreciate why the courts may be reluctant to grant them and consequently why such remedies are subject to additional bars which do not apply to the grant of other types of remedies.

Only private law remedies will be examined here. Remedies in public and international law will not be dealt with, though that is not to say that a similar analysis could not be conducted in those fields.

To recapitulate, three grave problems are addressed. First, the notion of a remedy lacks stability. The term 'remedy' is applied indiscriminately to a number of very different concepts. What we ought to call remedies are dealt with only sporadically and mixed with substantive rights. Secondly, the structure or taxonomy of the law of remedies is flawed. There is a tendency not to compare like with like and to mix different criteria for classification which results in overlapping categories. Thirdly, the law of remedies appears to be lost in substantive law and the law of civil procedure. There is no book which deals with remedies as a subject clearly distinct from substantive rights. There is insufficient focus on that which a book on contract, tort, or unjust enrichment will not reach. Nothing has been written systematically on the exclusive province of remedies.

The law of remedies is not part of the substantive law, nor of the law of civil procedure, though it is bounded and moulded by each. It is a unique subject worthy of independent study. This distinct area of law is discovered and mapped in this book.

2

Instability of 'Remedy'

A Introduction

This chapter will demonstrate that the concept of a remedy is unstable. The most obvious symptom of the lack of a stable concept is ambiguity. 'Remedy' is a very ambiguous word. It has multiple meanings, some of which overlap. Such a state of affairs is not conducive to clear thought and communication. We are in danger of misunderstanding what a speaker or writer means, of erring in our own thoughts, or leading our listeners or readers astray. Ambiguity leads to inconsistent usage. As will be shown, remedy is used in different senses by different users. To complicate things further, it is sometimes used in more than one sense by the same user. A Law Commission report provides an example:

> The second main problem which we identified in the consultation paper relates to the efficiency and cost of the remedy which is most widely used by minority shareholders to obtain some personal remedy in the event of unsatisfactory conduct of a company's business.[1]

Here remedy is used in two entirely different senses in the same sentence. Shareholders are said to be using a remedy in the sense of a court action to obtain a remedy presumably in the sense of a court order. Although experienced lawyers may be able to draw a distinction between these two different senses of remedy intuitively, a layperson is likely to be bewildered.

Another illustration is to be found in the English Civil Procedure Rules.[2] Rule 25.1 states that:

> The Court may grant the following interim remedies:
>
> (a) an interim injunction;
> (b) an interim declaration;

[1] Law Commission *Shareholder Remedies* Report No 246 (London: The Stationery Office, 1997) para 1.5. In a similar vein, Orde JA stated that 'nothing will be done to interfere with the paramount remedy of the first mortgagee to pursue his remedy against either of the two estates': *Ernst Bros Co v Canada Permanent Mortgage Corp* (1920) 47 DLR 362, 368.

[2] SI 1998/3132 with subsequent amendments.

(c) an order for:
(i) for the detention, custody or preservation of relevant property;
. . .
(iv) for the payment of income from relevant property until a claim is decided;
(d) an order authorising a person to enter any land or building in the possession of a party to the proceedings for the purposes of carrying out an order under sub-paragraph (c);
(e) an order. . .[the rule goes on to list 12 other orders]

The reader infers that a remedy is an order of the court. But then rule 25.2 states: 'An order for an interim remedy may be made at any time. . .'. If one attempts to apply the previous definition, this rule provides that 'an order for an order for X may be made at any time'. Obviously, something other than a remedy in the sense of an order is intended in the second rule. The sense of the word has been switched.

As Hohfeld stated, 'in any closely reasoned problem, whether legal or non-legal, chameleon hued words are a peril both to clear thought and to lucid expression'.[3] Remedy is a chameleon. At the very least, it is well to know that this is its nature and the different hues that it may take. Again, as Thayer wrote over a century ago:

> As our law develops, it becomes more and more important to give definiteness to its phraseology; discriminations multiply, new situations and complications of fact arise, and the old outfit of ideas, discriminations and phrases needs to be carefully revised. Law is not so unlike other subjects of human contemplation that clearness of thought will not help us powerfully in grasping it. If terms in common legal use are used exactly, it is well to know it; if they are used inexactly, it is well to know that, and to remark just how they are used.[4]

This chapter aims to demonstrate that the term 'remedy' is used inexactly and to illustrate how it is used. The first step will be to consider the literal and non-legal meanings of remedy. This will provide the basis for an inquiry into the broad functional definitions of a legal remedy, definitions which attempt to cover all or nearly all of its legal usages. The disparate specific meanings of the term will then be put under the spotlight. The next chapter will continue this theme in the context of five leading works on remedies.

B Literal and Non-Legal Meanings of Remedy

The first meaning of remedy given in the *Oxford English Dictionary*[5] is '[a] cure for a disease or other disorder of the body or mind; any medicine or treatment which alleviates pain and promotes restoration to health'. Remedy is a word that

[3] W. N. Hohfeld, 'Some Fundamental Legal Conceptions As Applied in Judicial Reasoning' (1913) 23 *Yale LJ* 16, 29.
[4] J. B. Thayer, *Preliminary Treatise on Evidence at the Common Law* (London: Sweet & Maxwell, 1898), 190.
[5] J. Simpson, J. and E. Weiner (eds) *Oxford English Dictionary* (2nd edn., Oxford: Clarendon Press, 1989).

is clearly connected with medicine. That connection becomes stronger when we examine its etymology. The Latin original of remedy is *remedium* which consists of *re* and *mederi*. The latter means to heal. To remedy an ailment is to heal the person afflicted; to restore him or her to health. A remedy is simply a means of healing or curing an ailment or disease. The word has also come to be applied figuratively to a much wider range of 'ailments'. The second meaning given in the *Oxford English Dictionary* is a very general one, namely '[a] means of counteracting or removing an outward evil of any kind; reparation, redress, relief'. It can be brought into play whenever the medical metaphor linking illness and means of relief is applicable. In its literal meaning, a remedy may be preventive as well as corrective. A preventive remedy is prophylactic; it operates pre-emptively to prevent an illness or disease from developing.

Even in its non-legal meaning 'remedy' is quite unstable. There are broad and specific senses that overlap. This can be illustrated with a simple example. Suppose *X* suffers indigestion and visits a doctor seeking a remedy. The doctor examines *X* and prescribes the following remedy, *X* should take a teaspoon of tonic three times a day. *X* leaves the doctor's surgery and goes to the pharmacy where he purchases the remedy. In the first sentence of this example, remedy may refer to either some means of obtaining relief from a disorder generally (that is, relief from indigestion), or more specifically a treatment, or a medicine. In the second sentence, it seems to refer to a treatment (that is, taking tonic three times a day) and in the third it refers to a medicine (that is, the tonic itself). The doctor might have told *X* to eat less and take more exercise—a remedy but neither a treatment nor a medicine.

Considering the dictionary definitions and the example above, one may conclude that when used in its non-legal sense, remedy may denote one of the following: (1) any means of preventing or obtaining relief from or redress of some evil; or, more specifically (2) a treatment leading to such relief or the process of bringing about such relief; or (3) something forming part of or applied in the treatment or process. Of course, it is often difficult to determine which sense is intended, as in the first sentence of the example. As will be seen, the legal senses of remedy reflect this inherent ambiguity.

C Broad Functional Definition of Legal Remedy

The notion of a remedy is easily extended into the legal context. An instance where a person is aggrieved by a perceived injustice, usually due to an actual or apprehended breach of duty, is seen as an injury or evil which requires treatment or removal. Hence the medical metaphor is invoked and the means of curing the ailment is called a remedy.[6] Consequently, 'remedy' is often used in legal

[6] P. B. H. Birks, 'Rights, Wrongs and Remedies' (2000) 20 *OJLS* 1, 9.

discourse simply to refer to any means provided by the law for obtaining redress or relief from a grievance.[7]

Where a grievance arises from an actual breach of duty, that which removes the grievance is a *corrective* remedy. Where it arises from a threatened or apprehended breach of duty, that which makes the claimant better is a *preventive* remedy.[8] A remedy, whether corrective or preventive, is often seen as a means of converting the 'ought' inherent in a legal duty into an 'is'; a means of converting a norm into a fact. It has been said that 'the function of a remedy is to "realize" a legal norm, to make it a "living truth".'[9]

A breach of duty is a wrong. Thus Lord Nicholls observed in *Attorney General v Blake* that 'Remedies are the law's response to a wrong (or, more precisely, to a cause of action).'[10] Viewed another way, an actual or apprehended breach of duty constitutes an actual or apprehended infringement of its correlative right.[11] Remedies may be seen as responses to infringements of rights.[12] Thus Gaudron J stated in *ABC v Lenah Game Meats Pty Ltd* that 'Because [an injunction] is a remedy, it is axiomatic that it can only issue to protect an equitable or legal right or, which is often the same thing, to prevent an equitable or legal wrong.'[13]

Most situations where a legal remedy is called for do involve a breach of duty, but it must be noted that although a grievance calling for a remedy *usually* involves a legal wrong, it is not so limited. Sometimes such grievances arise not from breaches of duties but from other events. For example, the receipt of a mistaken payment does not involve a breach of duty. Yet it is considered to give

[7] For example, Campbell defines contractual remedies as 'the courses of action open to a claimant, C, who wishes to take some step to cope with the consequences of the defendant, D's, (threatened) failure to perform his contractual obligation': D. Harris, D. Campbell, R. Halson, *Remedies in Contract and Tort* (2nd edn., London: Butterworths, 2002) 3.

[8] W. N. Hohfeld, 'The Relations between Equity and Law' (1913) 11 *Michigan L Rev* 537, 550.

[9] P. Gerwitz, 'Remedies and Resistance' (1983) 92 *Yale LJ* 585, 587.

[10] [2001] 1 AC 268 (HL) 284; Tilbury, Noone and Kercher adopt a broad definition of a remedy as a response to a wrong: M. Tilbury, M. Noone and B. Kercher *Remedies: Commentary and Materials* (3rd edn., Sydney: Law Book Co, 2000), 1, 422. Now in its 4th edition.

[11] In *Letang v Cooper* [1965] 1 QB 232, 247 (CA) Lord Diplock stated that '[i]n the context of civil actions a duty is merely the obverse of a right recognised by law. The fact that in the earlier cases the emphasis tended to be upon the right and in more modern cases the emphasis tends to be upon the duty merely reflects changing fashions in approach to juristic as to other social problems, and must not be allowed to disguise the fact that right and duty are but two sides of a single medal.' But although a duty always correlates with a right, it is not always the case that a right correlates with a duty for as Hohfeld showed the term 'right' also applies to privileges (liberties), powers, and immunities—each of which does not correlate with a duty: W. N. Hohfeld, 'Some Fundamental Legal Conceptions As Applied in Judicial Reasoning' (1913) 23 *Yale LJ* 16, 30.

[12] Barker asserts that remedies constitute the law's response to the violations of private law rights, or what he calls 'primary injustices': K. Barker, 'Rescuing Remedialism in Unjust Enrichment Law: Why Remedies are Right' [1998] *CLJ* 301, 319.

[13] (2001) 185 ALR 1, 17–18 (HCA) (footnote in relation to a possible exception in Australian public law omitted).

rise to an injustice which, applying the medical metaphor, requires a remedy.[14] A contracting party may be aggrieved where the counter-party insists that a contract has not come to an end. Again, the first party's grievance does not originate in a breach of duty. Yet, again, the first party can seek and obtain a legal remedy.[15] Similarly, no breach of legal duty is involved where a testator has made inadequate provision for a dependant in a will but the aggrieved dependant may obtain a legal remedy to improve that situation.[16]

Thus, at its broadest, a legal remedy is more than just a response to a breach of duty or a means of realizing a pre-existing right. A fully inclusive definition of a legal remedy in its broadest sense is some means provided by the law for redressing a grievance.

D Narrow Meanings of Legal Remedy

Apart from its broad meanings, the term 'remedy' is also used in more specific senses in legal discourse. These will now be identified, illustrated, and briefly discussed.

1 An action or cause of action as a remedy

As we have seen in the non-legal context, the word 'remedy' may be used to refer to a treatment or process that will lead to a cure. In the legal context, this is treatment in the sense of a suit or action leading to the redress of a grievance. The statement 'Your remedy is an action for breach of contract' involves the use of remedy in this sense. Here it refers to an avenue for realizing contractual rights. This usage is frequently encountered.[17] For example, Maitland used remedy in the sense of an action for damages when he wrote:

> To an action for damages delay is no defence unless the case has been brought within one of the Statutes of Limitation. Either the plaintiff is still entitled to the remedy or it has been taken from him by Statute, and you can fix the precise moment of time at which the statute takes effect — one moment he has a remedy, the next moment he has none.[18]

[14] Hence the right arising from an unjust enrichment is sometimes labelled a remedy. See p 16 below.

[15] In *Guaranty Trust Co of New York v Hannay & Co* [1915] 2 KB 536 (CA) a party to a contract was held to be entitled to seek a declaration that it was not liable under the contract. See Chapter 9 p 161.

[16] Inheritance (Provision for Family and Dependants) Act 1975 (UK), s 1. See Chapter 13 pp 211 and 213.

[17] Samuel appears to use remedy in the sense of an action in G. Samuel, *Law of Obligations and Legal Remedies* (2nd edn., London: Cavendish, 2001), 113–42.

[18] F. W. Maitland, *Equity: A Course of Lectures* (Cambridge: Cambridge University Press, 1936), 326. Limitation statutes have been held not to extinguish the substantive right to the payment of a debt: see Chapter 4 p 60.

Atiyah states that 'the seller's proper remedy is an action for damages for non-acceptance'.[19] Similarly Tettenborn writes:

> The old actions for *quantum meruit*, money had and received, money paid for a consideration that totally fails, and account of profits, for instance, all constitute pecuniary relief for unjust enrichment; but, at least as yet, they have not been regarded as anything other than separate remedies.[20]

This usage originates from the forms of action. The early common law was driven by forms of action. These were essentially sets of winning words.[21] If the plaintiff, as the claimant was then called, could bring his or her case within the requisite winning propositions, that is, prove the facts that substantiated those propositions, he or she would obtain the relief that he sought. It became common to refer to the forms of action as remedies because their availability bettered the plaintiff's grievance.[22] Rights later emerged as conceptualizations of the availability of a suitable form of action.

The term 'remedy' is also used in a way which is closely related to its sense of action or suit, namely, to refer to the availability or existence of a cause of action. Certain combinations of facts are actionable. This means that they have the potential to generate a particular legal consequence. There may be judicial intervention in the parties' affairs if an action is brought and they can be proved to exist. The law conceptualizes the actionability of these facts into what is generically known as a cause of action.[23] Lord Escher MR held in *Read v Brown* that a cause of action is 'every fact which it would be necessary for the plaintiff to prove, if traversed, in order to support his right to the judgment'.[24]

This notion of a particular set of actionable facts is conveyed by expressions such as conversion, money had and received, or breach of contract. If an aggrieved person's situation involves facts that are actionable, that is, a cause action, that person has a means of obtaining the court's assistance to make his or her predicament better. Hence the term 'remedy' is sometimes applied to a cause of action. In this way even conversion or negligence could be referred to as a remedy. For example, Lord Wilberforce said, 'conversion is a remedy, alternative to, or (to some extent) cumulative with, the remedy of damages for infringement'.[25]

[19] P. Atiyah, *Introduction to the Law of Contract* (5th edn., Oxford: Clarendon Press, 1995), 432.

[20] A. Tettenborn, *Law of Restitution in England and Ireland* (3rd edn., London: Cavendish, 2002), 43.

[21] Birks (n 6 above), 10. See generally F. W. Maitland, *The Forms of Action at Common Law* (Cambridge, Cambridge University Press, 1936).

[22] Birks (n 6 above), 10.

[23] P. B. H. Birks, 'Three Kinds of Objection to Discretionary Remedialism' (2000) 29 *Western Australian L Rev* 1, 4.

[24] (1889) 22 QBD 128, 131 (CA), following *Cooke v Gill* (1872–1873) LR 8 CP 107, 116. Compare *Letang v Cooper* [1965] 1 QB 232, 242–3 (CA), see Chapter 4 n 34.

[25] *Infabrics Ltd v Jaytex Ltd* [1982] 1 AC 1, 17 (HL).

2 A substantive right as a remedy

The term 'remedy' is often used in the legal context to refer to some kind of substantive right. In this book, a 'substantive right'[26] is taken to be a right that exists prior to the commencement of legal proceedings and the making of an order or pronouncement of a court in those proceedings.[27] For instance, it includes a contractual right to a payment, a right to the return of a mistaken payment or a right to a payment of damages for negligence. Each of these rights arises out of a different event that occurs prior to a judicial determination in the particular case.[28] A substantive right is a means or a stepping stone to relief and hence it is sometimes seen as a remedy. For example, Edwards and Stockwell write:

> Where a trustee holds property for the benefit of another, that other, the beneficiary, has a proprietary remedy, that is the right to the property and its fruits, or the profit made from it, since the trustee may not profit from the trust.[29]

(a) Kinds of substantive rights: primary and secondary

Substantive rights are of two kinds: primary and secondary (or, more descriptively, 'remedial').[30] A secondary right arises from a legal wrong, a breach of a primary duty. An example is the right to the payment of damages for negligence which arises out of a breach of a primary duty to take reasonable care.[31] A primary right is a right which exists independently of a wrong. Examples include the contractual right to the payment of an agreed sum and the right to the return of a mistaken payment.[32] The distinction between primary and secondary rights is based on the origin of the right.

This two-tiered structure was given prominence in the law of contract by Lord Diplock over a twenty year period beginning in the 1960s.[33] In *Lep Air Services*

[26] The term 'institutional' is also used to denote 'a relationship which arises and exists under the law independently of any order of a court' *Muschinski v Dodds* (1985) 160 CLR 583, 614 (HCA) (Deane J).

[27] 'A substantive real right is one which is vested in a person at law independently of any court order': R. Goode, 'Property and Unjust Enrichment' in A. Burrows (ed.), *Essays on the Law of Restitution* (Oxford: Clarendon Press, 1991), 222–3. See also D. M. Walker, *The Oxford Companion to Law* (Oxford: Clarendon Press, 1980), 1195.

[28] In this book, a substantive right is not taken to include a right against a court (if such a 'right' may be said to exist). Thus rights to obtain an *award* of damages or, perhaps, to a *decree* of specific performance are not treated here as substantive rights.

[29] R. Edwards and N. Stockwell, *Trusts and Equity* (5th edn., Harlow: Longman, 2002), 388.

[30] Walker (n 27 above), 1195. Birks (n 6 above), 12. For further discussion of the primary-secondary distinction see A. Pretto, 'Primary Rights and Rights *in Rem*' in P. B. H. Birks and A. Pretto (eds), *Themes in Comparative Law in Honour of Bernard Rudden* (Oxford: Oxford Universtiy Press, 2002).

[31] See Chapter 10 p 174.

[32] See Chapter 7 pp 109 and p 114.

[33] For example, *Hardwick Game Farm v Suffolk Agricultural and Poultry Producers Association Ltd* [1966] 1 WLR 287, 341 (CA), affirmed [1969] 2 AC 31 (HL); *C Czarnikow Ltd v Koufos* [1966] 2 QB 695, 731 (CA), affirmed [1969] 1 AC 350 (HL); *Robophone v Blank* [1966] 1 WLR 1428, 1446 (CA); *Ward v Bignall* [1967] 1 QB 534, 548 (CA); *London and Thames Haven Oil*

Ltd v Rolloswin Investments Ltd, Lord Diplock stated that, on a termination of a contract, by the acceptance of a repudiation:

> for [the contract-breaker's] primary obligations there is substituted by operation of law a secondary obligation to pay to the other party a sum of money to compensate him for the loss he has sustained as a result of the failure to perform the primary obligations.[34]

Lord Reid also stated in the same case, in the context of repudiation of contracts:

> For the breach of any contract the normal remedy is damages in money. The contract may have been to deliver, say, 100 tons of wheat. If the party fails to deliver somehow that obligation disappears and by operation of law is replaced by an obligation to pay money. So it appears to me that when a contract is brought to an end by repudiation accepted by the other party all the obligations in the contract come to an end and they are replaced by operation of law by an obligation to pay money damages.[35]

In *Photo Production Ltd v Securicor Transport Ltd*,[36] Lord Diplock made it clear that secondary rights arise by implication of the law from any breach of contract, not only when a repudiatory breach is accepted.[37]

More recent decisions of the House of Lords show that this distinction has had a lasting impact on English law. In *Alfred McAlpine Construction Ltd v Panatown*[38] Lord Clyde referred to a secondary obligation to compensate[39] and Lord Millett also spoke of 'a secondary obligation to pay damages'.[40] In *Attorney General v Blake*[41] Lord Hobhouse observed that 'This is not a claim to the performance of any obligation save in the sense used by Lord Diplock that contractual obligations are correctly understood as being the obligation to perform or pay damages for failing to do so — the primary and secondary obligation.'[42]

Austin was responsible for the first appearance of the distinction between primary and secondary rights in English jurisprudence over a century before

Wharves Ltd v Attwooll [1967] Ch 772, 815 (CA); *Lep Air Services Ltd v Rolloswin Investments Ltd* [1973] AC 331, 350–1 (HL); *Photo Production Ltd v Securicor Transport Ltd* [1980] AC 827, 848–50 (HL); *Paal Wilson & Co v Partenreederi* [1983] 1 AC 854, 915 (HL). This achievement is traced in B. Dickson, 'The Contribution of Lord Diplock to the Law of Contract' (1989) 9 *OJLS* 441.

[34] [1973] AC 331, 350 (HL). [35] Ibid 345.

[36] [1980] AC 827, 848–50 (HL), see also quote reproduced in Chapter 7 text to n 40. In *Photo Production* Lord Diplock drew a distinction between 'general secondary' and 'anticipatory secondary obligations'. The former arise on any breach of contract. The latter arise only on a breach of contract which entitles the innocent party to terminate.

[37] It must be noted that although Lord Diplock's position is very closely followed in this work, it is not entirely adopted. Lord Diplock's view (expressed in *Photo Production* at 850) that liquidated damages clauses in contracts give rise to secondary rights is not adopted here. Rights arising from such clauses will be treated as primary. The reasons for this are outlined in Chapter 7 p 110.

[38] [2001] 1 AC 518 (HL). [39] Ibid 534. [40] Ibid 595.

[41] [2001] 1 AC 268 (HL).

[42] Ibid 297–8. Lord Hobhouse dissented on the point that the secondary obligation could be non-compensatory.

the courts expressly adopted it.[43] He had written:

> Those [rights] which I call primary do not arise from injuries, or from violations of other rights and duties. Those which I call secondary or sanctioning (I style them sanctioning because their proper purpose is to prevent delicts or offences) arise from violations of other rights and duties, or from injuries, delicts or offences.[44]

Although Lord Diplock developed his analysis in the context of breach of contract, following Austin's lead, this work applies the distinction between primary and secondary rights in the field of private law generally.

(b) Confusion as to secondary rights

It must be noted that there is some confusion as to the content of secondary rights. A secondary right may be a right to an act by the defendant, such as a right to the payment of compensation.[45] Secondly, it may be a right to an order of the court, such as a right to an order for compensation. Barker appears to take the latter view when he writes:

> [T]he theoretical distinction between primary and secondary right still holds. . .The plaintiff's (secondary) entitlement to a court order for the restoration of the money is not the same as his (primary) entitlement to it without such an order. . .In truth, the right to an order is a subtle *substitute* for the primary right, albeit a clever and, to the casual eye, indistinguishable one.[46]

Thirdly, a right that arises out of the order of the court is sometimes called a secondary right.[47] Barker appears to slip into this third sense on occasion. He writes: 'whether the court in the mistake case grants an order for the return of money had and received, a constructive trust, a *quantum meruit* or a *quantum valebat,* it is dispensing secondary, not primary rights.'[48] As will be seen, Tilbury conflates rights of the third type with rights of the first type under the label secondary rights.[49] It is submitted that the label secondary right should be limited to the first sense—a right to an act by the defendant arising out of a breach of duty, or more broadly a jural relationship arising out of such a breach. Secondary rights in this sense will be discussed in further detail in Chapters 10 to 13.

[43] Austin was probably influenced by Pothier in this regard whose *Traité des Obligations* was translated by Evans and first published in English in 1806. See B. Rudden, 'Correspondence' (1990) 10 *OJLS* 288 where Rudden suggests that the source of Lord Diplock's distinction was Pothier.

[44] J. Austin, *Lectures on Jurisprudence Vol II* (R. Campbell (ed.) (5th edn., London: John Murray, 1885), Lecture XLV, 763.

[45] This was the view of Lord Diplock. See *Hardwick Game Farm v Suffolk Agricultural and Poultry Producers Association Ltd* [1966] 1 WLR 287, 341 (CA).

[46] Barker (n 12 above), 321.

[47] Austin's considered view was that rights arising from judgments are primary: Austin (n 44 above), 64–5.

[48] Barker (n 12 above), 322.

[49] Chapter 3 p 34.

(c) A secondary right as a remedy

Secondary rights are commonly called remedies. As Birks observes, 'secondary rights are also remedies for the wrong. Here there is no contrast between "remedy" and "right", except that the two words take different positions in relation to the same phenomenon.'[50] Austin himself appeared to equate secondary rights with remedies when he wrote:

> In most systems of law, a vast number of primary rights and duties are not separated from the secondary; That is to say; The primary right and duty is not described in a distinct and substantive manner; but it is created or imposed by a declaration on the part of the legislature, that such or such an act or such and such a forbearance or omission, shall amount to an injury: And that the party sustaining the injury shall have such or such a remedy against the party injuring; or that the party injuring shall be punished in a certain manner.
>
> Nay, in some cases, the law which imposes the primary right or duty, and which defines the nature of the injury, is contained by implication in the law which gives the remedy, or which determines the punishment.[51]

A number of contemporary writers on remedies appear to follow Austin's lead and treat secondary rights as forming part of the law of remedies.[52]

(d) A primary right as a remedy

The great majority of primary rights such as the rights protected by the law of tort or most of the rights arising from consent cannot be described as remedies for they cannot be said to be means of obtaining relief from a particular grievance. However, a limited number of primary rights are often referred to as remedies. For example, rights to 'liquidated damages' which have been expressly agreed under a contract are sometimes called remedies and discussed in books on remedies.[53] They are primary rights as they do not arise out of the wrong of breach of contract but through the consent of the parties.[54] Similarly, a holder of a security is often given express rights under the security agreement to facilitate the recovery of money lent. These primary rights are also frequently called remedies. The decision in *Alliance and Leicester Plc v Slayford* provides examples of this usage:

> [A] mortgagee has a number of remedies all designed to enforce payment of what is due to him under the mortgage, which may be pursued concurrently as soon as the mortgagor is in default or successively, until payment in full is recovered or the mortgagee acts in a way

[50] P. B. H. Birks, 'Equity in the Modern Law: An Exercise in Taxonomy' (1996) 26 *U Western Australia L Rev* 1, 11.

[51] Austin (n 44 above), Vol II, Lecture XLV, 767 (footnote omitted but idiosyncratic punctuation unaltered).

[52] W. Covell and K. Lupton, *Principles of Remedies* (Sydney: Butterworths, 1995), 1; Tilbury et al (n 10 above), 1, 4.

[53] For example, Harris, Campbell and Halson (n 7 above), Chapter 9.

[54] See Chapter 7 p 110.

which amounts to an election. Thus if the mortgagee chooses to sue the mortgagor on his personal covenant and obtains a money judgment, abandons his security and brings bankruptcy proceedings, he cannot thereafter exercise remedies as a secured creditor. . .[T]here is no abuse of process in a mortgagee, who has been met with a successful *Barclays Bank Plc v O'Brien*[55]-type defence taken by the wife of the mortgagor, merely choosing to pursue his remedies against the mortgagor by suing on the personal covenant with a view as an unsecured creditor to bankrupting him. . .[56]

Rights born of other events which do not involve a breach of duty such as unjust enrichment can also fall within this category. For instance, the recipient of a mistaken payment does not commit a wrong, yet the restitutionary right which arises against him can nonetheless be seen as providing relief from the payer's grievance and is therefore capable of being called a remedy.[57]

3 A court order as a remedy

The term 'remedy' is frequently applied to an order of the court. In *Broome v Cassell & Co Ltd* Lord Diplock stated that 'The award of damages as the remedy for all civil wrongs was in England the creature of the common law.'[58] Similarly, in *Kuddus v Chief Constable of Leicestershire,* Lord Scott stated that 'The remedies the court can provide include awards of damages, declarations of right and, in most cases, injunctions.'[59] Cane adopts the same meaning when he writes that 'The law of tort does sometimes award non-monetary remedies: injunctions and orders for the return of specific goods. . .'.[60] Similarly Jones and Goodhart write that 'Specific performance is a decree of the court. . .Specific performance is then a discretionary remedy.'[61] As will be made clear in the next chapter, this appears to be the core meaning of the term. It is most commonly expressly adopted by those who write on remedies. Further illustrations of its use will not be provided here to avoid duplication. However, it is appropriate at this stage to refer to the distinction Birks draws between a remedy as an order of the court obtained as of right and as an order given by the court in its discretion.[62]

(a) An order made 'as of right'

In his *Commentaries on the Laws of England,* Blackstone clearly equated remedy with an order of the court which is obtained as of right:

The judgment, though pronounced or awarded by the judges, is not their determination or sentence, but the determination or sentence of *the law*. It is the conclusion that

[55] [1994] 1 AC 180 (HL).
[56] [2001] 1 All ER 1, 8 and 11 (CA) (Peter Gibson LJ).
[57] Birks (n 6 above), 14.
[58] [1972] AC 1027, 1127 (HL).
[59] [2002] 2 AC 122, 156 (HL).
[60] P. Cane, *Tort Law and Economic Interests* (2nd edn., Oxford: Clarendon Press, 1996), 4.
[61] G. Jones and W. Goodhart, *Specific Performance* (London: Butterworths, 1986), 1. Contrast text to n 77.
[62] Birks (n 6 above), 15–17.

naturally and regularly follows from the premises of law and fact. . .Which judgment or conclusion depends not therefore on the arbitrary caprice of the judge but on the settled and invariable principles of justice. The judgment, in short, is the remedy prescribed by law for the redress of injuries; and the suit or action is the vehicle or means of administering it.[63]

Here Blackstone wrote of an order which the court could not choose not to award. Once a case had been made out, the order—the law's remedy—could not be refused. Birks also identifies a contrasting usage of 'remedy' in the sense of an order that has developed in contradistinction to the term 'right'.

(b) An order given in court's 'strong' discretion

Birks points out that:

> The genuine opposition between 'right' and 'remedy'. . .contradistinguishes entitlements inhering in individuals independently of judicial pronouncements ('rights') and, on the other hand, discretionary judicial pronouncements which, if they confer rights on an individual, do so by their own virtue and not merely by way of declaration or realization of a pre-existing entitlement ('remedies').[64]

Some orders of the court are granted in the court's strong discretion.[65] The claimant has no right to the order and no prior right to what the order confers.[66] In deciding what form the order is to take, the judge must balance numerous factors such as the claimant's substantive rights, the effect of the order and other issues of policy. The judge is said to fashion such a remedy. Hammond J uses 'remedy' in the sense of such an order in the following passage:

> Legal craftsmanship of a high order is required to see that entitlement, on the one hand, is recognised and supported, and the idea (of the "right") advanced. The remedy, on the other hand, both supports that right and is appropriate to the particular occasion. A "good" judgment is somehow a satisfying package which satisfies both the general, and the particular.[67]

The nature of the relationship between rights and remedies and the role of discretion in that relationship will be subjected to closer examination in subsequent parts of this book.

4 Means of enforcing a court order as a remedy

The problem of the instability of the term 'remedy' is not new. In the late eighteenth century, Bentham considered it in his *Comment on the Commentaries*,

[63] W. Blackstone, *Commentaries on the Laws of England Vol III* (16th edn., London: T. Cadell & J. Butterworth, 1825), 395. See Birks (n 6 above), 15–16.

[64] P. B. H. Birks, 'Proprietary Rights as Remedies' in P. B. H. Birks (ed.), *The Frontiers of Liability Vol 2* (Oxford: Oxford University Press, 1994), 217.

[65] See Chapter 6 p 97.

[66] See Chapter 13 for examples of such orders.

[67] G. Hammond, 'The Place of Damages in the Scheme of Remedies' in P. Finn (ed.), *Essays on Damages* (North Ryde New South Wales: Law Book Co, 1992), 200 (footnote omitted).

a trenchant and sustained attack on Blackstone's *Commentaries on the Laws of England*. After dividing a law into declaratory, directory, remedial, and sanctional parts, Blackstone had described the remedial part of a law as the part 'whereby a method is pointed out to recover a man's private rights, or redress his private wrongs'.[68] Bentham made an issue of the imprecision of Blackstone's definition of 'remedial'. The relevant passages in the *Comment* are enlightening because they show that Bentham, in searching for a more precise meaning to be given to the remedial part of a law, entertained and rejected the ideas that actions and secondary rights constituted such a part. Bentham begins by citing Blackstone's illustration of the remedial part:

'When the declaratory part of the Law has said that the field or inheritance, which belonged to Titius's father, is vested, by his death, in Titius; and the directory part has forbidden anyone to enter on another's property without the leave of the owner; if Gaius after this will *presume* (naughty presumptuous Gaius!) 'to take possession of the land, the remedial part of the Law will make Gaius restore the possession to Titius, and also pay him damages for the invasion.'[69]

Then after yet another of the personal attacks on Blackstone with which the *Comment* is replete, Bentham continues by surmising how Blackstone may have arrived at his notion of the remedial part of the law:

In the common language of the bar, *damages* is often spoken of as *a remedy*. And the restoring a man a thing he has a *right* to, comes within of a remedy (in part at least) to the *wrong* done him, by taking it away from him. Out of these two ideas he has patched up in the manner we have seen, that of the remedial part that is to be found, he told us, in *every* law.[70]

Bentham then upbraids Blackstone for his lack of precision in relation to the remedial part of the law:

Question upon question will here occur to those who see how far this account is from containing anything that is intelligible. Is it to appoint these damages that is the 'office' of the remedial part, or only to appoint the course to be taken for recovering them, or both? If the former only, then how differs this part from the Sanctional? If the latter only, then how comes it to appear before the sanctional which it speaks of? If both, then how came these two parts so different to be reckoned but as one? How is it that this part of the Law more than any other part makes Gaius restore the possession, and pay the damages: and what is it that it does to make him? Is it that this part and not the rest is the cause that he restores and pays? No, for that is an effect that belongs to the whole of the Law together. Is it that it says that he shall restore and pay? No, for that belongs to the sanctional part, if this sort of Law is understood to have a sanction belonging to it, and that sanction any meaning.[71]

[68] W. Blackstone, *Commentaries on the Laws of England Vol I* (16th edn., London: T. Cadell & J. Butterworth, 1825), 54. This is similar to the broad functional definition of 'remedy' posited above.

[69] J. Bentham, *Comment on the Commentaries* (C. W. Everett (ed.) Oxford: Clarendon Press, 1928), 86 (text and punctuation in this and the quotations which follow have not been altered).

[70] Ibid 87.

[71] Ibid 87.

Here Bentham has raised and rejected the view that secondary rights (that is, '[the part that] says that he shall restore and pay') are the remedial part of the law. He also rejects the view that the remedial part sets out the course to be taken for recovering possession or damages, that is, the law of actions or the law of procedure. What then did Bentham conclude was meant by the remedial?[72] He continued:

Or, to come at last to the truth of things, and to give this remedial part something of a sense (tho very inappositely indicated by the term). Is it not the case thus after all, that it bids a somebody else and not Gaius to take the field from Gaius and give it back again to Titius, and also to take money's worth from the same Gaius and give it to the same Titius, under the name of damages (that is, reparation of damages) sustained by him from being so long out of it? Whatever the Law does, whatever it 'makes' a man do, it does, it makes him do by speaking. It has a mouth. It has no hands. In the directory part it binds, in the sanctional part it prophecies. In the remedial part (of that complex apparatus I mean which our Author treats as if it were *one* Law) in the remedial part it bids other men than him whom it bad and prophesied before to fulfil such prophecy (I speak here of a Law with a penal sanction) upon the first man in case of his disobedience.[73]

Thus Bentham's view was that the remedial part of the law prescribed how the sanctional part was to be given effect. Unfortunately, due to his polemical rhetoric, his own statements are not free from ambiguity. He appears to have equated the remedial part of the law with enforcement. As Corbin states: 'The "enforcement" of A's right and B's duty means the application of the sanction — the penalty — by societal agents.'[74] These societal agents, sheriffs or bailiffs, are who Bentham appears to be referring to as the other persons who are to realize the claimant's rights. However, in his discussion Bentham seems to bypass the need for a judgment before enforcement can occur; and a judgment was the very thing which to Blackstone was the remedy.[75]

However, Bentham's suggested sense is not unknown. The term 'remedy' is at times applied to the means of enforcing a court order. Sir George Baker P in *Paton v Trustees of British Pregnancy Advisory Service*[76] stated: 'I ask the question, "If an injunction were ordered, what could be the remedy?" and I do not think I need say any more than that no judge could even consider sending a husband or wife to

[72] It may be that by the remedial part of the law Blackstone meant the part relating to the obtaining of a remedy which to him was a judgment. See text to n 63 above. The obtaining of a judgment would generally 'make Gaius restore the possession to Titius, and also pay him damages for the invasion.' Only in rare cases would the further step of enforcement need to be taken.

[73] Bentham (n 69 above), 87–8.

[74] A. Corbin, 'Rights and Duties' (1922–24) *Yale LJ* 501, 516.

[75] Blackstone never had the opportunity to answer these points made by Bentham as the *Comment* was not published until 1928. However, even if it had been published during his lifetime, Blackstone would most likely have remained silent. When asked if he would respond to Bentham's *Fragment on Government* (Payne et al, London 1776), he is said to have replied, 'No, not even if it had been better written.': L. Stephen (ed.), *Dictionary of National Biography Vol V* (London: Smith, Elder & Co, 1886), 137.

[76] [1979] QB 276, 280.

prison for breaking such an order.' Likewise Jones and Goodhart write: 'If the defendant disobeys [a decree of specific performance], the court has adequate remedies to compel compliance; for example it has power to nominate a person to execute an instrument if the defendant refuses to do so, and, in the last resort, he may be punished by being committed for contempt.'[77]

5 Final outcome as a remedy

In this final sense, a remedy is used to mean the actual act, thing, or occurrence that effects or amounts to the redress or relief that the claimant obtains. Pomeroy subscribed to the view that a remedy is an act or thing which brings about the relief:

> Remedies, in their widest sense, are either the final means by which to maintain and defend primary rights and enforce primary duties, or they are the final equivalents given to an injured person in place of his original primary rights which have been broken, and of the original primary duties towards him which have been unperformed. Remedial rights, or rights of remedy, are rights which an injured person has to avail himself of some one or more of these final means, or to obtain some one or more of these final equivalents.[78]

Pomeroy provides examples to elucidate his definitions. The first concerns the situation where *X* contracts to buy goods from *Y* and *Y* fails to deliver them. 'The remedy given under such circumstances is a pecuniary compensation, a sum of money in the place of the goods, which in our legal nomenclature is termed damages. In this instance, the remedy is plainly an *equivalent*.'[79] Here the remedy is a thing. The second example is the case where *X* contracts to buy land from *Y* and *Y* fails to convey the land. Here the remedy is the conveyance of the land itself, an act. It is effected by specific performance and is of the 'final means' variety.

Some further examples of the use of remedy in the sense of an act may be given. 'The remedy for the plaintiff's pain and suffering was the payment of $10,000 to the claimant by the defendant' or 'The remedy for the defendant's refusal to vacate the premises was the bailiff's ejectment of the defendant and delivery of vacant possession to the claimant'. Similarly Lord Clyde stated in *McAlpine (Alfred) Construction Ltd v Panatown Ltd* that 'a consequential right arises in the innocent party to obtain a remedy from the party who repudiated the contract for his failure in performance.'[80] This seems like Pomeroy's usage. His Lordship cannot be taken to be referring to a remedy in any of the other narrow senses identified above.

[77] G. Jones and W. Goodhart, *Specific Performance* (London: Butterworths, 1986), 1 (footnote omitted). Contrast text to n 61.

[78] J. N. Pomeroy, *Remedies and Remedial Rights by the Civil Action* (Boston: Little, Brown and Co, 1876), 2, 42.

[79] Ibid 2.

[80] [2001] 1 AC 518, 534 (HL).

Remedy in the sense of an act would also include an exercise of self-help. For example, it is sometimes said that in the case of nuisance the remedy may lie in the victim's own hands.

E Conclusion

Having covered the disparate senses in which the term 'remedy' is used, the works of a number of leading writers on remedies will be examined in the next chapter to determine whether the writers are sensitive to the term's instability, which sense of the term each prefers, whether each writer's usage is consistent, and how and on what basis the subject matter is categorized. This will further illustrate the problems with the term 'remedy' and assist us in selecting a stable core meaning in Chapter 4.

3

Writers on 'Remedies'

A Introduction

'Remedies' is treated as a subject in its own right by many scholars. There are numerous books on legal remedies. More are appearing each year. But what is it precisely that each work is focusing on? If the concept of a remedy were a stable one, the answer would be simple. Are the leading texts sensitive to the instabilities identified in the previous chapter? Is there consistency in the usage of the term 'remedy'? How are remedies classified? These and other related questions will be answered in this chapter.

B Lawson — Remedies of English Law

1 The work

The first edition of Lawson's seminal book on remedies, *Remedies of English Law*, was published in 1972. According to its author, a great comparative lawyer, it 'for the first time attempted to provide an outline of the full apparatus of legal remedies available in England'.[1] Until its appearance, remedies were covered as part of works on contract, tort, and equity. Of course they have continued to be treated in this way too. However, the work's originality and achievement lay in demonstrating that there was value in looking at different types of remedies side by side. Given Lawson's accomplishments in comparative law, it was fitting that he should bring his skills of comparative analysis to bear upon the notion of a remedy that appeared so often in English civil law and had not yet been closely examined. The second edition of the work was published in 1980. It was prepared by Lawson with the assistance of Harvey Teff. As the title indicates, both editions of the text focus exclusively on English law.

[1] F. H. Lawson, *Remedies of English Law* (2nd edn., London: Butterworth & Co, 1980), v.

2 Scope of the concept of a remedy

Lawson attempted to set out the scope of the concept of a remedy in the preface to the first edition, which was reproduced in the preface to the second:

> The notion of a 'remedy' is not easily defined, or even disengaged from its surroundings in the substantive law of rights, duties, powers and liabilities, or from the procedural steps that have to be taken in order to obtain a remedy or, if necessary, to enforce it. Moreover, the character and sometimes even the existence, of a remedy are often determined by the means of enforcing it; to disregard those means entirely would be to leave everything 'in the air'. Although, therefore, this is not a book about substantive law or about procedure, pleading, execution or bankruptcy, I have judged it necessary to deal with all of them summarily in an introduction. But my main purpose is to set out *what* redress a person can obtain, not *how* he can obtain it.
>
> Within these limits I have tried to cover the ground completely, including all kinds of remedies, judicial and non-judicial, legal and equitable, public and private, specific and in the 'substitutional' form of a money award, coercive and non-coercive.[2]

Although the author tells us what a remedy is not, he does not suggest a working definition beyond stating that it is difficult to define, suggesting that it is 'what redress a person can obtain' and listing a number of dichotomies into which remedies can be classified.

A close look at the introductory chapter allows us to garner what Lawson considered a remedy to be. It starts 'If you have been wronged by another person, the first step you will take will probably be to ask him for reparation. Only if you fail in this or do not arrive at a settlement will you seek a remedy.'[3] Thus a remedy is something other than a mere request for and receipt of reparation. The author then asserts that 'remedies are cures for wrongs'.[4]

According to Lawson, a 'wrong' is an infringement of an 'interest' protected by law.[5] Interests which are protected by law include rights *in rem* (rights which need to be respected by persons generally) such as rights to property, personal integrity, reputation which give rise to torts,[6] and rights *in personam* (rights which need to be respected only by certain persons) such as rights arising out of contracts and trusts. However, there are other interests 'of a vague character' which are protected in the absence of a tort or breach of contract or trust. These include the right to the return of a mistaken payment, the interests protected through complaints to public officers rather than civil actions, or the interests at stake in family law matters where it is difficult to identify infringed rights.[7] Thus Lawson's definition of a wrong is far broader than the generally accepted notion of a breach of duty. Lawson's definition of a remedy may be said to be a cure for or means of

[2] F. H. Lawson, *Remedies of English Law* (London: Butterworth & Co, 1972), 10.
[3] Lawson (n 1 above), 1. [4] Ibid 3. [5] Ibid 4.
[6] Lawson adopts a broad concept of a right *in rem*. In contrast, this work takes a right *in rem* to simply mean a property right. See Chapter 4 n 30. [7] Lawson (n 1 above), 4.

redressing an infringement of an interest protected by law. This is similar to the broad definition discussed in Chapter 2.[8] It does not clearly differentiate remedies from substantive rights.

Notwithstanding the above, it is apparent that Lawson often uses the term remedy in narrower senses. 'Judgment' and 'remedy' are frequently used interchangeably. 'The execution of judgments calls for closer attention. . .remedies of which execution is easy will be preferred to those where it is difficult or even troublesome.'[9] More explicitly: 'We must now pass to the main subject of this book, the judgments of courts and the various substitutes for them'[10] or 'An award of damages, the commonest of all remedies. . .'.[11] The author also uses remedy in the sense of the rights arising from a judicial command stating 'all the necessary remedies. . .can be awarded in a single judgment by a judge of either the Queen's Bench or the Chancery Division of the High Court.'[12]

Lawson is not consistent and at times, albeit rarely, lapses into remedy in the sense of an action or cause of action. Thus he writes: 'Considered exclusively as a remedy, the action for debt hardly needs comment.'[13] Similarly, when he speaks of the extinction of remedies by lapse of time, he does not mean the extinction of court orders or rights arising therefrom but rather must be referring to the extinction of rights of action.[14]

Lawson asserts that criminal prosecution is not a remedy but he treats it as an alternative to civil action and devotes a chapter to it.[15] He also excludes requests to Members of Parliament for assistance from the concept of a remedy.[16] However, he does include a chapter titled 'Administrative remedies' on requests to administrative authorities to take action such as to prosecute for an offence under an enactment.[17]

3 Taxonomy of remedies

Despite the occasional instabilities noted above, Lawson's work contains a very sophisticated taxonomy of remedies which has not been superseded by later works. Lawson first divides remedies into self-help remedies, judicial remedies and non-judicial remedies.[18] Our focus is on judicial remedies and their classification.

Lawson begins with the German division of actions into *Leistungsklagen, Feststellungsklagen*, and *Gestaltungsklagen*.[19] The first is an action for performance

[8] See p 9. [9] Lawson (n 1 above), 7. [10] Ibid 12. See also 13.
[11] Ibid 14. See also other similar uses at 14 and 15. [12] Ibid 3. [13] Ibid 50.
[14] Ibid 17. See also Chapter 21 'Limitation of actions'.
[15] Ibid 16 and Chapter 18 'Administration of criminal justice'. But note that at 260 the author refers to criminal prosecution as an 'indirect remedy'. [16] Ibid 18.
[17] Ibid 21.
[18] Non-judicial remedies appear to include aspects of the administration of criminal justice and administrative remedies in the form of action by administrative authorities. Ibid viii, 257ff, 264ff.
[19] Ibid 12.

leading to a coercive judgment which can be executed. The second is an action for a declaration, a judgment that cannot be executed but may lead to another, this time coercive, remedy. The third is an action for a constitutive judgment, that is, a judgment that automatically changes the legal positions of the parties and cannot and need not be executed. An example of a constitutive judgment is an order dissolving a marriage.[20] He then moves away from the language of actions and judgments and begins to write in terms of remedies.[21]

According to Lawson, coercive remedies can be either positive, requiring positive conduct, or negative, requiring abstention. Positive coercive remedies can take the form of orders to give (that is, transfer ownership or possession in any way), orders to do (that is, to provide a service or to do an act other than to give) or orders to undo (which are closely related to orders to do). Orders to give are subdivided into orders to give money and anything else. The former, money judgments, are subdivided according to whether they are liquidated or unliquidated, that is, whether the sum due is ascertained or needs to be quantified by the judge.

Representing Lawson's formal taxonomy of judicial remedies diagrammatically, we have:

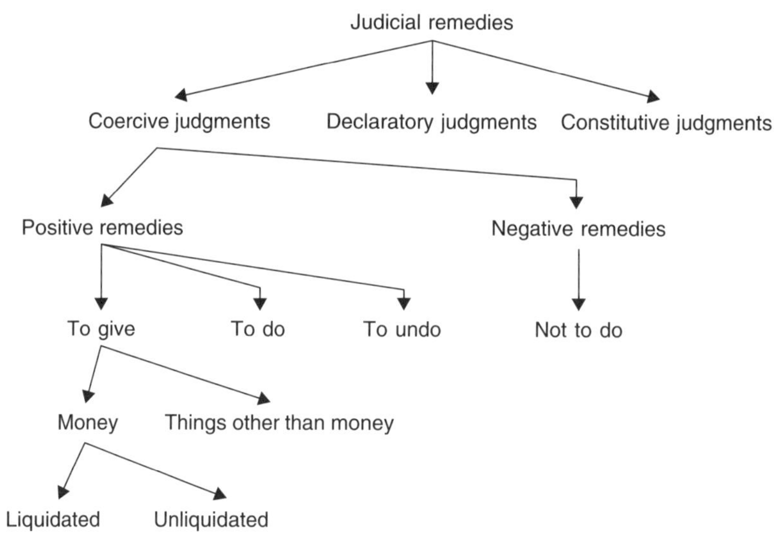

Figure 3.1

After outlining this taxonomy, Lawson moves on to explain the distinction between substitutional and specific remedies.[22] Substitutional remedies are substitutes for performance, for example, an award of damages. Specific remedies include orders to restore a specific object, orders for specific performance

[20] See Chapter 13 for further examples. [21] Lawson (n 1 above), 12–14. [22] Ibid 14.

of a contract (including orders to pay a sum due pursuant to a loan or a sale). Substitutional remedies are generally as of right and available at common law whereas specific remedies are generally discretionary and available only in equity.

Lawson next states that, as a matter of practicality, it is best to adopt a distinction which separates money and non-money judgments.[23] He observes that money judgments which give rise to judgment debts could be less valuable than specific remedies as most—but not all—specific remedies were not subject to the risk that their enforcement could be frustrated by the defendant's bankruptcy.[24] However, the author also points out that some money judgments operate *in rem*[25] and hence can also have full effect despite the defendant's bankruptcy. He thus decides that it is best to divide coercive remedies into money remedies *in personam* which produce judgment debts, money remedies *in rem* and specific remedies other than money remedies.[26]

Lawson then proceeds by splitting money remedies into those which relate to liquidated debts and unliquidated damages. The latter are subdivided into nine classes according to the sum awarded: (a) a sum representing the value of goods or services supplied by the plaintiff; (b) a sum representing the loss suffered by the plaintiff; (c) a nominal sum; (d) a derisory or contemptuous sum; (e) a penal sum; (f) a sum representing an unjustified enrichment; (g) a sum representing the profit derived by the defendant; (h) a sum that the defendant cannot conscientiously retain because it belongs to the plaintiff; and (i) a sum awarded according to a judge's discretion. He then points out that some of these judgments may be obtained through personal and some through proprietary actions.[27]

Lawson then discusses (b), (c), (d), and (e) under the sub-section titled 'damages', (f) and (g) under the sub-section titled 'restitution', (h) under the sub-section titled 'money remedies *in rem*', and (i) under a sub-section titled 'discretionary monetary awards'.

When discussing specific remedies, Lawson draws a distinction between those that can be performed by someone other than the defendant (he calls these 'fungible' orders) and those which only the defendant can perform. The former include all orders *to give* and *to undo* and some orders *to do*, the latter include orders *not to do* and orders *to do* which would require the defendant's personal skills or judgment.[28] He divides his discussion of specific remedies as follows: prohibitory orders which specifically enforce obligations *not to do*, mandatory injunctions which specifically enforce obligations *to*

[23] Ibid 15. [24] Ibid 15.

[25] That is, the money is treated as property and not currency (ibid 148) and claimant is held to be the owner of the money and not to merely be owed the money (ibid 15). [26] Ibid 16.

[27] Ibid 49–53. This may be taken to be a classification of primary and secondary rights to payment rather than of remedies. See Chapter 5 p 76. [28] Ibid 175.

undo and orders of specific recovery, specific restitution, specific substitution, and specific performance which specifically enforce obligations *to give* or *to do*.[29]

Thus Lawson, taking into account the distinctions and practical considerations discussed above, ultimately structures the text[30] on the basis of the following taxonomy:

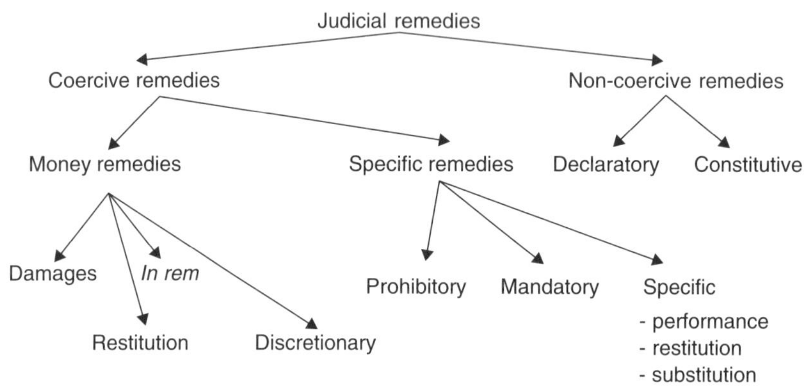

Figure 3.2

4 Summary

Lawson's very detailed taxonomy of remedies in the sense of judgments is illuminating. However, as he does not restrict himself to that meaning the ambit of the text is very wide, frequently delving into substantive law. Apart from discussing various types of judgments that were enumerated above, the author engages in an extensive discussion of the assessment of damages.[31] The chapter on restitution is one of the least structured chapters in the work. Lawson discusses the action of money had and received, waiver of tort, account, constructive trusts, and frustration.[32] He discusses tracing in considerable detail.[33] The lack of structure in some areas and the extremely wide sweep of the work are perhaps partly due to the infancy of the common law in many of these areas at the time and partly due to the author discussing remedies in a broad and unstable sense. The main shortcoming of the work is a failure to clearly separate remedies from substantive rights.

[29] That is, the money is treated as property and not currency (ibid 148) and claimant is held to be the owner of the money and not to merely be owed the money (ibid 15), 177.

[30] Lawson (n 1 above), vii–viii (diagram derived from the Table of Contents).

[31] Ibid Chapter 4. [32] Ibid Chapter 5. [33] Ibid Chapter 6.

C Burrows — Remedies for Torts and Breaches of Contract

1 The work

One of the most widely read textbooks on remedies in English law today is *Remedies for Torts and Breach of Contract* by Burrows. The first edition of this accessible work was published in 1987. Although primarily aimed at students, it became popular with practitioners. The book's goal was to treat the principles relating to remedies for breach of contract and remedies for torts as a coherent whole so that the similarities and differences between them could be better appreciated. The book was not intended to cover self-help remedies or remedies for unjust enrichment. The third edition, published in 2004, was unavailable at the time of writing, hence references contained herein are to the second (1994) edition.

2 Scope of the concept of a remedy

The work focuses on judicial remedies. On the first page it sets out what judicial remedies are:

> Judicial remedies are remedies given by the courts. . .[The book] examines what the courts can do to counter an infringement (or threatened infringement) of the plaintiff's legal rights, by a tort or breach of contract. . .A judicial remedy may be either coercive or non-coercive, that is, it may be either a court order to do or not to do something, backed up by enforcement procedures, or a court pronouncement indicating or altering what the parties' rights or duties are or were. Examples of the former are damages, specific performance, injunctions and the award of an agreed sum while the declaration is the most obvious example of the latter.[34]

The definition which Burrows gives is clear and he applies it in a very consistent manner.[35] With few exceptions, he speaks of remedies being 'awarded' which can only refer to remedies in the sense of court orders or pronouncements.[36]

Burrows clearly separates remedies from causes of action. '[T]raditional contract and tort courses. . .concentrate on the cause of action rather than the remedies side of the law'.[37] He also distinguishes remedies from adjectival law which determines the procedure for obtaining remedies and from the enforcement or execution of remedies.[38] However, unfortunately Burrows does not expressly separate the concept of a secondary right, as defined in Chapter 2,[39]

[34] A. Burrows, *Remedies for Torts and Breach of Contract* (2nd edn., London: Butterworths, 1994), 1 (footnotes omitted).

[35] For example, 'An award of damages is almost always a common law remedy and by it a sum of money assessed by the court is ordered to be paid by the defendant to the plaintiff for a tort or breach of contract.': ibid 16. For arguably inconsistent usage see 322 ('the promise enforced represents the parties' agreed remedy').

[36] 'In general there is no objection to a plaintiff being awarded more than one remedy for a tort and/or breach of contract.' Ibid 11. See also 14 and 291.

[37] Ibid ix.

[38] Ibid 2.

[39] See p 13.

from the concept of a remedy. This would have the advantage of clearly differentiating the discussion of remedies from the discussion of secondary rights.

Burrows, as Lawson before him, devotes a significant portion of the work to secondary rights rather than 'remedies' within the meaning of the term expressly adopted by him at the beginning of the first chapter. Thus, although it is said to be a work on 'remedies' for torts and breach of contract, a great deal of its content comprises an analysis of the secondary rights that arise upon a breach of contract and the commission of a tort. This part of the book is a comparative study of various secondary rights predominantly with the goals of compensation and restitution. Approximately half of the book is concerned with secondary rights to compensation. The word 'remedy' is almost not mentioned in these chapters at all. The author therefore does not fall into the error of using the term 'remedy' synonymously with a secondary right.

3 Taxonomy of remedies

Burrows prefers to classify remedies according to 'function'.[40] He states that at a particular level the functions of remedies can be said to be: compensation, restitution, punishment, compelling performance of positive obligations, preventing wrongful acts, compelling the undoing of a wrong, declaring rights. Remedies are then placed in these categories according to their function as follows:[41]

Primary function	Remedies
Compensation	Compensatory damages.
Restitution	Restitutionary damages. Account of profits. Award of money had and received.
Punishment	Exemplary damages.
Compelling performance of positive obligations	Specific performance. Award of an agreed sum. Mandatory enforcing injunction. Appointment of a receiver.
Preventing wrongful acts	Prohibitory injunction. Delivery up for destruction or destruction on oath.
Compelling the undoing of a wrong	Mandatory restorative injunction. Delivery up of goods.
Declaring rights	Declaration. Nominal damages. Contemptuous damages.

Figure 3.3

Burrows attempts to play down the historical division between legal remedies, which are generally available as of right, and equitable remedies, which are generally discretionary, pointing out that they often perform the same functions.[42]

[40] Burrows (n 34 above), 7–8. [41] Ibid 8 (table reproduced). [42] Ibid 9.

The author develops the above classification further in a chapter titled 'Judicial Remedies' in *English Private Law*.[43] He retains the categories of compensation, restitution, punishment, declaring rights, and prevention. He renames the category of compelling performance of positive obligations and compelling the undoing of a wrong as specific enforcement and (specific) restoration respectively.[44]

4 Summary

Burrows' definition of a judicial remedy is clear and consistently applied. His classification, which is similar to that of a number of other writers, is examined in detail in Chapter 5.

D Meagher, Gummow and Lehane — Equity: Doctrines and Remedies

1 The work

Equity: Doctrines and Remedies is, without doubt, the leading Australian textbook on the law of equitable remedies and general equitable doctrines and principles. Its initial three authors were Meagher, Gummow and Lehane. The text is primarily aimed at practitioners, though it has also proved popular with students. The book does not, as befits the title, deal with remedies traditionally available in common law courts. It focuses primarily on Australian law but also contains extensive coverage of English law. The first edition of the work was published in 1975, the second edition in 1984, the third edition in 1992,[45] and the fourth edition, prepared by Meagher, Heydon and Leeming, in 2002.[46] The commentary that follows relates to both the third and fourth editions as they are not materially different for the purposes of this work. References to the third edition have been retained as it was the last edition directly from the hand of the initial three authors who have been described as 'judges widely acknowledged to be among the greatest masters of equity in the modern world'.[47]

2 Scope of the concept of a remedy

Unfortunately the authors do not proffer a definition or description of what they consider to be a remedy, whether generally or as opposed to a doctrine. Thus

[43] A. Burrows, 'Judicial Remedies' in P. B. H. Birks (ed.), *English Private Law Vol II* (Oxford: Oxford University Press, 2000), Chapter 18.
[44] Ibid 818.
[45] R. P. Meagher, W. M. C. Gummow and J. R. F. Lehane, *Equity: Doctrines and Remedies* (3rd edn., Sydney: Butterworths, 1992).
[46] R. P. Meagher, J. D. Heydon and M. J. Leeming, *Meagher, Gummow and Lehane's Equity: Doctrines and Remedies* (4th edn., Sydney: Butterworths, 2002).
[47] P. B. H. Birks, 'Equity in the Modern Law: An Exercise in Taxonomy' (1996) 26 *U Western Australia L Rev* 1, 3.

some concepts come to be described as both a doctrine and a remedy. There are references to: 'doctrine of rectification' and 'remedy of rectification';[48] 'doctrine of specific performance' and 'remedy of specific performance';[49] 'doctrine' of subrogation and 'remedy of subrogation';[50] and 'doctrine of marshalling' and 'remedy of marshalling'.[51] In relation to the latter, that is, marshalling, the phrases 'exercise of remedies' and 'exercise of rights' are used interchangeably.[52] Also reference is made to a 'doctrine of rescission' but rescission is treated elsewhere as a remedy.[53]

In structuring their text, Meagher, Gummow and Lehane treat the following as remedies: declarations, specific performance, injunctions, specific restitution,[54] damages in equity, rescission, account, rectification, delivery up, and cancellation of documents and receivers.[55]

They often use the term 'remedy' in the sense of an order of the court. For example, they write that '[a]t law. . .all remedies consisted of either an unconditional verdict for the plaintiff in a specified sum of money or an unconditional verdict for the defendant'[56] or that 'the remedies in equity included orders obliging the defendant to make restitution to the plaintiff'.[57]

Sometimes remedy is used in the sense of an action or cause of action. It is stated that: 'the legal remedy was an action for damages in deceit';[58] 'the previous legal remedy was in deceit';[59] 'the remedy was to sue at law using X's name';[60] and 'the common law action of money had and received is often sufficient remedy'.[61]

Remedy also appears to be used in the sense of a substantive right. It is stated that: 'equity would permit the lender to stand in the place of the supplier and use his legal remedy to recover from the husband';[62] '[t]he surety is also entitled to relief where his remedies upon the principal obligation have been affected as a result of dealings between the creditor and debtor';[63] and 'the endorser should have the remedies of a surety to the securities of the creditor'.[64]

The following are also referred to as remedies: discovery, interlocutory receivers, interrogatories, a suit for the perpetuation of testimony,[65] a Mareva (freezing) injunction,[66] and 'tracing remedies'.[67]

[48] Meagher et al (n 46 above) [3-160], [26-010], [26-030], etc contrast [26-035], [26-055]; 3rd edn. [331], [2602], [2606], etc contrast [2607], [2611].

[49] Ibid [11-140] contrast [20-005], [20-030], etc; 3rd edn. [1128] contrast [2001], [2006], etc.

[50] Ibid [9-005] contrast [11-025]; 3rd edn. [901], [916] contrast [1105].

[51] Ibid [11-015], [11-020], etc contrast [11-280]; 3rd edn. [1103], [1104], etc contrast [1156].

[52] Ibid [11-175]–[11-200]; 3rd edn. [1136]–[1140].

[53] Ibid [1-095] contrast [13-095]; 3rd edn. [119] contrast [1318].

[54] But there is a reference to the 'doctrine of specific restitution'. Ibid [1-070]; 3rd edn. [114].

[55] Ibid ix–x (Table of Contents) and xiii (Preface).

[56] Ibid [3-055]; 3rd edn. [311].

[57] Ibid [12-015]; 3rd edn. [1203].

[58] Ibid [15-005]; 3rd edn. [1501].

[59] Ibid [12-015] also [12-055]; 3rd edn. [1203] also [1211].

[60] Ibid [9-020]; 3rd edn. [904].

[61] Ibid [9-0250]; 3rd edn. [949].

[62] Ibid [9-080]; 3rd edn. [915].

[63] Ibid [9-230]; 3rd edn. [945].

[64] Ibid [10-050]; 3rd edn. [1010].

[65] Ibid [10-230]; 3rd edn. [148].

[66] Ibid [3-040]; 3rd edn. [308].

[67] Ibid [4-015], [4-080]; 3rd edn. [403], [416].

The authors seem to intend to exclude doctrines ('e.g. estoppel, subrogation, marshalling, contribution, set-off, election, satisfaction and performance'[68]) from the concept of a remedy. They also exclude grounds on which equity intervenes to rescind transactions ('e.g. fraud and undue influence').[69]

3 Taxonomy of remedies

The taxonomy of equitable remedies is not discussed in the work. Part Five is titled 'Remedies' and the exposition is broken down into the following chapters: declarations, specific performance, injunctions, specific restitution, damages in equity, rescission, account, rectification, delivery up and cancellation of documents, and receivers.[70] This must be taken to be the authors' preferred classification of equitable remedies.

4 Summary

There is a wide-ranging use of the term 'remedy' throughout the text. This is not surprising given that three authors were involved in its preparation. However, it aptly illustrates the instability of the term and the difficulties that arise in the absence of a clear definition.

E Tilbury — Civil Remedies

1 The work

The leading general Australian work on remedies is Tilbury's two-volume treatise *Civil Remedies*. The first volume was published in 1990 and the second in 1993. Volume I *Principles of Civil Remedies* deals with general issues such as the structure of Australian remedial law, the choice of remedies, and general principles of remedial law. The general principles are considered in chapters devoted to compensation, restitution, punishment, coercion, urgent relief, and declarations. Volume II *Remedies in Particular Contexts* applies the general principles in chapters devoted to personal injury, death, injury to reputation, feelings and liberty, injury to property, breach of contract, and injury to economic interests.[71] The works focus on Australian law but make frequent reference to English decisions. They are stated to be primarily intended for practitioners.

2 Scope of the concept of a remedy

Tilbury commences by describing 'the general idea of a remedy' as 'redress, normally for an anticipated or, more usually, an antecedent 'wrong', that is,

[68] Ibid xiii (Preface). But as we have seen above, they also at times refer to some of these as remedies.

[69] Ibid xiii (Preface).

[70] Ibid ix–x (Table of Contents).

[71] Where possible, each of these sections is divided into compensation, restitution, punishment, coercion, and declaration: M. J. Tilbury, *Civil Remedies Vol II Remedies in Particular Contexts* (Sydney: Butterworths, 1993), v–x.

for the infringement or breach of a right which is recognized and protected by law.'[72] This is similar to the broad definition of a remedy identified in the previous chapter. He asserts that:

For the purposes of this book *the law of remedies is that branch of substantive law which deals with the types of redress available in response to the imposition of liability on a party in civil litigation.* These remedies are, principally, damages, compensation in equity, restitution, injunction, specific performance and declaration.[73]

The above definition seems to suggest that remedies are court orders. However, the author also intends to include the law of secondary rights, as defined in Chapter 2,[74] within the law of remedies. He refers to the Austinian distinction between primary and secondary rights and suggests that it approximates to the distinction between rights and remedies.[75] But he adds that rights arising from unjust enrichment are remedial (although primary) and suggests that the law relating to their content or 'the measure of recovery', though not their creation, belongs in the law of remedies.[76]

In the following passage, Tilbury asserts that remedies are rights and describes the kinds of rights that they are:

There is no jurisprudential distinction between 'right' and 'remedy'. A 'remedy' is as much a 'right' as that 'right' which it seeks to protect. The characteristic of a legal right, in Hohfeld's classical analysis, is that there is a correlative duty on some other person(s) to respect that right. Thus, if A has a right to the delivery of goods sold to him by B, the jural correlative is that B is under a duty to deliver those goods. Now, if B fails to deliver, A has a right to damages or to specific performance, and B is then under a duty to pay damages or to perform. Similarly, in tort A may have a right not to be injured in circumstances in which B is under a duty of care to A; should B breach that duty, A has a right to damages, and B has a duty to compensate A. Again, T may be under a duty to administer trust property in accordance with certain standards for the benefit of B; if T breaches that duty, B has a right to compensation, restitution and/or injunctive relief, and T is under a duty to compensate, make restitution or comply with the injunction. It is, therefore, clear that a remedy is of the same nature as a right and that both belong to the substantive law.[77]

Rights and duties of a very different nature are not distinguished in this passage. The third example refers to T's duties, the first two of which are expressed to arise immediately on breach (thus being secondary rights as defined in Chapter 2), but

[72] M. J. Tilbury, *Civil Remedies Vol 1 Principles of Civil Remedies* (North Ryde New South Wales: Butterworths, 1990), [1001]. The author adheres to the broad definition of remedy in his more recent work: 'For the purposes of this Chapter, "remedy" is the legal response to events that constitute a wrong or to events that, while not constituting a wrong, still give rise to legal liability. If we adopted Birksian terminology, we would put this shortly as: a remedy is a legal response to a wrong or a not-wrong': M. Tilbury, 'Remedies and the Classification of Obligations' in A. Robertson (ed.), *Law of Obligations: Connections and Boundaries* (London: Cavendish, 2004), 14–15.

[73] Ibid [1006] (author's emphasis retained). [74] See p 13. [75] Ibid [1003].

[76] Ibid [1004] and [4001]–[4002]. That Tilbury takes primary and secondary not to be mutually exclusive is also illustrated at [6055] 'the interlocutory injunction. . .is, in itself, both a primary and secondary right'. [77] Ibid [1002] (footnotes omitted).

the last of which can only arise out of an order of the court. This is symptomatic of the fact that Tilbury conflates rights existing before court orders and the rights arising from the making of court orders under the label of 'secondary rights'.

The failure to distinguish between these different concepts is reflected in the usage of the term 'remedy' throughout the work. For example, remedy is used in the sense of a secondary right: 'the word "right" does not imply the existence of a remedy (i.e. a secondary right) to enforce that right'.[78] Remedy is also used in the sense of a court order: '[t]he nominate coercive remedies of Australian law are: the injunction, specific performance. . .' and then '[t]he injunction is a coercive order. . .'[79] and 'specific performance is a remedy. . .Specific performance is. . .a decree of the court. . .'.[80] On occasion Tilbury also lapses into the use of remedy in the sense of an action stating, '[t]he nominate coercive remedies of Australian law are:. . .the action for an agreed sum. . .'.[81]

Tilbury also frequently refers to 'damages' as a 'remedy'[82] and yet defines damages as 'the sum of money which is awarded by a court to a successful plaintiff as compensation in the case of certain wrongs.'[83] In those instances the author may be taken to be using remedy in the sense of a final outcome, that is, a physical thing that cures the claimant's grievance.

Tilbury suggests that liquidated damages, rectification and much of rescission relate to primary rights.[84] But he includes liquidated damages in the law of remedies because of its practical relevance to breach of contract.[85] He also treats remedial law as part of the substantive as opposed to procedural law.[86] But he includes a discussion of some matters of procedural law such as Mareva injunctions[87] and Anton Piller orders.[88]

3 Taxonomy of remedies

Tilbury observes that the relief that a claimant can obtain in civil proceedings is of three basic types:

> declaratory relief, where the plaintiff seeks an authoritative judicial statement of the legal relationship(s), if any, between the parties; substitutionary relief, which consists of a

[78] Ibid [8002]. See also [2009] and [6055]: '[A]n injunction seems always a secondary right. . .'. Contrast *Law Debenture Trust Corporation v Ural Caspian Oil Corporation Ltd* [1995] Ch 152, 170 (CA) (quoted in Chapter 4 n 37).

[79] Ibid [6001]–[6002].

[80] Ibid [6003]. See also [1020] and [6004].

[81] Ibid [6001]. See also [2001], [3013], [6026], and [6040]. Tilbury also seems to assert that a remedy can be a cause of action. At [8001] he states '[t]he declaration. . .is a remedy of general application' then at [8002] 'the declaration can itself be a cause of action'.

[82] Ibid [3001]: 'At law, the remedy is "damages" '. See also [3013], [3243].

[83] Ibid [3012].

[84] Ibid [1003].

[85] Ibid Chapter 13.

[86] Ibid [1006].

[87] The Mareva (now freezing) injunction is treated as a means of enforcing remedies and a remedy itself: 'the Mareva injunction is essentially concerned with the enforcement of monetary remedies' [7003] and 'the Mareva is. . .a discretionary remedy' [7029].

[88] Ibid [1008].

judgment in money as a substitute: and specific relief, where the plaintiff seeks by the judgment to coerce the defendant in some particular way.[89]

The author then goes on to observe that:

Substitutionary and specific relief are further classifiable by reference to the plaintiffs remedial objectives. In substitutionary relief; these are compensation, restitution and/or punishment. In specific relief, the species of the genus are identified rather differently. For while the plaintiff's overall objective remains constant, it is practically important to know whether he is seeking relief on a permanent, as opposed to an interim or urgent basis.

Now, if we hereafter refer to 'specific relief' as 'coercion' (which brings out the essential characteristic of such relief), we can then say that the remedial objectives which a plaintiff may seek to achieve in civil litigation are: compensation, restitution, punishment, coercion, interim and urgent relief and declaratory relief. . .These plaintiffs' objectives then become the goals of our remedial law. And it is these remedial goals which, it is submitted, form the core of remedial law and give coherence to remedies as a legal subject.

This classification according to 'remedial goals' is reflected in the table of contents of the first volume of the work. Tilbury's classification may be represented as follows in a tabular form:[90]

Remedial goal	Remedies
Compensation	Damages. Compensatory relief in equity (compensation in equity, equitable damages, specific performance with compensation).
Restitution	Quasi-contractual claims. Rescission. Account of profits. Proprietary claims. Constructive trust.[91]
Punishment	Exemplary damages. Statutory penalties
Coercion	Injunctions. Specific performance. Action for an agreed sum. Specific recovery of chattels and of land. Delivery up and destruction or cancellation of materials or documents.[92]
Interim and urgent relief	Interlocutory injunctions. Interim injunctions. Mareva injunctions. *Ne exeat regno.* Anton Piller orders.
Declaratory relief	Declarations. Nominal damages.

Figure 3.4

[89] Tilbury (n 72 above), [1028].

[90] This table is derived from the table of contents. Ibid v–ix. The format is adopted from Burrows, see text to n 41 above.

[91] Under the heading 'Restitution', Tilbury focuses on claims rather than remedies. Tilbury (n 72 above), Chapter 4. The various types of restitutionary claims are listed at [4010]–[4014].

[92] Ibid [6001].

The second volume, which examines remedies in particular contexts, is ordered according to the nature of the claim and the interests sought to be protected.[93]

4 Summary

Tilbury's classification and the criterion on which it is said to be based are very clearly set out. Both will be further discussed in Chapter 5. However, what forms part of the law of remedies is not set out with clarity. This is then reflected in a fairly inconsistent use of the term remedy. Furthermore, large areas of substantive law are included in the work. The chapter on restitution is noteworthy in this respect.[94] The discussion is conducted in terms of claims and actions, covering much the same ground (namely, the content of restitutionary rights) covered by writers on the substantive law of restitution. As in the work of Burrows, the term 'remedy' hardly features in the discussion of damages, except in the discussion of equitable compensation.[95]

F Walker—The Law of Civil Remedies in Scotland

1 The work

Walker is one of the most prolific writers on Scottish private law. He first published a book on damages in 1955 and has written extensively in the field of private law since. His encyclopaedic dictionary *The Oxford Companion to Law* published over twenty years ago has not been superseded.[96] Walker's work on remedies *The Law of Civil Remedies in Scotland*[97] was published in 1974, just two years after Lawson's *Remedies of English Law*. According to Walker, prior to his work, remedies had not been regarded as a branch of private law in Scotland and had not been dealt with as a group. They had been separately dealt with as part of Scottish texts on substantive law such as contract or delicts and in texts concerned with procedure.[98] Walker introduces his work by stating that:

> In modern times more thorough analysis of legal concepts. . .justifies distinctions between on the one hand the rights and duties attaching to particular relationships and the consequences of their not being implemented, and on the other between the remedies which the legal system may grant, and the procedural forms and machinery whereby those remedies may be sought and, if the court is satisfied, granted. Remedies, in short, can, and should be, studied separately both from the obligations, breaches of which call for remedies, and from the rules of procedure whereby rights and duties are stated and declared, and remedies awarded for infringement of rights and non-implement of duties.[99]

[93] Ibid [1030]. [94] Ibid Chapter 4. [95] Ibid Chapter 3.
[96] D. M. Walker, *The Oxford Companion to Law* (Oxford: Clarendon Press, 1980).
[97] D. M. Walker, *The Law of Civil Remedies in Scotland* (Edinburgh: W. Green & Son, 1974).
[98] Ibid 3. [99] Ibid 4.

2 Scope of the concept of a remedy

Walker points out that whereas 'remedy' is often used in statutes, books, and cases, it is not defined anywhere. It is merely assumed that everyone knows what it means. He observes that 'the essential idea is redress for a grievance. . .the essence of remedy is the idea of redress of wrong or breach of duty'.[100] This is similar to the broad definition of a remedy that was identified in Chapter 2.

Walker defines a remedy more narrowly when distinguishing remedies from procedure. We may take the following to be his definition of a judicial remedy:

> Remedies are those judicial awards which entitle a pursuer or petitioner to some right which, at least to some extent, corrects the results of the misconduct of the defender and renders to the pursuer or petitioner what is deemed justly due to him.[101]

However, he appears to move away from that definition when he writes: '. . . remedies, such as claims to interdict against threatened injury or damages for breach of contract. . .'[102] and '. . .a common law remedy such as a claim of damages. . .'.[103] He also writes: 'do remedies, such as claims for implement of an obligation or for damages for non-implement, fall into the category of substantive law or of procedure (in the broad sense) or of adjective law?'[104] and '. . .remedy, such as a claim for damages. . .'.[105] Thus the author treats remedies not only as orders or awards but also as claims.[106] It is unclear whether he is using 'claim' here in the sense of a substantive right[107] or in the sense of an action.[108]

Walker's discussion of secondary or remedial rights is also unclear and does not serve to clarify his concept of a remedy. He writes that secondary or remedial rights 'confer consequential legal rights, such as to obtain divorce, or damages or such other remedy as may be prescribed by law as competent and appropriate'.[109] This suggests that they are rights to obtain a remedy. But he also writes that civil remedial rights include:

> those remedial rights which can be granted only by a competent civil court on application being made to it according to its jurisdictional and procedural rules and, so far as necessary, after satisfying it by legal argument and evidence of disputed facts. This category comprises judicial declarations of rights, orders prohibiting breaches of duty, compelling performance of duties, ordering payment, compensating for loss caused by breach of duty, and various other cases.[110]

[100] Walker (n 97 above), 10. [101] Ibid 7. [102] Ibid 7. [103] Ibid 13.
[104] Ibid 5. [105] Ibid 24.
[106] But elsewhere he speaks of 'a claim to the remedy': ibid 8.
[107] He states that '[r]emedies are. . .not distinct from rights, but kinds of legal rights': ibid 7.
[108] He clearly uses remedy in the sense of an action when he states 'A person who is creditor. . . has the remedies of action for payment or *ad factum praestandum*. . .': ibid 337.
[109] Ibid 8. [110] Ibid 8.

Here the author equates remedial or secondary rights with judicial awards or rights conferred in judicial awards. But, as quoted above,[111] he had earlier equated some judicial awards with remedies. Putting these quotations side-by-side, it seems that, confusingly, remedial rights are both (1) rights to remedies *and* (2) remedies or rights conferred in remedies.[112]

Walker distinguishes civil remedies from other judicial and non-judicial orders or means of seeking relief, in particular, from penalties imposed by criminal courts, from 'administrative' remedies (which he does not consider to be remedies in the strict sense of the term) such as legal claims or benefits awarded by administrative tribunals or officers and from political remedies such as the petitioning of a politician.[113] Later, he again stresses that insurance claims, claims for social security benefits, and criminal compensation are not claims for civil remedies.[114] The author also distinguishes civil remedies from other pronouncements made by courts in response to applications for 'for assistance, guidance, authority or sanction'.[115] Thus he states that he does not consider the appointments of judicial factors, grants of powers to trustees, decisions on the interpretation of wills, or appointments of executors to be remedies.

3 Taxonomy of remedies

Walker does not discuss the basis for the classification of *remedies* that he chooses to adopt. Nor does he set it out in the body of the text in any detail.[116] The reader is left to discover it from the structure of the book. It will be taken that the table of contents represents the author's taxonomy of remedies. This is in fact expressly presented by Walker as his taxonomy of remedies in a later work.[117]

Walker first discusses 'remedies not requiring resort to a court' which he divides into three sub-categories: self-help, rescission, and rights of retention or lien and of compensation[118] and the right of stoppage in transitu. The next category is 'contractually stipulated remedies' which include irritancy provisions[119]

[111] See text to n 101 above.

[112] McCracken makes the same point: 'There is, however, a fundamental distinction, which Professor Walker did not specifically address, between on the one hand *a right to a remedy* and on the other hand *the remedy itself*': S. McCracken, *The Banker's Remedy of Set-Off* (London: Butterworths, 1998), 139.

[113] Ibid 10.

[114] Ibid 15.

[115] Ibid 18.

[116] He only lists categories of 'remedial rights' and 'actions': ibid 17–18.

[117] D. M. Walker, *Principles of Scottish Law: Volume IV* (4th edn., Oxford: Clarendon Press, 1989) 261 where he states that 'The main classes of remedies recognized are:' and then lists what is essentially the table of contents of his 1974 text with minor changes.

[118] Confusingly for common lawyers, 'compensation' is the equivalent of set-off in the language of civilian systems.

[119] An 'irritancy clause' is a clause permitting the termination of a contract for default.

and 'liquidate' damages and penalty provisions. The remaining categories—apart from the last—seem to primarily deal with judicial remedies. The last category of 'miscellaneous remedies' comprises: appeal to the *Nobile Officium*;[120] application for Lawburrows;[121] rectification of registers; judicial powers to resolve partnership and company disputes; sequestration;[122] ranking and sale; division or division and sale of property, division of commonty;[123] march fences; competing claims; indemnity provisions and relief; remedies ancillary to procedure; exclusion, limitation, and prescription of claims for remedies.

Judicial remedies appear to be implicitly divided into the following categories: judicial declaration of rights consisting of declarator and reduction;[124] prevention of infringement of rights consisting of suspension and interdict;[125] possessory remedies for securing rights of possession; enforcing performance of duties; substitutional redress—damages; consistoral remedies;[126] admiralty remedies and statutory remedies.

'Enforcing performance of duties' is a major category which consists of various sub-categories including decrees *ad factum praestandum*;[127] claims for restitution, payment of debt, action of constitution;[128] count, reckoning and payment;[129] petition for sequestration or liquidation, landlord's sequestration for rent, poinding of the ground;[130] maills and duties;[131] remedies of secured creditors[132] and claims for interest. 'Substitutional redress—damages' is the other major category of remedies. It includes damages for breach of contract, for delict, for breach of the obligation of restitution, for breach of trust, and for damages for breach of statutory duty.

[120] This is an equitable jurisdiction to grant a remedy where there is none.

[121] This is a process whereby a person who fears bodily harm may have the court order the person causing the threat to provide security.

[122] This is the removal of property from the possession of litigants pending trial.

[123] This process allows tenants in common to obtain a division of the property.

[124] 'Declarator' is the equivalent of a declaration of a right. 'Reduction' is the equivalent of a declaration of the non-existence of a right under a deed or document—it is judicial annulment.

[125] 'Suspension' is the equivalent of an order stopping proceedings, particularly the execution of judgments. 'Interdict' is the equivalent of an injunction.

[126] 'Consistoral remedies' include declarators of marriage, nullity, legitimacy, and bastardy, and decrees of separation, adherence, divorce, and putting to silence.

[127] A 'decree *ad factum praestandum*' is the equivalent of an order for specific performance of an obligation to do an act other than to pay money.

[128] An 'action of constitution' is an action for a declaration that a debt is still owing. It may be brought by a creditor against the personal representatives of a deceased estate.

[129] 'Count, reckoning and payment' is the equivalent of an account.

[130] 'Poinding of the ground' is a declaratory real action available in special circumstances which creates a right over moveables present on the land.

[131] The action of 'maills and duties' is a special action to recover rent from tenants available in special circumstances.

[132] This should have been placed under the heading 'remedies not requiring resort to a court' because it covers a secured creditor's powers of sale and to appoint a receiver.

Thus Walker's scheme for classifying judicial remedies may be represented as follows:

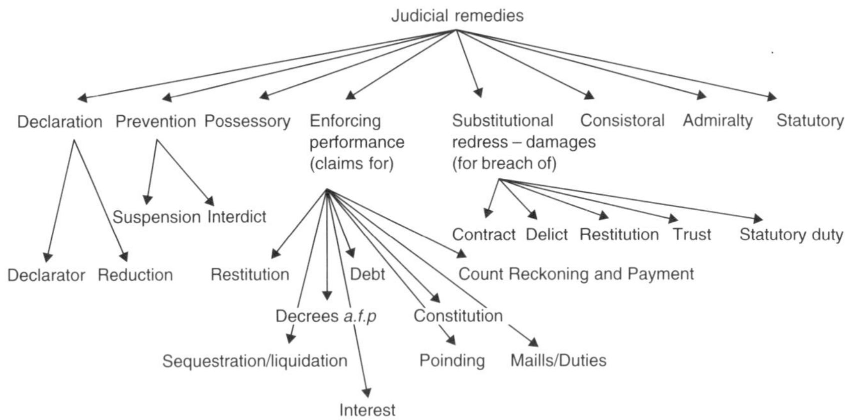

Figure 3.5

4 Summary

Walker's definitions of and use of the term 'remedy' are difficult to pin down. His conceptual discussion of remedies and remedial rights is not clear and at times appears to be inconsistent. As pointed out above, there is no discussion of the basis on which remedies are classified.

Despite the author's caveat at the beginning of the work that remedies are separate from civil procedure and substantive obligations, much of what the book contains concerns actions and primary and secondary rights rather than remedies. For example, Chapter 14 which is titled 'Claims for Restitution' hardly touches on remedies at all. It is concerned with 'claims' and discusses the causative events (that is, the facts) from which substantive rights to restitution arise.

G Conclusion

All the writers whose work was discussed in this chapter treat remedies as a separate subject worthy of independent study. However, some do not define, or do not define with precision, what they consider 'remedies'—the subject matter of their work—to be. Some authors, after giving a definition, are not rigorous in their respect for their definition, for at times they appear to move away from it. The principal instabilities involve: (1) wandering from remedies in the sense of orders to remedies in the sense of substantive rights and (2) not keeping at bay the use of remedy as 'cause of action'. Consequently, the reader can never be sure what is the particular province of the law of remedies as perceived by the writer.

All authors adopt some kind of taxonomy of remedies, it would be impossible to structure a book on remedies without one. However, not all discuss the taxonomy and the criterion or criteria on which it is based.

4

Stable Core Meaning of 'Remedy'

A Introduction

With the instability of 'remedy' demonstrated, this chapter identifies and explains the stable core concept of a remedy. As Dobbs states, 'the field of remedies needs suitable boundaries.'[1] These boundaries are demarcated in the first section by making a commitment to use the term 'remedy' only in the sense of the rights arising from certain court orders or pronouncements. The only relaxation which will be permitted is that the court order itself may be referred to as the remedy so long as this is understood as nothing more than a convenient shorthand for the rights born of such a judicial command or statement.

The broad functional definition of a legal remedy is then rejected. Of course, anything that makes a bad situation better can be called a remedy. But this colloquial usage simply cannot form the basis of a discrete area of law. It is a meaning which cannot be defended as setting the boundaries of the subject. Next, the various narrower meanings of the term which were identified in Chapter 2 are examined and reasons for not adopting them as the core meaning are set out. The matter which is removed from the law of remedies in this way is not lost, for the truth is that it is covered elsewhere and its treatment under the name of 'remedy' merely creates confusion. Finally, aspects of the relationship between substantive rights and remedies are discussed in light of the stable meaning.

The reader must not forget that that the aim of the definitional exercise which this chapter engages in is not and cannot be to capture every usage of 'remedy' in a legal context as one would if one were writing a legal dictionary. It is to find the stable concept which the term should denote if it is to have a precise technical legal meaning on the basis of which a separate legal subject can be constructed.

[1] D. Dobbs, *Law of Remedies Damages-Equity-Restitution Practitioner Treatise Series Vol 1* (2nd edn., St Paul Minnesota: West Publishing Co, 1993), 24.

B Stable Core Meaning of Remedy

1 Core usage of remedy

As was seen in Chapters 2 and 3, remedy is commonly used in the sense of a judgment or order of the court.[2] It is used in this sense, though not necessarily consistently, by all the writers on remedies whose work we examined in the previous chapter: Lawson, Burrows, Meagher, Gummow and Lehane, Tilbury, and Walker. Furthermore, when many scholars set out an advised definition of a remedy, they define it in just this way. As we have seen, Burrows has taken this position writing that 'A judicial remedy may be either coercive or non-coercive, that is, it may be either a court order to do or not to do something, backed up by enforcement procedures, or a court pronouncement indicating or altering what the parties' rights or duties are or were.'[3] Jacob stated in his Hamlyn lecture that '[Remedies] take the form of a judgment or order of the court under which the legal rights and interests of the parties relating to the particular matters in controversy are thenceforth determined and regulated.'[4] In a similar vein, Andrews defines a remedy as '(a) any final or interlocutory order of the court which entitles the successful party to further recourse (such as damages, debt, specific performance or injunctions); or (b) a procedure or judicial order which disposes of the action without trial'.[5]

These definitions identify the core usage of the term 'remedy' in a legal context. As a starting point for further analysis, a remedy will be taken to be a court order. For convenience and unless the context otherwise dictates, the term 'order' will be used generically to include judgments, decrees, orders, and pronouncements.[6] The assertion that 'remedy' refers to an order requires a slight, but immediate, qualification. Although every 'remedy' can be taken to be a court order, not every court order ought to be taken to be a remedy. To remain within conventional usage as far as possible and to avoid straying into the law of civil procedure, only orders which a party obtains to redress a grievance existing before an action is

[2] Chapter 2 p 17.

[3] A. Burrows, *Remedies for Torts and Breach of Contract* (2nd edn., London: Butterworths, 1994), 1 (footnotes omitted).

[4] J. Jacob, *Fabric of English Civil Justice* (London: Stevens, 1987), 169–70.

[5] N. Andrews, *Principles of Civil Procedure* (London: Sweet & Maxwell, 1994), 456 (footnote omitted). Andrews includes declarations within (a) noting that they can be supported by further proceedings. See Chapter 9 p 164.

[6] A judgment is usually used to mean a final as opposed to an interlocutory order, a decree to mean a judgment given by a court of equity, and a pronouncement to mean a non-enforceable judicial statement of parties' rights. The term 'judgment' is not used as the generic term because: (1) it is closely connected with the common law jurisdiction; (2) it is widely used to refer to 'reasons for judgment'; (3) the court forms approved in the CPR state 'It is ordered that' rather than 'It is adjudged that'. See, for example, Form No 45 'Judgment after trial before judge without jury' listed in CPR Part 4 PD Table 2.

brought (a 'pre-suit' grievance) and which are available at trial,[7] together with their pre-trial equivalents,[8] will be equated with remedies. This includes orders such as decrees of specific performance, injunctions, judgments requiring the payment of money (such as awards of damages or restitutionary awards), and pronouncements such as declarations. Such orders are intended to finally (or, in the case of interim remedies, temporarily pending a full trial) settle a dispute between the parties arising out of a pre-suit grievance, usually—but not always—an actual or threatened infringement of a substantive right.

This qualification excludes orders which merely assist in the preparation for a trial such as disclosure, interrogatories, and search (Anton Piller) orders. It also excludes orders which merely assist in the present or future enforcement of another order such as attachment of earnings orders, garnishee orders, charging orders, freezing (Mareva) orders,[9] and contempt orders. Orders which merely assist in preparation for a trial are excluded as they do not address a pre-suit grievance. That is, they themselves are not intended to remove the grievance which brought the claimant to court in the first place. Orders which relate to the future or present enforcement of another order are excluded because they can be said to respond to and cure a very specific grievance, namely, actual or apprehended non-compliance with a court order. All of these orders are of an ancillary nature. Even in traditional treatments of the subject they are usually excluded in an attempt to prevent overlap with the law of civil procedure.

2 The nature of a court order or pronouncement

Given that the core usage of 'remedy' identified above involves a reference to a court order or pronouncement, the nature of court orders and pronouncements needs to be examined. A court order is often used to refer to a command directed to one of the parties. A pronouncement is used to refer to an authoritative statement that is not a command, in other words, a declaratory statement.[10]

[7] The idea of pre-trial, available at trial and post-trial orders is derived from the classification of remedies in A Burrows 'Judicial Remedies' in P. B. H. Birks (ed.), *English Private Law Vol II* (Oxford: Oxford University Press, 2000), 814–15.

[8] Some, but not all, interim orders function by giving direct effect to what are perceived at a preliminary hearing to be the substantive rights of claimants. This is akin to final remedies which give direct effect to (replicate) what are found at trial to be the substantive rights of claimants. Interim orders of this nature ought to fall within the law of remedies because they purport to give effect to substantive rights, albeit for a limited period of time, rather than to adjectival or procedural rights. See also Burrows (n 3 above) 423, 445 and *ABC v Lenah Game Meats Pty Ltd* (2001) 185 ALR 1 (HCA). Thus some interim injunctions, awards of damages, orders for delivery up and declarations are taken to be remedies in this work. See CPR Rule 25.1 for a list of possible interim remedies.

[9] The High Court of Australia has held that the phrase 'Mareva orders' (per Gaudron, McHugh, Gummow, and Callinan JJ) or 'asset preservation order' ought to be used in preference to 'Mareva' injunctions: *Cardile v LED Builders Pty Limited* (1999) 198 CLR 380 (HCA) 393, 401, and 411.

[10] Just as 'order' will be used generically in later chapters to include pronouncements so 'command' will be used generically, for convenience, to include such declaratory statements.

The giving of a command or the making of a statement is an event that happens in the world. This event usually takes the form of an utterance of a judge which is later reproduced in an official document.[11] This document is also called a court order or a judgment. The event—the making of the command or statement—generates rights, usually with immediate effect.[12] Thus Corbin states:

> The judgment or decree of the court is a new and additional operative fact. It is sufficient of itself to create a right and duty. Generally it serves to liquidate and make certain that which before was unliquidated and uncertain.[13] Sometimes the performance required by the judgment is different from that required by either the primary or the secondary duty.[14] Even if not, it has a legal operation in other respects different from that of the pre-existing facts.[15]

We use 'court order' to refer to (1) the event, (2) the command or statement, (3) the order document, and (4) the rights that are generated. But in many instances when we use the phrase 'court order', we mean only the latter. For example, we refer to a jural relationship when we speak of a court order being granted, breached, enforced, in force, suspended, or discharged. In these instances, we cannot sensibly be referring to an event or a mere set of words, whether uttered or written in a document. We must be referring to a jural relationship involving a right in the claimant and, usually though not necessarily, a correlative duty on the defendant. It is this right which may be granted and this duty which may be breached, enforced, or discharged. Therefore a court order is not necessarily the words that the judge utters or the official document, just as a contract is not a piece of paper and property is not a physical object.[16] Like contract and property, court order can refer to a jural relationship.

Thus defining remedies as certain court orders is equivalent to saying that remedies are certain jural relationships. Like contract and property, a remedy is best characterized as a jural relationship.[17] Remedies are the rights that arise from a particular class of events, namely, the making of certain judicial

[11] Sometimes, as with judgments by default, there may be no judicial utterance but merely the issue of a document: CPR Part 12.

[12] CPR Rule 40.7(1) 'A judgment or order takes effect from the day when it is given or made, or such later date as the court may specify.'

[13] 'Liquidation' of substantive rights is discussed Chapter 5 p 79.

[14] These types of remedies, to be labelled 'transformative', are discussed in Chapter 13.

[15] A. Corbin, 'Rights and Duties' (1922–24) *Yale LJ* 501, 516–17. The same point was made by Austin and Hohfeld: J. Austin, *Lectures on Jurisprudence Vol I* (R. Campbell (ed.) (5th edn., London: John Murray, 1885), 64–5; W. N. Hohfeld, 'The Relations between Equity and Law' (1913) 11 *Michigan L Rev* 537, 551.

[16] Failure to draw these distinctions blurs legal and non-legal conceptions. Hohfeld showed that legal discussions are confused through the failure to differentiate legal relations from the mental and physical facts that give rise to or are connected with them: W. N. Hohfeld, 'Some Fundamental Legal Conceptions as Applied in Judicial Reasoning' (1913) 23 *Yale LJ* 16, 20–5.

[17] 'Remedies are. . .not distinct from rights, but kinds of legal rights': D. M. Walker, *The Law of Civil Remedies in Scotland* (Edinburgh: W. Green & Son, 1974), 7.

commands or statements. To avoid confusion, we must be conscious that these events from which remedies arise can themselves be called 'court orders' though in a different sense. It is this non-jural sense of 'court order' as a command that is intended when remedies are sometimes said to be rights *arising from* 'court orders'.

In short, remedies are rights, powers, liberties, or immunities. As Robert Walker LJ stated in *Oliver Ashworth Ltd v Ballard Ltd*, 'every remedy is in one sense a right, even if its grant is discretionary, but not every right is a remedy.'[18] These rights may entitle the claimant to have the defendant act or refrain from acting, usually under the direct threat of state force, in the way set out in the order document.

We call these particular rights 'remedies' as there is no other distinct name for such rights in our jurisprudence. By calling them remedies, we can distinguish them from substantive rights. The term 'tertiary' rights has been used[19] but it is submitted that it is inappropriate as sometimes primary rights are given direct effect.[20] In such a case, the label 'tertiary' would cause confusion as one would proceed directly from primary rights to 'tertiary' rights with no secondary rights necessarily having arisen.

3 A note on self-help 'remedies'

So far the discussion has focused on judicial remedies but it is apposite to briefly discuss the notion of self-help 'remedies' at this point. Like judicial remedies, self-help 'remedies' should also be characterized as jural relationships. What is usually referred to as a self-help remedy is a privilege or immunity which permits the aggrieved person to act in a particular way.[21] A self-help 'remedy' enables the claimant to realize his or her rights through his or her own acts.[22] A self-help 'remedy' simply negates the duties and liabilities that would otherwise exist. Examples include the privilege of self-help in tort which, for example, entitles the possessor of land to eject a trespasser or an owner to recapture his or her stolen goods, or the 'right', or more accurately immunity, of set-off. It should be noted that self-help 'remedies' are also closely aligned with the powers for enforcing judicial remedies in that their exercise realizes rights in the same manner as the actions of sheriffs and bailiffs realize judicial remedies.[23]

Self-help 'remedies' and judicial remedies as defined above are only loosely related. They are only related through the broad functional definition of a

[18] [2000] Ch 12, 28 (CA).

[19] P. B. H. Birks and A. Pretto, 'Introduction' in P. B. H. Birks and A. Pretto (eds), *Breach of Trust* (Oxford: Hart, 2002), xi.

[20] See Chapters 7 to 9.

[21] A privilege is an absence of a duty, an immunity is an absence of a liability: Hohfeld (n 16 above), 32 and 55.

[22] As opposed to a judicial remedy which is often a right of the claimant to have the defendant act, under the direct threat of state force, in a particular way.

[23] For a discussion of the enforcement of remedies see, in particular, Chapters 7 and 8.

remedy as both are means provided by the law for the redress of a grievance. In fact, self-help 'remedies' are substantive rights in that they arise independently of a trial. They are often secondary (or remedial) rights as they often arise from breaches of primary duties. For consistency, they will not be referred to as remedies in this work.[24] It is preferable to label them 'rights of self-help'. For example, in *Cargill v Gotts*, Lord Templeman speaks of the exercise of a 'right of self-help'.[25] Similarly, Tettenborn writes: 'Examples [of self-help] include the right to peaceably retake one's own property, and the right to self-defence'.[26] An examination of self-help falls well outside the scope of this book. It is an altogether different field of study. As Tilbury notes: 'the general issue of the extent to which the law does, and ought to, permit recourse to self-help raises questions which obviously have little in common with the principles and policies applicable to judicial remedies.'[27] Despite trying to force the two together, writers on remedies usually end up marginalizing rights of self-help, or ignoring them altogether without any satisfactory explanation. In this book there is no mystery in their exclusion. They are not 'remedies' as that word should be understood.

C Rejection of Various Definitions

1 Broad definition of remedy not adequate

A broad functional definition of 'remedy' was identified in Chapter 2,[28] namely that a remedy was some means provided by the law for redressing a grievance. Although such a broad definition cannot be faulted on the basis that it does not cover a particular usage of the term, it is an unsatisfactory basis for a disciplined study of remedies. A definition that covers almost all cases is part of the problem that this work is attempting to address and not a solution to it. Such breadth is a source of ambiguity.

The word 'right' suffers the same problem as the word 'remedy'. Hohfeld showed that '[t]he word "right" is used generically and indiscriminately to denote any sort of legal advantage, whether claim, privilege, power or immunity.'[29]

[24] The broad functional definition which links self-help 'remedies' and judicial remedies is rejected in the next section.

[25] (1981) 1 WLR 441, 450 (CA). However, some authors use this phrase interchangeably with 'remedies of self-help'. There is similar instability in relation to particular modes of self-help, for example, 'right of set-off' and 'remedy of set-off' are frequently used interchangeably. This causes unnecessary confusion.

[26] A. Tettenborn, *An Introduction to the Law of Obligations* (London: Butterworths, 1984), 211.

[27] M. Tilbury, *Civil Remedies Vol 1 Principles of Civil Remedies* (North Ryde New South Wales: Butterworths, 1990), [1007]. See also J. Carter and M. Tilbury, 'Remedial Choice and Contract Drafting' (1998) *Journal of Contract Law* 5, 8–9.

[28] See p 9.

[29] W. N. Hohfeld, 'Fundamental Legal Conceptions as Applied in Judicial Reasoning' (1916–17) 26 *Yale LJ* 710, 717.

Hohfeld's insightful solution to the problem, even if not universally accepted in all respects,[30] has been invaluable in helping to clear up thinking and communication. It would be unsatisfactory to stop after identifying a right to be a legal advantage, for one would then fail to see that rights can be claims, liberties, powers, or immunities. In the same way, it is also unsatisfactory to stop after identifying a remedy to be some means provided by the law for redressing a grievance.

As we have seen, the term 'remedy' is used indiscriminately to denote any means provided by the law for redressing a grievance, whether an action or a right of action, a substantive right arising from a wrong or another event, an order or pronouncement of the court, a means of enforcing an order, or a final outcome. All of these concepts satisfy the broad definition. This is problematic. As Hohfeld wrote:

> Anyone who has seriously observed and reflected on the interrelation of ideas and language must realize how words tend to react upon ideas and to hinder or control them. More specifically, it is overwhelmingly clear that the danger of confusion is especially great when the same term or phrase is constantly used to express two or more distinct ideas.[31]

With 'remedy' we have a term that is unhappily being used to express more than six related but distinct ideas. This is a serious problem if the law of remedies is to be a coherent subject with clear boundaries. A subject based on the broad functional definition of a remedy can be no more than a miscellany of disparate topics, some of which overlap with other areas of law.

2 Rejected narrow meanings of 'remedy'

The rejected narrow meanings of remedy will now be briefly discussed. It would be unreasonable to restrict the term 'remedy' exclusively to any of these meanings as they are relatively infrequent as compared to the core meaning identified above.[32] Using them alongside the core meaning involves a serious blurring of the line between various concepts and often demonstrates insensitivity as to the existence of such a line.

[30] Hohfeld's deconstruction of rights *in rem* into 'multital' relations is particularly out of favour at the moment. See J. W. Harris, *Property and Justice* (Oxford: Clarendon Press, 1996), 120–5; J. E. Penner, *The Idea of Property* (Oxford: Oxford University Press, 1997), 23–5; P. B. H. Birks, 'Definition and Division: A Meditation on *Institutes* 3.13' in P. B. H. Birks (ed.), *The Classification of Obligations* (Oxford: Oxford University Press, 1997) 1, 9–10.

[31] W. N. Hohfeld, 'Fundamental Legal Conception as Applied in Judicial Reasoning' (1916–17) 26 *Yale LJ* 710, 715.

[32] All writers on remedies surveyed in Chapter 3 used remedy in the sense of a court order at some time, particularly in relation to injunctions, decrees of specific performance, and declarations.

(a) *An action or cause of action ought not to be called a remedy*

The term 'remedy' should not be used as a synonym for 'action' or 'cause of action'.[33] There are words in legal discourse which clearly and precisely convey this meaning. It is preferable to use 'action' or 'suit' when referring to the court process or 'cause of action' when referring to the set of facts that empower the court to grant relief.[34] This usage is a hangover from the time when forms of action were thought to be remedies in themselves.[35] It is a relatively uncommon usage. Works on remedies, such as those surveyed in Chapter 3, are not concerned with actions or causes of action.[36] Modern works on civil procedure deal with the former and works on substantive law deal with the latter.

(b) *A secondary right ought not to be called a remedy*

There are a number of reasons why secondary rights should not be called remedies. First, the term 'remedy' is very often attached to concepts that simply cannot be said to be secondary rights. For example, injunctions and decrees of specific performance are always called 'remedies'. Every discussion of remedies includes references to them. Every lawyer would enumerate them if asked to give examples of remedies. However, they are very different to secondary rights.[37] Secondary rights are rights that arise from wrongs prior to a court order being made.[38] Injunctions and decrees of specific performance are court orders. If we rigorously restricted the term 'remedy' to secondary rights, we would have to conclude that orders such as injunctions and decrees of specific performance are not remedies.

The difference between secondary rights to damages existing prior to a court order and rights to damages arising out of such a judicial command is sometimes overlooked as both are indiscriminately called 'damages' in practice. The distinction between the two is very fine because the courts give effect to secondary rights by restating them in the court order. But there is also a subtle difference apart from their origin. The former are unliquidated but the latter are usually liquidated.[39] This means that secondary rights to damages are usually rights

[33] Chapter 2 p 11.

[34] 'A cause of action is simply a factual situation the existence of which entitles one person to obtain from the court a remedy against another person': *Letang v Cooper* [1965] 1 QB 232, 242–3 (CA) (Lord Diplock). Compare Chapter 2 p 12.

[35] Chapter 2 p 11.

[36] Dobbs expressly rejects this meaning: Dobbs (n 1 above), 27.

[37] As Beldam LJ stated in *Law Debenture Trust Corporation v Ural Caspian Oil Corporation Ltd* [1995] Ch 152, 170 (CA): 'Injunctions compelling the performance of positive obligations have much in common with specific performance, excluded from Lord Diplock's analysis. So have mandatory restorative injunctions which compel the undoing of a wrong. They are remedies which a plaintiff may seek from the court, either to compel performance of a primary obligation or to restrain the defendant from actions inconsistent with the primary obligations under the contract. In my view they are not themselves secondary rights arising by implication from the terms of the agreement.'

[38] Chapter 2 p 14.

[39] As noted previously, 'liquidation' is discussed Chapter 5 p 79.

to compensation, restitution, or punishment in the abstract with the actual amount due being unassessed[40] but rights to damages recast in a court order are usually assessed at a sum certain.[41] The former are substantive rights, not remedies as defined in this chapter. Only the latter ought to be called remedies.

Secondly, secondary rights should not be called remedies because not every infringement of a right generates secondary rights. Tilbury, Noone and Kercher recognize this difficulty stating that 'a definition of remedies simply in terms of secondary rights is, strictly, incomplete'.[42] Courts sometimes directly give effect to primary rights in court orders. For example, courts directly effectuate primary rights to restitution arising from unjust enrichment or primary rights arising from contract by replicating them in the court order.[43] If a rigorous commitment were made to restrict the term 'remedy' to secondary rights, the term 'remedy' would be simply inapplicable in those situations.

Thirdly, some of the features that we ascribe to remedies would become nonsensical. For instance, it does not make sense to speak of 'discretionary' remedies if remedy is a synonym for a secondary right. A discretionary secondary right is a contradiction in terms. If a wrongdoer's duty to pay compensation for a wrong were dependent on the court's discretion then it could not be said that there was a secondary 'right' to such compensation before an order were made. Any right to it would only exist once a court had exercised its discretion in favour of a claimant and it would arise out of the judicial command. It could not be a substantive right, that is, a right that exists prior to a court order.

Fourthly, if remedies were equated with secondary rights, existing patterns of understanding would be destroyed. In particular, the category of tort or, more widely, the category of civil wrongs, would be eviscerated. Unless duplication were accepted and with it the dangers of wasted effort and inconsistent rules,[44] the law of civil wrongs would have to exclude important issues such as remoteness or measures of recovery which would only belong in the law of remedies. More alarmingly, it would no longer be possible to subscribe to the proposition that obligations arise from contract, wrongs, unjust enrichment, and other events. The legal relations we currently classify as obligations arising from wrongs correlate with secondary rights. If those secondary rights were equated with remedies, and if duplication between the law of obligations and the law of remedies were not tolerated, only remedies could be said to arise from wrongs.[45] This would be

[40] These secondary rights are further discussed in Chapter 10.

[41] But this is not always the case. Sometimes a court makes an order for damages to be assessed, in which case it restates the claimant's unliquidated secondary right to damages. Then if the parties cannot agree on precise sum, the right is liquidated at a second hearing. See Chapter 10, text to n 11.

[42] M. Tilbury, M. Noone and B. Kercher *Remedies: Commentary and Materials* (3rd edn., Sydney: LBC 2000), 4.

[43] Chapters 7 and 8.

[44] P. B. H. Birks, 'The Law of Restitution at the End of an Epoch' (1999) 28 *U Western Australia L Rev* 1, 9.

[45] P. B. H. Birks, 'Rights, Wrongs and Remedies' (2000) 20 *OJLS* 1, 21.

confusing and unnecessarily damaging to this rational, longstanding, and useful taxonomy of obligations.[46]

(c) A primary right ought not to be called a remedy

As has been seen, primary rights are sometimes referred to and treated as remedies.[47] For example, the primary right to restitution arising from a mistaken payment or other similar unjust enrichment at the expense of the claimant is often discussed in books and courses on remedies.[48] This is due to the fact that the existence of rights such as this helps to remove a grievance that the right-holder has. Thus the right-holder has a remedy in the broad sense of the term. The medical metaphor comes into play. It is undesirable that primary rights be called remedies because few primary rights are capable of being called remedies in this way. For example, most contractual rights or the rights correlating with duties of care in tort cannot as they do not respond to a grievance. This usage is relatively infrequent outside the context of the law of restitution. It can be avoided without much difficulty.

(d) Means of enforcement of a court order ought not to be called a remedy

Although 'remedy' is sometimes used to refer to a means of enforcement,[49] this is an uncommon usage in leading texts on remedies as we saw in Chapter 3. Powers of execution are distinct from remedies because they arise from non-compliance with remedies. Some writers are sensitive to this and prefer to call such means of enforcement 'procedures',[50] 'devices',[51] 'modes', or 'measures'.[52] Furthermore, most writers on remedies expressly exclude enforcement from their compass.[53] But enforcement is not unimportant to the law of remedies. As will be seen when we examine particular remedies in Chapters 7 to 13, the means of enforcement is a very important characteristic of each remedy. It is a feature with which one must be familiar in order to have an adequate knowledge of a particular remedy.

[46] Although that is not to say that this taxonomy has not attracted criticism: D. Wright, 'Wrong and Remedy: A Sticky Relationship' [2001] *Singapore J of Legal Studies* 300, 305, and 306; S. M. Waddams, *Dimensions of Private Law* (Cambridge: Cambridge University Press, 2003) and G. Samuel, 'English Private Law: Old and New Thinking in the Taxonomy Debate' (2004) 24 *OJLS* 335.

[47] Chapter 2 p 16.

[48] Thus, for example Dobbs discusses the substantive rights to restitution (how they are generated and their content) in extensive detail in his work on remedies: Dobbs (n 1 above), Chapter 4 at 550–705 and parts of Chapter 5.

[49] Chapter 2 p 18.

[50] Andrews (n 5 above), 514–21.

[51] Dobbs (n 1 above), 17–20.

[52] J. Jacob, 'General Report' in J. Jacob and U. Jacobsson (eds), *Trends in the Enforcement of Non-money Judgments and Orders* (Deventer: Kluwer, 1988), 16 ('modes') and 20 ('measures').

[53] There are some exceptions such as B. Kercher and M. Noone, *Remedies* (2nd edn., Sydney: Law Book Co, 1990), 2, 5, 39–71, 229–32 who expressly treated means of enforcement as remedies, and Dobbs (n 1 above), 14–20, 186–219 who does not conflate remedies with means of enforcement but does discuss both.

(e) Final outcome ought not to be called a remedy

This is also a usage that is rarely encountered today. Although Pomeroy's definition of a remedy as the payment of money or other actual outcome of litigation[54] was insightful in that it distinguished secondary or, as he preferred to call them, remedial rights from the end products of litigation, his definition of remedy does not accord with modern usage and is best avoided.

If we treat 'remedy' as a legal conception, then calling acts or things 'remedies' involves an unnecessary and undesirable blurring of legal and non-legal conceptions. Hohfeld showed that legal discussions may become confused through the failure to differentiate legal relations from physical facts that are connected with those legal relations.[55] As already stated, an example of this problem is the use of the term 'property' to sometimes refer to a physical object and sometimes to the rights over that object.

D Relationship Between Substantive Rights and Remedies

It is now appropriate to take a closer look at the relationship that substantive rights bear to remedies and vice versa.

1 Line between substance and remedy

The line between substance and remedy could be drawn in various places. For example, any rights that arise following a breach of duty could be, and have been, considered to fall within the realm of remedies as in figure 4.1. However, it is a keystone of this work that secondary rights belong to the substantive law; that a more principled place to draw the line is as depicted in figure 4.2.

Primary rights	Secondary rights	Court orders
Substance	Remedy	

Figure 4.1

Primary rights	Secondary rights	Court orders
Substance		Remedy

Figure 4.2

It is axiomatic, given the definitions that have been adopted above, that substantive rights should not be referred to as remedies. Furthermore, rights arising from wrongs, such as the right to the payment of damages that arises when a contractual duty is breached, must be classed as substantive rights.

[54] Chapter 2, p 21. [55] See n 16 above.

2 Fitting substantive rights, remedies, and enforcement together

Birks divides the process of realising rights through litigation into three separate steps or phases.[56] The first phase is a claim which is 'the assertion of a right capable of being entertained and realised by a court'.[57] The second phase is the order that the court makes to realize[58] the right. The third phase is the enforcement of that order. As we have already seen and Birks points out, 'These three phases taken together can be called the remedy, and each separate phase can equally be referred to as a remedy.'[59] We have made the commitment to restrict the term 'remedy' to the rights arising at the second stage. When we ask how remedies in this sense fit with primary and secondary rights and powers of enforcement, we find that this work has already been done by Kocourek and by Hohfeld before him.

Though seemingly complicated, Kocourek's analysis illuminates the place of remedies in private law litigation:

> It is interesting to observe the complicated series of steps which follow a breach of a legally frangible[60] relation to the last stage of economic repose. The reactions of nature are immediate and concrete. In the legal field, except in the sphere of self-help, reactions are either not immediate or not concrete. If, for example, there is a breach of duty to perform a promise, the first reaction often is, a new legal relation involving a duty to repair the consequences of the first breach. This new relation is infrangible and, if not evolved[61] by performance, may be specifically enforced by an action. When the power to sue is exercised and carried to judgment, an officially formulated repetitive duty is substituted for the second duty. Upon failure to perform this latter duty in the form of a judgment, economic satisfaction, if possible, can be attained only by the application of a new sanction, the power of execution by a levy or attachment, leading in the normal case to a sale of property and a new duty in the executive officer to pay over the proceeds.[62]

Kocourek's terminology is difficult but the ideas are sound. It is helpful to restate the points made in his example in more familiar terms. When a duty to perform a promise is breached, it sometimes ceases to exist; take a non-specifically enforceable promise to provide personal services on a given date as an example. If the duty to provide services on that date is not performed, it is replaced with a secondary duty to pay compensation. As long as this secondary duty is not

[56] Jacob drew the same three-fold division: Jacob (n 52 above), 14.

[57] P. B. H. Birks, 'Personal Property: Proprietary Rights and Remedies' [2000] 11 *KCLJ* 1, 3.

[58] This work uses the term 'effectuate' in this context. Court orders are taken to give effect to or 'effectuate' rights. Enforced or voluntary performance is taken to 'realize' rights, that is, to convert norms into facts.

[59] Birks (n 57 above), 3.

[60] Kocourek attempted to introduce a number of new terms. They have not found favour with other writers and consequently reduce the readability of his work. By 'frangible' Kocourek meant a legal relation which may be violated—presumably one that ceases to exist on breach. An 'infrangible' relation on the other hand is meant to be one which cannot be violated in this way.

[61] By 'evolved' Kocourek meant extinguished by performance, fulfilled.

[62] A. Kocourek, *Jural Relations* (2nd edn., Indianapolis: Bobbs-Merrill, 1928), 348.

performed, the claimant may bring an action to compel its performance. If the action is successful, the court's command will give rise to a new duty to pay compensation (the remedy) that restates and thus authoritatively confirms the prior secondary duty. If this new duty is breached, the claimant's power of execution may be exercised to place the court's officer under a duty to sell the defendant's property and pay the proceeds to the claimant.

Such a restatement of a substantive right in an order will be called 'replication'.[63] Where the claimant's substantive right correlates with a duty on the defendant, a remedy may 'replicate' the right by restating the defendant's duty. For example, where D is under a duty to pay C £50, the court order may state 'It is ordered that the defendant pay the claimant the sum of £50'. This would be a replicative remedy.

It should be noted that the rights involved at each phase of the litigation process may be personal or proprietary. Hohfeld demonstrates this well with the following example:

> Suppose, once again, that A is owner of Blackacre, and that B drives his automobile over A's lawn and shrubbery. A's primary right *in rem* is thereby violated, and a secondary right *in personam* arises in favour of A and against B,—an "*obligatio*" to use the term of Mr Justice Holmes. A may sue B at law for damages and get as a result of the "primary stage" of the proceeding, an ordinary legal judgment *in personam* for (say) $500. Such judgment would "merge" or extinguish A's secondary right *in personam* together with B's secondary duty, and would create a (new) judgment obligation-right *in personam* and a correlative duty—for the payment of $500. Such judgment would be binding even though the judgment debtor, B, had no assets whatever. . .If. . .B has property either at the time judgment is rendered or at some later time, a "secondary stage" of the proceedings, beginning with the writ of execution, may be had. That is the sheriff, under such writ, has the power and the duty of selling sufficient property of B and applying the proceeds to the satisfaction of the judgment.[64]

He further points out that 'enforcement is said to be either *in personam*, as in the case of the typical contempt proceeding employed to coerce performance of a decree in equity, or *in rem*, as in the case of the typical execution sale following upon an ordinary legal judgment *in personam*.'[65]

Hohfeld's example shows that rights at various points of the litigation process may be either personal or proprietary. A violation of a proprietary right may give rise to a personal secondary right, as with a right to damages for conversion, or a

[63] Barker uses this term in the context of an order which gives direct effect to a right to the return of a mistaken payment, '[t]he order replicates the content of the primary right': K. Barker, 'Rescuing Remedialism in Unjust Enrichment Law: Why Remedies are Right' (1998) 57 *CLJ* 301, 321.

[64] W. N. Hohfeld, 'Fundamental Legal Conception as Applied in Judicial Reasoning' (1916–17) 26 *Yale LJ* 710, 760, see also 761–3. It should be noted that for Hohfeld a right *in rem* was more than just a proprietary right: see text to n 30. However, nothing turns on this in the quotations reproduced above as they still make their point if we read a right *in rem* to be only a proprietary right.

[65] Hohfeld (n 15 above), 714–15.

violation of a personal right may give rise to a proprietary secondary right, as with property acquired in breach of a fiduciary duty.[66] These substantive rights may then be restated or 'replicated' as remedies. At the enforcement stage, the remedy, whether personal or proprietary, may be enforced or realized through execution processes which operate on property or on the person.[67]

3 Existence of substantive rights

The value of giving a metaphysical 'existence' to certain kinds of rights has been denied. Some — most notably Holmes — have taken the view that certain primary rights are not a part of the law. Holmes famously stated, 'The duty to keep a contract at common law means a prediction that you must pay damages if you do not keep it — and nothing else.'[68] Some take the view that all substantive, that is primary and secondary, rights should not be considered law. Frank stated that:

> For any particular person, the law, with respect to any particular set of facts, is a decision of a court with respect to those facts so far as that decision affects that particular person. Until a court has passed on those facts no law on that subject is yet in existence.[69]

Thus Frank's assertion here was that the law consists *only* of remedies as defined in this chapter.

It would be a diversion for this chapter to venture into this debate. While we could speak only in terms of remedies, this would be very inconvenient as we have become used to thinking and communicating in terms of rights. In this book, it is expressly assumed that primary and secondary rights exist independently of and prior to the making of a court order in the particular case.[70] Such rights conceptualize conditions for the availability of remedies. And remedies, being a species of rights themselves, usually conceptualize conditions for the availability of various modes of enforcement, that is, the exercise of state force for the benefit of private individuals. All these concepts have a useful role to play in legal reasoning allowing us to explain adjudication, to organize our thoughts, and argue about the legal effects that certain events have or should have. They also have a useful hortatory function serving as guides for behaviour in the absence of, and without the need for, state interference in the particular case.[71]

[66] Chapter 12 p 201.

[67] Chapters 7 and 8 discuss the various modes of enforcement in some detail.

[68] O. W. Holmes, 'The Path of the Law' (1897) 10 *Harv L Rev* 457, 462. Tettenborn observes that confusion between obligation and remedy has led to the emergence of this view: Tettenborn (n 26 above), 3.

[69] J. Frank, *Law and the Modern Mind* (2nd edn., London: Stevens, 1963), 50.

[70] This is not to suggest that we *must* think of rights as having such an existence; it is merely an acknowledgement that in practice we do. Thus we often say that a right has arisen, come into existence, been transferred or assigned, been extinguished or that someone does or does not have one even though no court has ruled on the matter.

[71] P. Atiyah, 'From Principles to Pragmatism: Changes in the Function of the Judicial Process and the Law' (1979–80) 65 *Iowa L Rev* 1249.

4 Substantive rights before remedies or vice versa?

Accepting that it is meaningful to speak of rights that exist independently of the commands or statements of judges in the particular case, it is clear that these substantive rights are very closely connected to remedies. Goulding J stated in *Chase Manhattan Bank NA v Israel-British Bank (London) Ltd* that:

> Within the municipal confines of a single legal system, right and remedy are indissolubly connected and correlated, each contributing in historical dialogue to the development of the other, and, save in very special circumstances it is idle to ask whether the court vindicates[72] the suitor's substantive right or gives the suitor a procedural remedy as to ask whether thought is a mental or cerebral process. In fact the court does both things by one and the same act.[73]

The next question is whether substantive rights arise because remedies are granted or whether remedies are granted because substantive rights are thought to exist. Whether substantive rights come before remedies or vice versa seems like asking whether chickens existed before eggs. Friedman writes:

> A discussion of the classification of legal rights and remedies may place the emphasis upon either. Much depends on the basic approach. Does one believe that the remedy is meant to protect the legal right (and the corresponding duty) and that this is, in fact, its sole purpose, or does one assume that it is the other way around? Rights and obligations were created in order to justify the granting of a remedy. In any event the idea that the choice of one leads to the abandonment of the study and analysis of the other seems to be misplaced.[74]

Jacob also turned his mind to this issue and seemingly held both beliefs identified by Friedman. Jacob stated that 'remedies reflect the substantive rights and interests of the parties and, conversely, they constitute an essential foundation upon which the rules of substantive law have been and are being fashioned, constructed and enforced.'[75] The two beliefs do not appear to be mutually exclusive.

For the purposes of this work the following simple position will be adopted. Where a remedy is granted in circumstances where it was not previously available and it continues to be or is likely to continue to be granted in such circumstances, the conclusion may be drawn that there is a substantive right in existence that has been generated by the availability of the remedy. As Lord Dunedin stated in *Nocton v Lord Ashburton*, 'the common law (though there is no harder lesson

[72] It should be noted that in this work the term 'effectuation' is preferred to 'vindication' because of the civil law connotations of the latter term. In civil law systems, vindication is the direct assertion of a property right. Graham Virgo intentionally uses the term 'vindication' in a broader sense than civil lawyers: G. Virgo, *The Principles of the Law of Restitution* (Oxford: Clarendon Press, 1999), 16 and Part V. This usage is not adopted here because it is liable to lead to confusion.

[73] [1981] Ch 105, 124.

[74] D. Friedman, 'Rights and Remedies' (1997) *LQR* 424, 425.

[75] Jacob (n 4 above), 169.

for the stranger jurist to learn) began with the remedy and ended with the right'.[76] However, it is assumed that once a substantive right is recognized as existing then it is the substantive right which drives the remedy. The remedy usually follows because the substantive right has been infringed. A right in this sense may be said to be the conceptualization of the availability of a remedy. But once such a structure is built on the availability of a remedy, it determines whether and when the remedy should be available.

An example of a situation where a remedy was granted in new circumstances, and hence where it did not replicate a prior substantive right, is *Kleinwort Benson Ltd v Lincoln City Council*.[77] A bank, having paid sums of money to a local authority under a mistake of law, brought an action seeking an order that the local authority repay the sums in question. The English courts had previously held that a mistake of law could not be a basis for the recovery of a payment. Unless we entertain the fiction that the common law exists in all its splendour awaiting discovery,[78] we must conclude that the bank had no substantive right to a repayment prior to the decision to grant the remedy in that case.[79] But because of this decision which permitted recovery, it has become meaningful to speak of substantive rights to the return of payments made under mistakes of law which can be given direct effect by that remedy in similar circumstances in the future. *Woolwich Equitable Building Society v Inland Revenue Commissioners*[80] is another groundbreaking case where, as part of the development of the law, a remedy was first granted in the absence of a substantive right. Money paid pursuant to an ultra vires tax demand was held to be recoverable. Because of this decision and the operation of the doctrine of precedent, substantive rights can now be said to arise in similar circumstances. Remedies can now be said to be granted in similar circumstances because these substantive rights exist.

To recapitulate, the position taken here is that the dichotomy between (1) right and (2) remedy is a dichotomy between (1) a substantive right which is a structure built on the availability of a court order and (2) a right arising out of a certain judicial command or statement.[81] This raises the questions of whether it is possible to have rights without remedies and remedies without rights.

[76] [1914] AC 932, 964 (HL). [77] [1999] 2 AC 349 (HL).

[78] This is the position of the now defunct declaratory theory of law. See Lord Reid, 'The Judge as Law Maker' (1972) 12 *Journal of the Society of Public Teachers of Law* 22; *Kleinwort Benson Ltd v Lincoln City Council* [1999] 2 AC 349 (HL); A. Mason, 'Legislative and Judicial Law Making: Can We Locate an Identifiable Boundary?' (2003) 24 *Adelaide L Rev* 15, 16–20.

[79] This is so even though for years before this case, it was predicted that if the matter came up for decision, a right to the recovery of a payment made under a mistake of law would be recognized. This position was based on an interpretation of the law and the prevailing attitudes to the need for change. It demonstrates the truism that external principles impact on the development of the law and that we must understand them to fully understand the path that legal doctrine may take.

[80] [1993] AC 70 (HL).

[81] Which in itself is a structure built on the availability of a mechanism for the realization of the remedy, or, looking at it from the perspective of the duty, enforcement.

5 Remedies without substantive rights

Can there be remedies without substantive rights? Is the maxim *ubi remedium ibi ius*[82] ever false? The question can be reformulated as whether there can be remedies that do not replicate either primary or secondary rights. As we have seen above, this occurs when a remedy is granted for the first time, that is, where it is granted in circumstances in which it was not available before. But there is also a distinct class of remedies which differ from the rights of the parties which exist prior to the court's decision. These remedies will be called 'transformative' remedies because they inevitably modify or transform the parties' substantive rights to a significant extent. Such remedies are sometimes granted entirely at the court's discretion. They are different from most other remedies in that their availability does not generate *particular* substantive rights.[83] This class of remedies will be discussed in Chapter 13.

6 Substantive rights without remedies

Can there be rights without remedies? The common law position is that there can be rights which will not or cannot be replicated in court orders. There are primary rights that will not be replicated as a general rule. Examples include the right that correlates with a duty of care in tort or a contractual right to the performance of personal services. Such rights are usually given indirect effect through the imposition of secondary rights which are then replicated court orders.[84]

But it seems that there can be substantive rights which will not even be given such indirect effect in court orders. Examples of such rights include statute-barred debts, rights under contracts unenforceable for want of form[85] and rights under contracts with minors.[86] It seems that in some limited but firmly established cases,

[82] 'Where there is a remedy, there is a right.'

[83] However, the availability of such transformative remedies may indirectly support the existence of primary substantive rights. For example, the primary right created by section 52 of the Trade Practices Act 1973 (Cth) which correlates with a duty not to engage in misleading or deceptive conduct is supported by transformative remedies set out in section 87, as to which see Chapter 13 p 205. But not all transformative remedies support primary rights in this way, for example, remedies which provide family maintenance or property readjustment on divorce appear to neither generate nor indirectly support any substantive rights.

[84] Or, as observed in the above note, such rights may be indirectly supported by transformative remedies.

[85] A contract of guarantee is unenforceable unless it is evidenced in writing: Statue of Frauds 1677 (UK) s 4. This section was repealed in relation to other contracts by the Law Reform (Enforcement of Contracts) Act 1954 (UK). Another way of saying that a contract is unenforceable, as opposed to void, is to say that the replication of substantive rights arising from it is barred. Money paid under an unenforceable contract is not recoverable on the basis of total failure of consideration: *Thomas v Brown* (1876) 1 QBD 714, 723; see also *Head v Kelk* (1963) 63 SR (NSW) 340, 348.

[86] 'It is, however, a different question whether, if an infant pays money on the footing of a contract, he can afterwards recover it back. If an infant buys an article which is not a necessary, he

the maxim *ubi ius ibi remedium*[87] is false.[88] Let us take statute-barred debts as an example.

At common law, the effectuation of rights through remedies did not become barred by the mere passage of time. However, a policy of barring stale claims led to the introduction of statutes of limitations.[89] Generally, where the substantive right to a payment arises from a simple contract, the defendant will have a plea in bar which operates as a complete defence if the claimant seeks replication of that right more than six years after the cause of action in relation to it arose.[90] In the case of a right arising from a deed, the period is twelve years.[91] If the statutory bar is pleaded in relation to a statute-barred debt,[92] the replicative remedy must be refused.

A statute-barred debt is not extinguished. The common law position is that the right continues to exist. In *Ronex Properties Ltd v John Laing Construction Ltd*,[93] Lord Justice Donaldson stated that it is 'trite law that the English Limitation Acts bar the remedy and not the right'.[94] The continued existence of the jural relationship may have various consequences. Some of these were outlined by Gummow and Kirby JJ in *Commonwealth v Mewett*:

> Where a debtor makes a payment to the creditor without directing that it be paid in reduction of a particular debt, the right of appropriation which thereby devolves upon the creditor may be exercised by application to payment of the time-barred debt rather than to another debt which is still enforceable. A possessory lien may be exercised in respect of a statute-barred debt. Further, where the debtor approaches the court for equitable relief in aid of other rights against the creditor, the debtor will be required to do equity. Thus, a mortgagor seeking equitable relief in a redemption action is obliged to do equity by paying to the mortgagee all arrears of interest from the date of the mortgage, not merely that interest due and owing for less than six years. These latter considerations may not

cannot be compelled to pay for it, but if he does pay for it during his minority he cannot on attaining his majority recover the money back.': *Ex parte Taylor* (1861) 8 DM & G 254, 258 (Taylor J).

87 'Where there is a right, there is a remedy.'

88 However Hohfeld's stabilization of the concept of a right seems to suggest that such 'sanctionless' rights or 'duties of imperfect obligation' are not claims correlating with duties but rather rights in the sense of liberties or immunities.

89 *Cholmondeley v Clinton* (1820) 2 J & W 1; 4 Bli 1.

90 Limitation Act 1980 (UK) s 5. An acknowledgement or part payment of a debt, made within the limitation period, restarts the running of the limitation period: s 29(5); *Spencer v Hemmerde* [1922] 2 AC 507 (HL). In the case of certain loans, time begins to run only when a written demand is made: s 6. Time may commence to run later where the right-holder is under a disability (a minor or of unsound mind): s 28(2) or there has been concealment of facts relevant to the claim: s 32.

91 Limitation Act 1980 (UK) s 8.

92 If the defendant wishes to rely on the statutory defence to the claim, it must be pleaded. If it is not, the action will continue on its merits and the defendant may not be permitted to raise it at a later stage: *Ketterman v Hansel Properties* [1987] AC 189 (HL); *Commonwealth v Verwayen* (1990) 170 CLR 390 (HCA).

93 [1983] 3 WLR 875, 879.

94 But there are some situations where the Limitation Acts do extinguish rights, for example, proprietary rights in relation to land and chattels: Limitation Act 1980 (UK) ss 3(2) and 17.

bear upon the facts of the particular case [before the court], being but illustrations of the proposition that the existence of direct curial remedy is not co-extensive with the juridical existence of the right.[95]

Furthermore, because the right continues to exist even though the relevant limitation period has expired, it constitutes a cross-demand which allows an equitable set-off to be asserted.[96] Also, the payer of a statute-barred debt acquires no right to recover the sum paid.[97] The defendant is not unjustly enriched in such a case.

E Conclusion

A clear line between substantive rights and remedies has been drawn. It is apparent that the domain of remedies cannot include questions such as when substantive rights to compensation, restitution or punishment will arise, what their content is or what interests they protect. Such issues belong to a separate field of inquiry and not to the study of remedies in the strict sense.

Just as there are texts on restitution that focus on primary rights arising from unjust enrichment and secondary rights which have such a goal,[98] it is also appropriate to have texts devoted to compensation[99] and punishment[100] which focus on substantive rights with these kinds of goals. Maintaining the commitment made to the stable meaning of remedy, these would not be texts on remedies but texts on primary and secondary rights.

If remedies are defined as rights arising from certain judicial commands or statements, the law of remedies becomes narrower than the law of all responses to infringements of rights. The domain of the law of remedies becomes the generation, content, and effect of a certain class of rights. The manner of organizing this body of law, its taxonomy, is the subject matter of the next chapter.

[95] (1997) 146 ALR 299 (HCA). 'Remedy' is used here in the sense of a right of action.

[96] S. R. Derham, *The Law of Set-Off* (3rd edn., Oxford: Oxford University Press, 2003), 103.

[97] *Bize v Dickason* (1786) 1 Term R 286, 287; 99 ER 1097, 1098 (Lord Mansfield).

[98] For example, R. Goff and G. Jones, *The Law of Restitution* (5th edn., London: Sweet & Maxwell, 1998); A. Burrows, *The Law of Restitution* (London: Butterworths, 1993); Virgo (n 72 above).

[99] For example, H. McGregor, *McGregor on Damages* (16th edn., London: Sweet & Maxwell, 1997).

[100] See Chapter 10 p 176 for a discussion of 'rights' to punishment.

5

Classification of Remedies[1]

A Introduction

Lord Steyn started his speech in *Attorney General v Blake* by saying, 'My Lords, in law classification is important. Asking the right questions in the right order reduces the risk of wrong decisions. This truth is illustrated by the case before the House.'[2] This chapter focuses on the classification of remedies. As Kercher points out, 'The coherence of our study of Remedies does not come from its social, political or legal background. . .Our study's coherence comes from the ways in which we classify these remedies. . .'.[3] Unfortunately our current classifications of remedies are defective. Naturally this impacts on the coherence of the law of remedies.

In this chapter we will evolve a model of what might be called a dominant or received classification of remedies and we will ultimately conclude that the basic criterion for such a classification has to be totally different. The fundamental proposition should be that remedies either replicate antecedent (substantive) rights or transform them. In reaching this conclusion, and rejecting others, we have to observe a number of essential principles of classification. In particular the classifier's eye has to be kept on the following three questions.

First, what is being classified? Given the instability of 'remedy', what purport to be classifications of remedies may in fact not be comparing like with like. Foreign matter sometimes finds its way into classifications. Just as a classification of books must exclude newspapers and paintings, so a classification of remedies must rigorously exclude whatever does not fall within the definition of a remedy.

Second, what criterion operates? Every classification has a basis according to which different categories are distinguished. For example, book content and name of author are possible criteria for the classification of books. If a taxonomy uses more than one criterion it must be hierarchical; that is, composed of different levels. Only one criterion can operate at any one level of a hierarchy. We will see

[1] This chapter is substantially based on the author's paper 'The Classification of Judicial Remedies' delivered on 10 September 2002 at the SPTL Conference, De Montfort University, Leicester, and subsequently published in [2003] *LMCLQ* 477.

[2] [2001] 1 AC 268, 290 (HL).

[3] B. Kercher, 'Legal History and the Study of Legal Remedies' (2001) 39 *Brandeis L Rev* 619, 629.

that writers on remedies have not been sensitive to this requirement. Current classifications of remedies erroneously mix different criteria. This is as if books were classified into law books, chemistry books, art books, and books by English authors; that is, according to a series that mixed the criteria of content and nationality of the author.

Third, what could a disciplined classification of remedies look like? We will see that it diverges dramatically from the usual practice. A new classification primarily based on the relationship between remedies and the substantive rights to which they give effect will be outlined.

B Classifications of Remedies

1 Most common classifications

As was seen in Chapter 3, remedies are commonly, either expressly or impliedly, classified according to some variant of the following series of categories: compensation (or 'compensatory damages'), restitution, punishment (or 'exemplary damages'), specific enforcement (or coercion), declaration, and others (such as rescission). The terms that are actually chosen by different authors reflect a slightly different emphasis in distinguishing each category from the others.

As we saw in Chapter 3, Burrows adopts the following classification based on, as he says, 'function': compensation, restitution, punishment, compelling performance of positive obligations (specific enforcement), preventing wrongful acts, compelling the undoing of a wrong (specific restoration), and declaring rights.[4]

Tilbury bases his series on the following, as he says, 'remedial objectives' or 'goals': compensation, restitution, punishment, coercion, interim and urgent relief, and declaratory relief.[5] Tilbury's series is also applied by Kercher and Noone.[6] Wright's remedy continuum, which is divided into compensation, restitution, and coercion, seems to be derived from Tilbury's classification.[7]

[4] A. Burrows, *Remedies for Torts and Breach of Contract* (2nd edn., London: Butterworths, 1994), 8 and 'Judicial Remedies' in P. B. H. Birks (ed.), *English Private Law Vol II* (Oxford: Oxford University Press, 2000), 818. Chambers adopts a similar series based on goal in classifying 'liabilities' for breach of trust: 'At a lower level of generality, liabilities for breach of duty can be organised: according to the goals they are supposed to achieve: direct enforcement of the duty, compensation for loss, restitution of gain, punishment, or other goals.': R. Chambers, 'Liability' in P. B. H. Birks and A. Pretto (eds), *Breach of Trust* (Oxford: Hart, 2002), 2.

[5] M. Tilbury, *Civil Remedies Vol 1 Principles of Civil Remedies* (North Ryde New South Wales: Butterworths, 1990), [1029].

[6] In M. Tilbury, M. Noone and B. Kercher, *Remedies Commentary and Materials* (2nd edn., North Ryde New South Wales: Law Book Co, 1993) it is adopted expressly, 9. In the third edition M. Tilbury, M. Noone and B. Kercher, *Remedies Commentary and Materials* (3rd edn., North Ryde New South Wales: Law Book Co, 2000) the categories of interim and urgent relief and declaratory relief are omitted from the series, 9, 11–12.

[7] D. Wright, *The Remedial Constructive Trust* (Sydney: Butterworths, 1998), 283.

Dobbs divides remedies into four main categories 'according to the nature and purpose of the relief awarded'[8]: (1) damages remedies which include compensatory and punitive damages, (2) restitutionary remedies which include orders for payment of restitution and restitution *in specie* (recovery of property), rescission and reformation (rectification), (3) coercive remedies which include injunctions and specific performance, and (4) declaratory remedies.[9]

Harris, Campbell and Halson structure their discussion of contract remedies into four parts: first-step remedies (being forbearance, alternative dispute resolution, and settlement; self-help and consumer protection), compensation, literal enforcement, and restitution.[10]

2 Received classification

In the following sections it will be shown that the commonly used series are not composed of categories of the same nature. For the purposes of argument, the hypothetical or received classification that will be discussed is: compensation, restitution, punishment, specific enforcement or coercion, declaration, and others. In this classification, prevention, specific restoration, and interim and urgent relief will be placed in the 'others' category without consideration of whether they could constitute separate categories or whether they belong in the same series as the nominate categories at all. This is done because there is no advantage in unnecessarily complicating the discussion.

The aim of this chapter is not to focus on particular categories adopted by particular authors but rather to stress a point applicable to each of the taxonomies set out above, namely, that categories such as specific enforcement, coercion, and declaration do not belong alongside compensation, restitution, and punishment.

C What is Being Classified?

1 Effect of imprecise definition on taxonomy

Problems may occur in the construction and application of a taxonomy if foreign matter is included in the set of things that is to be classified. If one is constructing a taxonomy of books, one must be sure that one is actually categorizing books and that one does not inadvertently include paintings and newspapers. Efforts to include such foreign matter in the taxonomy may cause damage by skewing

[8] D. Dobbs, *Law of Remedies Damages-Equity-Restitution Practitioner Treatise Series Vol 1* (2nd edn., St Paul Minnesota: West Publishing Co, 1993), 11.

[9] Ibid 2–9.

[10] D. Harris, D. Campbell and R. Halson, *Remedies in Contract and Tort* (2nd edn., London: Butterworths, 2002), vii–xi.

the series of categories that is created. Categories such as landscapes or tabloids may emerge as major categories in the taxonomy—categories which have little to do with books but seem apposite in light of what is actually being examined. There is a risk of the inclusion of foreign matter where the classifier has no clear definition of what things are actually being classified.

2 Definition of 'remedy'

In order to classify remedies we must have a clear concept of a remedy. The stable core meaning of remedy identified and adopted in Chapter 4 provides just that. It allows us to focus on a single concept to the exclusion of others.

3 Foreign matter must be excluded

One must be vigilant to keep the taxonomy of remedies free of foreign matter such as substantive rights, both when constructing the taxonomy and when applying it.

Some categories included in the received classification may also function as categories for concepts which are not remedies, for example, substantive rights.[11] Substantive rights are clearly capable of being sorted into the first three categories of compensation, restitution, and punishment. Some primary rights belong in these categories. For example, a contractual right to the payment of liquidated damages, a right to the payment of a sum as restitution for unjust enrichment or a contractual right to the payment of a penalty[12] respectively. Secondary rights can be easily divided into these goal-based categories. A right to the payment of compensatory damages for a wrong, a right to a payment of a sum as restitution for a wrong or a right to the payment of exemplary damages belong in each of the respective categories.

These substantive rights can be erroneously assumed to belong in a taxonomy of remedies just because they fit neatly into these categories. It is easy to make this mistake. They do not belong just as paintings do not belong in a taxonomy of books, even though they may fit neatly into categories based on book content such as history, nature, or sport. The taxonomy of remedies, if it is not to be a jumble of various types of rights and categories, must be kept pure. It must be constructed by reference to, and applied only to, rights which fall within a precise definition of remedy.

[11] But not all categories in the received classification can apply to substantive rights. The categories of specific enforcement, coercion, or declaration cannot sensibly apply to primary or secondary rights, just as the categories of topic or date of publication cannot apply to animals. Only court orders can be placed in the categories of specific enforcement, coercion, or declaration.

[12] Although the contractual right to a penalty is not recognized as a matter of policy in common law systems, it is enforced in civil law systems: G. H. Treitel, *Remedies for Breach of Contract* (Oxford: Clarendon Press, 1988), 208–44.

D What Criterion Operates?

There are many ways to classify a set of things which fall within a particular concept. Continuing with our book example and assuming that we have a stable concept of a book, we could arrange our library according to the criterion of the first letter of the title with a shelf for books starting with A, another for B, and so on. An alternative would be to order it by the date of publication with a shelf for each year. Even the colour of the cover could provide the basis for another taxonomy. In fact, most of us find it most useful to arrange our books according to their content. Different taxonomies answer different questions. We choose criteria for them depending on what we want to know. For example, what books on a given topic we have in our library.

Whether we should classify according to one criterion rather than another varies with our activities and aims. If we are reading for a law course along traditional lines where the law is divided by topic then the classification of our books by content is the most sensible approach. However, if we are writing biographies of leading legal scholars, it would be more useful to arrange our library according to author. These are simple examples of the need to match the classification to the task at hand. Often the utility of good classification is more elusive. But is it clear that the nature of an entity can be revealed, or concealed, by the location where it is placed within a classification of similar entities. Classification plays an important role in the understanding of its subject matter.

If we do not know the criterion for a classification, that is, the basis on which the categories included in the classification are constructed and distinguished from each other, then problems may arise. It may be difficult to say whether and why something belongs in a particular category and not in another. The received classification of remedies suffers from this problem.

It is often treated as dogma that remedies for breach of contract fall into two groups, namely, damages (or, more broadly, compensation) and specific performance (or, more broadly, specific enforcement). Thus, a leading equity text states: 'The only remedy which the common law afforded for breach of contract was an award of damages. In equity, however, the due performance of the contract itself was in many cases enforced upon the ground of inadequacy of the damages recoverable for breach.'[13] However, this ignores the most common contractual remedy, the award of an agreed sum.[14] This remedy,

[13] J. McGhee, *Snell's Equity* (30th edn., London: Sweet & Maxwell, 2000), 649, [40–01].

[14] H. Beale, *Remedies for Breach of Contract* (London: Sweet & Maxwell, 1980), 144. In the year 2000, 1,157 claims for debt were issued in the Queens Bench Division of the High Court whereas only 1,050 claims for breach of contract (presumably for damages or specific performance) were issued at that time; in the county courts the disparity is much greater, 1,631,966 'money claims' were issued with only 13.1 per cent of them being unliquidated: Lord Chancellor's Department *Judicial Statistics England and Wales for the Year 2000* (Norwich: The Stationery Office, 2001), 29, 37–9.

which gives direct effect to a primary right to a payment under a contract, has been placed by leading scholars outside of each of these categories, and for conflicting reasons. 'Thus', as Rudden observes, 'in England the major specialist books—Fry on Specific Performance, McGregor on Damages—expressly decline to discuss the enforcement of a monetary obligation, the former on the ground that it is an action for damages, the latter on the ground that it is not.'[15] Either there is a third category of contractual remedy or the categories are so ill-defined that leading scholars cannot apply them or agree what they are. In either case, there is a classification problem that needs to be resolved.

The curious effects do not stop there. Sometimes the categories do not function in the under-inclusive way described in the preceding paragraph but have an over-inclusive operation. Take an award of an agreed sum which gives effect to a contractual right to the payment of agreed or liquidated damages. It may be counted twice. Arguably it may be placed under specific enforcement because it involves compelling the performance of a primary right. If categorized by its goal, it also belongs under compensation. This double-counting may be due to ill-defined categories or a more serious structural problem, mixed criteria. That problem will now be investigated.

1 What is the criterion for the categories of compensation, restitution, and punishment?

The first three categories of the received taxonomy—compensation, restitution, and punishment—classify remedies by reference to their goals. All rights can be classified according to goal into compensation, restitution, punishment, and other goals.[16] Remedies, themselves being rights, are also capable of being classified into these 'goal-based' categories, along with the primary and secondary rights that remedies give effect to.

What exactly are the goals represented by compensation, restitution, and punishment? First, we need to note that these goals are the goals of rights, say of A. They are also the goals of correlative duties, say of B. They represent the goal of a jural relationship between A and B. Compensation is the goal where B has a duty to transfer wealth to A which is equivalent to a loss suffered by A (where loss includes the non-receipt of a benefit under a contract). Restitution is the goal where B has a duty to transfer wealth to A which is equivalent to a gain made by B. Punishment is the goal where B has a duty to transfer wealth to A, or suffer

[15] B. Rudden, 'Some Thoughts on Monetary Obligations' (unpublished manuscript 19 May 1997) 5. The footnote states: 'Sir Edward Fry, A Treatise on the Specific Performance of Contracts §7, (6th ed. by George Russell Northcote MA, Sweet & Maxwell 1921, repr 1985). Harvey McGregor, McGregor on Damages p.2, §3(1) (15th edition, Sweet & Maxwell Ltd 1988).'

[16] P. B. H. Birks, 'The Law of Restitution at the End of an Epoch' (1999) 28 *U Western Australia L Rev* 1, 13 and 17.

another detriment, which is unrelated to A's loss or B's gain (for policy reasons of retribution, deterrence, or prevention). Each of these goals represents an intended effect of a different measure on the relative positions, in terms of wealth or wellbeing, of A and B.

There are many rights which do not fall within any of these categories including, for example, the right to the conveyance of land under a contract of sale or the right to the payment of a purchase price. The goals of these rights are not compensation, restitution, or punishment hence they must be placed in a miscellaneous category labelled 'others'. This residual category is extremely wide for it includes whatever diverse goals other than compensation, restitution, and punishment may be sought to be achieved by rights, whether they be substantive rights or remedies. It may be possible to group some of these rights under labels which summarize other goals, but it is unnecessary for the arguments developed in this chapter to engage in this task, other than making the following observation.

Birks includes 'perfection' as a goal of rights alongside compensation, restitution, and punishment.[17] But the goal of 'perfection' cannot be extracted from the 'others' category and aligned with these goals. 'Perfection' seems to have been first characterized as an 'aim' alongside such categories by Elias.[18] For the purpose of classifying constructive trusts, Elias identifies the following as the aims of the 'rules' of constructive trusts: compensation based on a 'theme' of repairing losses, restitution based on a theme of disgorging gains and perfection based on a theme of honouring commitments.[19] When using the term 'perfection' Elias appears to refer to the aim of fulfilling the duty arising from a 'choice to dispose of one's options'. When using 'restitution' he appears to refer to the aim of fulfilling a duty to give up a gain made through another's loss. When using 'reparation' he appears to refer to the aim of fulfilling a duty to repair a loss caused to another.[20]

The latter two categories are defined by reference to the measure of the intended effects on the relative positions of the parties, which are equivalent to those of the goal-based categories of restitution and compensation. They are not defined by reference to the origin of the duty,[21] which in the case of restitution may include an unjust enrichment, a wrong[22] or a 'choice to dispose of one's options',[23] or in the case of reparation or compensation may include a wrong or 'choice to

[17] Birks (n 16 above), 17.

[18] G. Elias, *Explaining Constructive Trusts* (Oxford: Clarendon Press, 1990).

[19] Ibid 1. [20] Ibid 4.

[21] Rights can be classified into the following categories according to their origin, that is, the causative events from which they arise: consent, wrongs, unjust enrichment and others: P. B. H. Birks, 'Introduction' in P. B. H. Birks (ed.), *English Private Law Vol 1* (Oxford: Oxford University Press, 2000), xli.

[22] For example, *Attorney General v Blake* [2001] 1 AC 268 (HL).

[23] For example, *Sebel Products Ltd v Customs and Excise Commissioners* [1949] Ch 409; *Nurdin & Peacock plc v DB Ramsden & Co Ltd* [1999] 1 WLR 1249, 1266–9.

dispose of one's options'.[24] On the other hand, perfection is defined by reference to its origin—a choice or, putting it another way, consent. The problem with aligning these three categories now becomes clear. The aim of fulfilling a duty arising from consent (i.e. honouring commitments) belongs alongside the aim of fulfilling a duty arising from an unjust enrichment (i.e. returning unjust enrichments) and the aim of fulfilling a duty arising from a wrong (i.e. redressing wrongs). That is, it belongs in a series based on causative event. It does not belong in a series based on what Birks characterizes as a goal or response.

It is important to keep causative events and responses apart, especially because one kind of event may give rise to more than one response.[25] In short, Elias's perfection aim is concerned with giving effect to a particular causative event ('disposal of choices') whereas his restitution and restoration aims focus on giving effect to particular goals or responses to causative events (disgorging gains and repairing losses). Clearly, perfection does not belong alongside compensation, restitution, and punishment. An example of a taxonomy that is mixed in a similar way would be a classification of books into books written by Guenter Treitel, books which aim to explain contract, and books which aim to explain tort.

2 Are specific enforcement, coercion, and declaration goal-based categories?

Remedies are not only placed into the categories of compensation, restitution, or punishment but also into categories such as specific enforcement, coercion, or declaration. Yet specific enforcement, coercion, or declaration cannot be said to be a purpose, objective, or goal of a right in the same way that compensation, restitution, or punishment are. The latter three represent goals in the sense of outcomes that any type of right, whether a substantive right or a remedy, may aim to bring about.

Specific enforcement, coercion, or declaration do not represent goals of a similar nature. They are not goals that can be expressed in terms of the intended change of the relative positions of the parties, like compensation, restitution, or punishment were in the previous section. If they are not based on such goals, what are they based on? The criteria for these categories of remedies will now be identified.

3 What are the criteria for the specific enforcement category?

What are the common features that distinguish remedies placed in the specific enforcement category from those in the compensation, restitution, and

[24] For example, a liquidated damages clause in a contract: *Dunlop Pneumatic Tyre Co Ltd v New Garage and Motor Co Ltd* [1915] AC 79 (HL).

[25] P. B. H. Birks, *Introduction to the Law of Restitution* (Revised edn., Oxford: Clarendon Press, 1989), 39–44.

punishment categories? It cannot be merely that these orders give direct effect to or 'replicate' the claimant's substantive right. If this were the sufficient feature for inclusion in the specific enforcement category, the goal-based categories of compensation, restitution, and punishment would overlap significantly with it. This is because a remedy in all but exceptional circumstances purports to replicate either a primary right or, more usually, a secondary right. These rights, especially the latter, may often have a goal of compensation, restitution, or punishment.[26] Such a notion of specific enforcement is obviously too broad and cannot be taken to be intended by those who use it as a category alongside the goal-based categories. Thus, if one wants to retain specific enforcement as a category alongside compensation, restitution, and punishment one must attempt to restrict it by requiring the remedies that belong to it to have additional features which remedies in the goal-based categories do not share. One must introduce additional criteria.

A narrower meaning of specific enforcement is preferred, namely, a right arising from an order compelling a person to perform the very *positive primary* duty that the person is under. Thus Burrows writes (in the context of remedies for wrongs):

> In this section, we examine what may be termed 'specific' remedies for wrongs. In general, these are orders requiring a defendant to comply with his primary duty not to commit a wrong. Where the duty in question is a positive one (as, for example, with most contractual duties) the remedies (for example, specific performance or the award of an agreed sum) order the defendant to perform his positive duty. In other words, the remedies seek specific enforcement.[27]

This introduces a second and a third feature for membership in the specific enforcement category, namely, the need for the replicated duty to be a primary one and for it to be positive, that is, to do something. However, this does not solve the problem that the received series faces. Although generally compensation, restitution, and punishment deal with secondary rights and specific enforcement deals with primary rights, this is not invariable. As already stressed, a primary right can be a right to compensation, restitution, or punishment. For example, even if we adopted these qualifications, a remedy replicating a right to restitution arising from an unjust enrichment (a positive primary right) would still belong both in the restitution category and the specific enforcement category.

The introduction of a fourth feature requiring the right to arise from consent leads us to the generally accepted definition of 'specific performance', namely, 'a decree of the court which compels the defendant to personally do what he

[26] For example, an award of money due under a contract may replicate a primary contractual right to the payment of an indemnity (goal of compensation); an award of restitution for unjust enrichment may replicate a primary right to the return of a mistaken payment (goal of restitution); or, an award of damages may replicate a secondary right to the payment of damages for a breach of a duty of care (goal of compensation).

[27] Burrows 'Judicial Remedies' (n 4 above), 863.

promised to do'.[28] This also does not remove the possibility of overlap. For example, a remedy replicating an express contractual right to compensation would belong both in the compensation and the specific enforcement categories.[29] If the goal of a contractual right to the conveyance of land were characterized as specific enforcement, why should the goal of a contractual right to compensation not only be characterized as compensation but also as specific enforcement? What makes it so different from a right to the conveyance of land? It cannot be that a right to liquidated damages requires the payment of money. Duties for the payment of money can be and are specifically enforced. For example, in *Beswick v Beswick*[30] the nephew who had agreed to make payments to his aunt, a third party to the contract, was compelled to specifically perform his duty to pay the sum of money.

Furthermore, the reference to consent or a promise introduces an event-based criterion as occurred with the category of 'perfection'. As already shown above, such an event-based category cannot align with compensation, restitution, and punishment which are founded purely on a goal-based criterion. They are neutral as to event. Specific performance always has an element of event because it deals with promises or, more generically, consent. Finally, the difference between these categories should not lie in the enforcement mechanisms (a fifth criterion) for the reasons that will be set out in the next section.

4 What is the criterion for the coercion category?

In an attempt to eliminate the double-counting encountered in the previous section, one may seek to distinguish (or further distinguish) certain remedies from remedies in the goal-based categories on the basis of their enforcement mechanisms. One may argue for a 'coercion' category consisting only of remedies embodied in orders enforceable by punishment of the defendant for contempt.[31] It would include decrees of specific performance and injunctions. This definition of coercive remedies is adopted by Dobbs who writes: 'The coercive order is sometimes also called an *in personam* order, meaning mainly that it is a personal directive enforceable "against the person" by the use of the contempt power...'.[32] This may also be the rationale behind the category

[28] G. Jones and W. Goodhart, *Specific Performance* (London: Butterworths, 1986), 1.

[29] *Dunlop Pneumatic Tyre Co Ltd v New Garage and Motor Co Ltd* [1915] AC 79, 86–87 (HL); *Phillips Hong Kong Ltd v A-G of Hong Kong* (1993) 61 Build LR 41 (PC).

[30] [1968] AC 58 (CA). See also Chapter 8 p 141.

[31] Contempt may be punished not only by committal (imprisonment) but also by sequestration (whereby possession of all the contemnor's real and personal assets is taken until he has purged his contempt) or by a fine: Chapter 8 p 000.

[32] Dobbs (n 8 above), 7. Contrast Lawson and Burrows who use the term 'coercive' to mean any remedy which is capable of enforcement whether by punishment for contempt or direct recourse to the defendant's assets: see Chapter 3 p 26 (Lawson) and p 29 (Burrows). To avoid confusion, the terms 'enforceable' and 'non-enforceable' will be used in this work to distinguish those remedies which are capable of enforcement by any such means from those remedies which are not enforceable and require an additional enforceable remedy for their realization.

adopted under the same name by Tilbury.[33] However, he does not make the reasons for the use of this label explicit.

One may argue that coercion aligns with the categories of compensation, restitution, and punishment which group remedies executable by recourse to the defendant's assets without the need to prove contempt. In contrast to the coercion category, these three goal-based categories could be said to group remedies executable by means of the seizure and sale of the defendant's goods, garnishee proceedings in relation to debts owed to the defendant, attachment of earnings, charging orders in relation to land or shares, or the appointment of a receiver in relation to other property. However, a closer consideration of the resulting series — compensation, restitution, punishment, and coercion — shows it to be unsatisfactory.

First, the different goals of remedies which are executable by direct recourse to the defendant's assets are distinguished into compensation, restitution, and punishment. This has the effect that particular instances of a remedy such as an award of an agreed sum must be placed in different categories depending on whether the effectuated primary right aims to provide compensation or restitution.[34] However, an order for the payment of a debt will fall outside of these categories altogether where its aim is do something other than to effect compensation, restitution, or punishment, such as to achieve payment of a purchase price or repayment of a loan. It cannot fall in the coercion category if that is limited to remedies enforceable through contempt proceedings.[35]

Secondly, the different goals of remedies that are enforceable by punishment of the defendant for contempt are ignored in this classification. Such remedies could also be distinguished into those with a goal of compensation, restitution, punishment, and other goals. Of course, the vast majority would fall into the 'others' category. But, for example, specific performance of a contractual right to a transfer of possession or ownership of property on breach of contract could be ordered, provided that its value was a genuine pre-estimate of the loss and not a penalty.[36] In such a case, the remedy would belong in the compensation category if classified by goal.

Thirdly, there is no reason in logic why all remedies which have the goal of compensation, restitution, or punishment could not be enforced by committal.

[33] Tilbury (n 5 above), [1029].

[34] Thus an award of an agreed sum giving effect to a contractual right to a refund would belong in a different category from an award of an agreed sum giving effect to a right to liquidated damages.

[35] Tilbury chooses to include an award of an agreed sum in the coercion category for reasons of convenience: Tilbury (n 5 above), [6001].

[36] In *Ex parte Newitt* (1881) 16 Ch D 522 (CA) a right to forfeit a contract-breaker's property was granted by contract 'as and for liquidated damages' though in this case no judicial remedy was required as the right-holder had exercised his right to take possession. A similar right was held to be a floating charge and void for want of registration in *Smith (Administrator) of Cosslett (Contractors) Ltd v Bridgend County Borough Council* [2002] 1 AC 336 (HL). The penalty issue in this context was considered in *Forestry Commission of NSW v Stefanetto* (1976) 133 CLR 507 (HCA).

Money remedies were enforceable by committal of the defendant in the bad old days of debtor's prisons. The choice between permitting such enforcement or only execution by recourse to assets is a policy choice. Hyde J's infamous statement in *Manby v Scott*[37] reflects the attitudes that prevailed when the enforcement of money remedies by imprisonment was the norm:

If a man be taken in execution, and lie in prison for debt, neither the plaintiff at whose suit he is arrested, nor the sheriff who took him is bound to find him meat, drink or clothes, but he must live on his own, or on the charity of others; and if no man will relieve him, let him die, in the name of God, says the law; and so say I.

There are limited circumstances where imprisonment for debt is still possible in some jurisdictions.[38]

Fourthly, remedies such as specific performance or an injunction are not always enforced by punishing the defendant for contempt. Sometimes they may be executed by direct recourse to the defendant's assets or by a substituted act of a third party.[39] In the case of obligations to pay money, this is the means of enforcement in most cases. Thus specific performance of such obligations could fall outside of the coercion category.

In short, there is no incompatibility between remedies having goals such as compensation, restitution, or punishment and enforcement by imprisonment or other types of punishment for contempt. Some remedies which have these goals are or were enforceable by imprisonment or punishment for contempt. Similarly, there is no necessary correlation between such goals and execution by direct recourse to assets. The root of the problem is that coercion is not a goal of the nature of compensation, restitution, and punishment. Coercion, through punishment for contempt, or the threat of such coercion is simply one of the methods for bringing about a goal such as compensation, restitution, or punishment.

5 What is the criterion for the declaration category?

The 'declaration' category comprises remedies that cannot be enforced, at least not without further applications to court.[40] 'Declaration' is a clear illustration of a category based on something other than a goal in the nature of compensation, restitution, and punishment. Remedies which cannot be enforced can also be placed into these categories. A court can declare rights to compensation, restitution, punishment, or other goals without actually providing the claimant with an enforceable remedy. Money judgments against the Crown provide an example of such unenforceable orders.[41]

[37] (1659) 1 Mod 124, 132, 84 ER 781, 786.

[38] For the position in England see G. Envis, *Enforcing Money Judgments* (London: Butterworths, 1995), 134–5 and for Australia see Tilbury, Noone and Kercher 3rd edn. (n 6 above), 797.

[39] Chapter 8 p 134.

[40] Chapter 9 p 158 discusses declarations of primary rights and Chapter 12 p 201 discusses declarations of secondary rights. See also Chapter 9 p 164.

[41] Crown Proceedings Act 1947 (UK) s 25(4).

6 Criteria must not be mixed

If a classification mixes criteria, then trouble may arise. Suppose we decide to arrange our books according to their content into categories of contract, tort, and jurisprudence and according to the first letter of the surname of their author into the categories of F, G and H. Clearly some books, but obviously not all, will then belong on two shelves. *The Concept of Law*[42] by Hart would belong on the shelf with books on the topic of jurisprudence and also on the shelf with authors' surnames beginning with H. Our classification will suffer from overlapping categories because of the mixed use of two criteria.

The received classification of remedies represents a series which purports to classify according to two or more criteria at the same time. The categories of compensation, restitution, and punishment classify remedies according to features they have *as rights*, namely, according to goal. The categories of specific enforcement, coercion, and declaration classify remedies according to features they have when viewed *as court orders*. By focusing on different types of features and hence criteria, overlapping categories have been created. These categories cut across each other with the consequence that some remedies may belong in two categories.

So far as a taxonomy includes two or more criteria, the combination must be hierarchical. In other words, mixed classifications must be avoided. Each level of the hierarchy must classify according to one criterion. As Tudge observes:

> Whatever criteria we adopt, however, and whatever we are classifying and for whatever purpose, all classifications tend to follow a common pattern. The items in question are first divided into big categories, and then each big category is divided into smaller categories, and so on. The result is a series of nesting groups called a hierarchy: little ones grouped within bigger ones within bigger ones still. All classifications, in short, are hierarchical.[43]

The remainder of this chapter will begin the process of constructing a hierarchical classification of remedies.

E What Could a Disciplined Classification of Remedies Look Like?

1 First principles of taxonomy

Tudge identifies the first principles of any taxonomy:

> Aristotle. . .spelled out the key idea — that in order to classify in a formal, reproducible manner, you have to rely on something more than the gestalt[44] that enables songbirds to

[42] H. L. A. Hart, *The Concept of Law* (2nd edn., Oxford: Clarendon Press, 1994).

[43] C. Tudge, *The Variety of Life* (Oxford: Oxford University Press, 2000), 19. Tudge writes about the classification of living creatures but his remarks are equally applicable to all taxonomies, including to the classification of the metaphysical constructs with which lawyers deal.

[44] Defined in J. Simpson and E. Weiner (eds), *Oxford English Dictionary* (2nd edn., Oxford: Clarendon Press, 1989) as 'A "shape", "configuration", or "structure" which as an object

differentiate between pigeons and hawks. You have in fact to define the criteria of your classification. In practice, you have carefully to describe the things in question, and then create groupings according to features that they have in common...You can produce quite different classifications depending on which features...you choose to focus on. But he also showed (another crucial insight) that some sets of characters seem to give more satisfactory results than others...Aristotle...confront[ed] crucial issues: the need to state clearly the criteria for classification; the fact that different criteria produce different results; and the inescapable need, therefore, to choose between different criteria.[45]

The features which are used to place certain remedies within the categories of compensation, restitution, punishment, specific enforcement, or coercion and declaration have been identified and discussed in the preceding sections. These and other characteristics of remedies will now be summarized. This will facilitate the choice of the main criteria for a new classification and the further development of that classification.

2 Features of remedies and possible criteria

The distinctions that might be drawn between remedies can be divided into distinctions based on, first, features that are common to all rights and, secondly, features that can only be ascribed to remedies because they can be viewed as court orders. These features are revealed by different questions. Each question identifies a different criterion which could be used to order one level of our hierarchical classification.

Features that are common to all rights, and hence may also be ascribed to remedies, include the historical source of the right, the content of the right, and the goal of the right. These features are revealed by questions which include: whether the right originated in common law courts or equity courts; whether it is personal or proprietary; whether the right is positive or negative — that is, to do or not to do; if positive, whether it requires a payment of money or some other act; and whether the right has a goal of compensation, restitution, punishment, or another goal. These are the features that remedies have simply because they are rights.

There are also a number of features that can only be ascribed to remedies and not all rights. These are the features that remedies have because they can be viewed as court orders.[46] These features are revealed by questions which include: whether the order is preventive or corrective — that is whether it is to prevent

of perception forms a specific whole or unity incapable of expression simply in terms of its parts'.

[45] Tudge (n 43 above), 20–1. Tudge is referring to Aristotle's work on the taxonomy of animals, see Aristotle Parts of Animals *De partibus animalium* (A. L. Peck (trans), Cambridge Massachusetts: Harvard University Press, 1961), Book I.

[46] Chapter 4 p 45.

a substantive right being infringed in the future[47] or whether it is made to redress or correct a past infringement of such a right; the order is the same as (replicates) or is different from (transforms) the substantive rights which the parties had before coming to court; whether the order was originally given in the common law or the equity courts—consequently, whether it is traditionally said that the claimant has a right to the order or that it is discretionary; and whether the order is in itself enforceable or non-enforceable; if enforceable, whether it is enforceable by punishment for contempt or by direct recourse to the defendant's assets.

Finally, there are features that may be ascribed to remedies by association with or derivation from the substantive rights that they effectuate. These features are revealed by questions which include: whether the remedy gives effect to a right that is equitable or legal; a primary or a secondary right; a right arising from consent, unjust enrichment, wrong, or another event; a personal or proprietary right; a positive or negative right; a right to a payment of money or to some other act; or a right with the goal of compensation, restitution, punishment, or another goal. Where the substantive right is replicated in the court order, these features become the features of the remedy. But where the claimant is given a remedy fashioned in the court's broad or strong discretion, some or all of these features will differ as between the substantive right and the remedy.

Some of these features are of less interest than others, at least for the purposes of a general taxonomy. We must select the criteria most satisfactory for our taxonomy, starting with the criterion for the highest or first level, what the Romans used to call the *summa divisio*.

3 The *summa divisio* or first level

The received classification uses the criteria which leading writers have treated as the most important for a general taxonomy. Its defect is that it mixes them. Three candidates for the basic criterion for a hierarchical taxonomy arise from our analysis of the received classification. The competing criteria might be labelled, by way of shorthand, as goal-based, enforcement-based, and effectuation-based. These labels are not self-explanatory. More fully, the goal-based criterion focuses on the goal of the remedy in terms of the measure of the change of the relative positions of the parties.[48] The enforcement-based criterion focuses on whether

[47] There are two kinds of preventive orders: (1) those which are intended to stop *another* from infringing the *claimant's* rights in the future, including some decrees of specific performance, injunctions, and declarations; and (2) those which are intended to eliminate the risk of the *applicant* infringing *another's* rights. It is trite to say that it is in a person's own interests not to infringe the rights of others. The elimination of this danger may be achieved by a remedy such as a declaration, rectification, probate of a will, or directions to trustees as to the administration of a trust. In such cases there is the danger of another person's rights being infringed if the situation is not judicially clarified and often consequent liability for the infringer (who may have acted entirely in good faith) as a result.

[48] See p 68.

and how the remedy may be enforced. The effectuation-based criterion focuses on whether and how substantive rights are given effect or effectuated in the remedy.

The first option is to classify according to the goal of the remedy. So the series would be: compensation, restitution, punishment, and other goals. This is a classification based on the goal of the remedy which itself is usually derivative of the goal of the substantive right to which the remedy gives effect. This is inadequate. The final miscellany category is too large because the multifarious primary rights arising out of contract or protected by tort that may be replicated in decrees of specific performance, injunctions, or declarations have numerous goals. Thus, the goal-based criterion cannot be utilized because one cannot construct an adequate goal-based series to cover all remedies. Primary rights, and hence the remedies which replicate them, have goals which are too diverse. Furthermore, remedies such as an award of damages or an agreed sum would need to be counted in many categories if a goal-based classification were adopted.

The second possibility is to classify remedies according to the potential consequences of recalcitrance or, putting it another way, the means by which they may be enforced. This series would be: enforceable and non-enforceable (or declaratory/constitutive). The first category could be subdivided according to whether the remedy is enforceable by punishment for contempt (coercive) or by direct recourse to the defendant's assets. However, the enforcement of remedies is generally not taken to be a core part of the law of remedies. Most texts on remedies refrain from dealing with the enforcement of court orders at all. As we saw in Chapter 4,[49] the enforcement of remedies if they are not complied with is a further and distinct step in the litigation process which can be, and usually is, treated separately to the grant of remedies.

The third possibility is to classify remedies not according to goal-based categories nor according to their potential effect on a recalcitrant defendant but by their relationship to the rights which existed before the parties found themselves in court. The most important and illuminating thing about remedies is their relationship to and effect on these substantive rights.[50] This will therefore be used as the *summa divisio* or the basic criterion. Focusing on this relationship between substantive rights and remedies, the main question is whether remedies are simply restatements of substantive rights existing independently before them or whether the court's order generates something which is quite different from the rights and duties which already pertained between the parties. With this question in mind, judicial remedies can be broken down into two broad classes: those which restate or replicate substantive rights

[49] See p 54.

[50] Scholars have long been making calls for analysis of and debate on this relationship. For example, D. W. M. Waters, 'Liability and Remedy: An Adjustable Relationship' (2001) *Saskatchewan L Rev* 429.

(replicative remedies[51]) and those which do not replicate any substantive rights (transformative remedies[52]). As we have seen, transformative remedies are remedies that differ extensively from the substantive rights which the claimant brought into court.

Some examples of replicative remedies include a decree of specific performance which may replicate a contractual right to a conveyance, an injunction which may replicate a right not to have one's possession of land interfered with, an award of restitution for unjust enrichment which may replicate a right to the return of a mistaken payment, an order for the recovery of land which replicates a right to recover possession of land, an award of an agreed sum which may replicate a contractual right to the payment of a purchase price or an award of damages which may replicate a right to the payment of damages for a breach of a duty of care, or a declaration which may replicate any right.[53]

A remedy which replicates a substantive right, such as a secondary right to the payment of damages, may sometimes need to 'liquidate',[54] that is, quantify or render certain, an amount which the claimant is entitled to recover from the defendant. The maxim *certum est quod certum reddi potest*[55] applies here. The claimant's substantive right is a right to be paid a sum to be determined by a formula, the formula being the rules relating to the quantification of the sum due, for example, the rules as to the assessment of damages. In that sense the right does exist prior to its replication in a quantified form in a court order. Thus the remedy in such an instance is best characterized as a replicative remedy rather than as a transformative one.

Say, in the case of a *quantum meruit* award, the claimant comes to court with a primary right to the reasonable value of the services he rendered, when he or she obtains a properly assessed award for £1,000, he or she receives nothing more nor less than a right to the reasonable value of the services he rendered. This is taken to be within the notion of replicating a right. The substantive right is given direct effect, in so far as is practically possible given the imprecise nature of the substantive right, in the court order. By force of necessity, the remedy renders the imprecise, precise. Such mere quantification is not taken to transform the claimant's substantive right in a significant way. Comparing the content of the remedy and the substantive right, the claimant is not getting anything to which he or she did not have a substantive right before coming to court.

[51] The term 'replicative' has been chosen for the situation where the rights whether primary or secondary are given direct effect in the order. 'Specific' seems to be too closely linked with the idea of giving direct effect to primary rights (only) and hence liable to lead to confusion if used more generically.

[52] The term 'transformative' has been chosen because where substantive rights are not replicated, the order necessarily alters or 'transforms' the pre-existing rights of the parties.

[53] These examples are developed in Chapters 7 to 12.

[54] 'A claim is said to be "liquidated" when it is for a fixed, inelastic sum or one which is calculable by the mere process of arithmetic': W. V. H. Rogers, *Winfield & Jolowicz on Tort* (15th edn., London: Sweet & Maxwell, 1998), 12 (footnotes omitted).

[55] 'That is certain which can be rendered certain.'

It is not only substantive rights to the payment of compensation that are imprecise and in need of 'liquidation' by the court. Other broadly expressed substantive rights may also need to be rendered more precise when replicated in a court order. For example, the rather abstract substantive right to enjoy quiet possession of land which is protected by the tort of nuisance had to be rendered precise in an injunction to restrain power-boat racing in *Kennaway v Thompson*.[56] The substantive right in its 'liquidated' form, and hence the remedy, restrained the club from engaging in 'motor-boat racing, water skiing and the use of boats creating a noise of more than 75 decibels on the club's water' but this was qualified as follows:

> the club is allowed to have, each racing season, one international event extending over three days, the first day being given over to practice and the second and third to racing. In addition there can be two national events, each of two days but separated from the international event and from each other by at least four weeks. Finally there can be three club events, each of one day, separated from the international and national events and each other by three weeks. Any international or national event not held can be replaced by a club event of one day. No boats creating a noise of more than 75 decibels are to be used on the club's water at any time other than when there are events as specified in this judgment. If events are held at week-ends, as they probably will be, six week-ends, covering a total of ten days, will be available for motor-boat racing on the club's water. Water skiing, if too many boats are used, can cause a nuisance by noise. The club is not to allow more than six motorboats to be used for water skiing at any one time.[57]

This is taken to have been a replicative remedy. In effect, the court merely rendered the claimant's imprecise substantive right more precise and restated it in an injunction. If the court had merely ordered the power-boat club not to interfere with the claimant's quiet possession, it would have failed to resolve the dispute which was essentially as to the extent of the claimant's substantive right to enjoy quiet possession.

Examples of transformative remedies include orders made under statutes which confer a broad or strong discretion to fashion remedies that do not resemble any substantive rights which the claimant can be said to have had before the order was made. One example is a family provision order under the Inheritance (Provision for Family and Dependants) Act 1975 (UK). Another example is an order under section 87 of the Trade Practices Act 1974 (Cth). An example of a non-statutory transformative remedy would be the 'remedial constructive trust', a remedy which is a proprietary right given in the court's broad or strong discretion in circumstances where the claimant did not have any proprietary rights before the order was made.[58]

The basic criterion which has been chosen reflects an aim of better understanding how remedies come into existence (i.e. the causative event of adjudication).

[56] [1981] QB 88 (CA). [57] Ibid 94–95 (Lawton LJ).

[58] Transformative remedies are discussed in further detail in Chapter 13.

Just as studies of contract begin by focusing on how a contract is made, studies of restitution begin by focusing on different events that constitute unjust enrichment, and studies of torts begin by focusing on the different events that give rise to torts, it is congruous that studies of remedies should begin by focusing on the event that brings remedies into existence. Of course in the present case there is only one event, namely, the judge's utterance or the issue of a document. Nevertheless the chosen criterion relates closely to that event, in that it divides the remedies that arise according to whether, in granting them, the judge replicates or transforms the substantive rights which the claimant brought into court.

In order to further distinguish remedies in each of the two main categories we must add additional levels to our classification.

4 Lower levels of the hierarchy

Replicative remedies may be further broken down into two sub-classes: those which replicate primary rights (specific remedies) and those which replicate secondary rights but thus only give *indirect* effect to primary rights (substitutionary remedies). Remedies which replicate primary rights include awards of an agreed sum (or, more broadly, money due under a contract), awards of restitution for unjust enrichment, decrees of specific performance, prohibitory injunctions, and orders for the recovery of land from trespassers. Remedies which replicate secondary rights include awards of damages and some mandatory injunctions. This second level of the classification focuses on a feature of the substantive right that is replicated.

At the next level, each category of replicative remedies may be further subdivided according to jurisdictional origin. Remedies originated either in the common law courts, the courts of equity, or are creatures of statute. Although law and equity are no longer administered in different courts, this has created differences that have persisted until the present day. Judges continue to adopt different approaches in awarding the relevant remedies. It is traditionally said that common law remedies are awarded 'as of right' whereas equitable remedies are awarded as a matter of discretion. 'As of right' is taken to mean that upon finding liability the courts are compelled to make an order which replicates the claimant's right. If the remedy originated in equity then a wider range of grounds for refusal of replication and hence more discretion is said to be at play than in the case of a remedy which originated at common law. For instance, remedies which originated in equity, such as specific performance and injunctions, may be refused on broad grounds such as the adequacy of damages, unclean hands, or hardship.

The reasons for the differences in approach may be found in history and in policy concerns surrounding the deployment of the relevant enforcement mechanisms. Common law and equitable remedies generally have different consequences if they are not complied with, in terms of the enforcement mechanisms that are available. Remedies which originated in the courts of equity are generally enforceable by contempt proceedings and those which originated in common law courts by direct recourse to the defendant's assets, such as by seizure and sale. Enforcement of the former type severely interferes with an individual's liberty; it is more drastic than the latter. Consequently courts seek to exercise more control over the grant of remedies which may lead to punishment for contempt. This seems to be the *raison d'être* for the so-called discretionary grounds for the refusal of such remedies. This element of discretion is further examined in the next chapter.

As the jurisdictional differences between remedies become less important, different criteria will become more important and hence it will also be desirable to structure the taxonomy of remedies differently. It may then be more preferable to adopt a taxonomy similar to Lawson's[59] which places greater emphasis on the content of remedies. One may wish to distinguish remedies according to what they confer on the claimant and require of the defendant. The main sub-division being between remedies which require the payment of money and hence are enforceable in one way (namely, by direct recourse to the defendant's assets) and remedies which require the doing of another act or forbearance, which are enforceable in different ways (namely, punishment of the defendant for contempt). One may also wish to sub-divide remedies according to their exigibility, that is, whether they are personal or proprietary. As stated above, the criteria that we focus on and the relative priority that we assign to them will depend on the aims of our taxonomy.

F Conclusion

The law of judicial remedies is the law associated with the effectuation of substantive rights by courts. Since remedies are themselves rights, the law of remedies is concerned with the generation of these particular rights — how they come to be, and the nature and the content of these rights — what they confer on the claimant and require of the defendant. The taxonomy of remedies proposed at the end of this chapter addresses these questions. The questions identify its key criteria.

The fundamental test is whether a remedy is a restatement of a substantive right or whether it is substantially different from all such prior rights. That is, whether it is replicative or transformative. The question is fundamental because it identifies a major divide in the subject matter. Different questions need to be asked of the two different classes of remedies that emerge. In the case of replicative remedies, the main questions are: first, what is the nature of the substantive right that the remedy replicates (as this settles the content of the remedy), in particular,

[59] Chapter 3 p 25.

whether it is a primary or a secondary right; and second, the jurisdictional origin of the remedy which determines the nature of the court's role in its replication. The latter determines the approach that the judge feels bound to adopt to the replication of the right and, in turn, whether replication may be refused on certain grounds. In the case of transformative remedies, the first question is what is the jurisdictional origin of the remedy; however, the most controversial issue is what content the remedy should have as this is not fully determined by the claimant's substantive rights but chosen by the judge from case to case.

After the element of discretion is examined in the context of remedies, the remaining chapters will give an account of remedies in private law within the analytical framework established in this first part of this book. The primary purpose will be to illustrate and stress the legitimacy of remedies as a discrete subject even though a large part of what has been considered to be included in the law remedies by many writers, namely secondary rights, has been taken away.

G Appendix

The proposed taxonomy can be represented diagrammatically as follows:

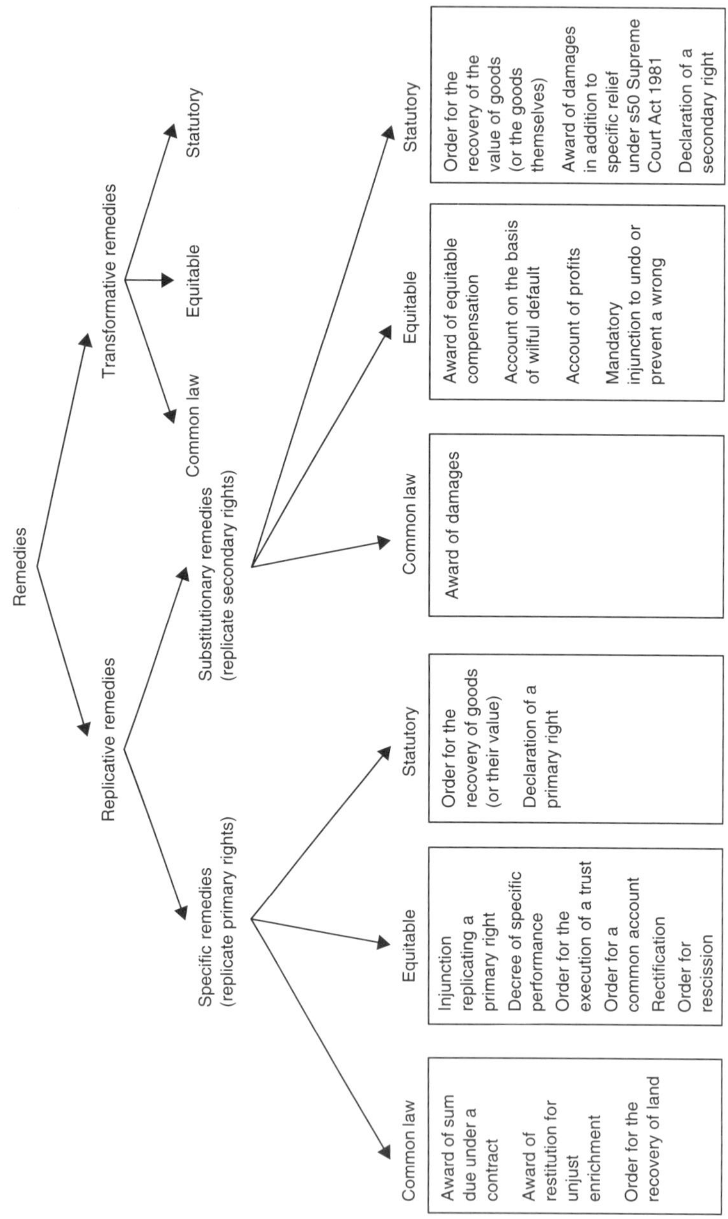

Figure 5.1

6

Discretion and Remedies

A Introduction

Although a claimant has a substantive right, it does not necessarily follow that a court must grant a remedy which replicates that right if it is infringed. Where, although the cause of action is established, the court exercises some choice as to whether to grant a particular remedy, it is traditionally said that the remedy is 'discretionary'. This label is usually attached to remedies which originated in the equity jurisdiction and some statutory remedies.

Discretion gives rise to two potential problems which need to be avoided in the construction of a taxonomy of remedies. First, it might be supposed that remedies should be classified as 'discretionary' or 'non-discretionary'. But, as we will see, there is often no significant distinction to be drawn. Nearly all remedies are to some extent discretionary but, in relation to equitable remedies, this element is exaggerated. Secondly, it might be thought, especially in relation to equitable remedies, that the presence of discretion means that a remedy must be classed as transformative rather than replicative. The labelling of remedies as discretionary might invite us to assume that more remedies are transformative than actually are. The role that discretion plays in relation to the grant of remedies must be studied to obviate these and other problems.

Much has been written about discretion. This chapter draws on the works of a number of scholars to overcome some stereotypical beliefs and in particular to highlight that: (1) the grant of replicative remedies which originated in the common law jurisdiction involves a degree of discretion; (2) the discretion in relation to replicative remedies which originated in the equity jurisdiction is discretion as to whether recognized bars operate so as to prevent the remedy being granted; (3) the degree of discretion in relation to such equitable remedies should not be exaggerated; and (4) the discretion traditionally involved in the refusal of equitable replicative remedies is quite different in type and scope from the broader and stronger discretion often involved in the grant of transformative remedies. A distinction must be drawn between the discretion that a court may have because it has to apply an open-textured standard to refuse a remedy and the discretion that a court may have to create an entirely new legal relationship between particular parties, that is, to grant a transformative remedy.

B A Closer Look at Discretion

1 Definition of discretion

At the core of the many definitions of discretion is the element of choice. Davis gave the classic academic definition: 'A public officer has discretion whenever the effective limits on his power leave him free to make a choice among possible courses of action or inaction.'[1] Discretion has been said to imply the power to choose from a number of alternatives. Barak writes that 'discretion is a power given to a person with authority to choose between two or more alternatives, when each of the alternatives is lawful.'[2]

2 Discretion and rules

Discretion may be contrasted with rules. But a dichotomy between rules and discretion is in some ways a simplification. Hawkins points out that the use of rules involves some discretion and the use of discretion makes some use of rules.[3] But as Gardner observes:

> It is important, however, not to allow this perception to lull us into thinking that there are therefore no further distinctions to be drawn, or choices to be made.
>
> In the first place, the blurring of the contrast between rules and discretions does not mean that everything reduces to a single point midway between the two. It is clear that some areas of decision are more constrained than others: that there remain separable ideas of 'rules' and 'discretion' as a matter of substance.[4]

Whereas discretion is present where the judge may make a choice in resolving the dispute before him or her, rules are institutional choices as to how such a dispute should be resolved in particular circumstances. If the conditions for their operation are satisfied, rules dictate a particular result.[5] Rules entrench particular policy choices made by a body with authority over the judge. Such choices are made by Parliament in legislation or by higher courts in decisions that set a binding precedent. Rules remove the necessity and authority for the judge to make a choice on the same issue.

[1] K. C. Davis, *Discretionary Justice: A Preliminary Inquiry* (Louisiana: Louisiana State University Press, 1969), 4.

[2] A. Barak, *Judicial Discretion* (New Haven: Yale University Press, 1989), 7.

[3] K. Hawkins, 'Using Legal Discretion' in K. Hawkins (ed.), *The Uses of Discretion* (Oxford: Clarendon Press, 1992), 3, 35.

[4] S. Gardner, 'The Element of Discretion' in P. B. H. Birks, (ed.) *The Frontiers of Liability Vol 2* (Oxford: Oxford University Press, 1994), 194.

[5] R. Dworkin, *Taking Rights Seriously* (London: Duckworth, 1977), 24.

3 Constraints on discretion

Discretion may be constrained to a greater or lesser extent; the number of alternatives which may be legitimately chosen and considerations which may be taken into account may be larger or smaller.

First, discretion may be constrained in that the alternatives which may be legitimately chosen may be circumscribed. For example, a judge in a criminal case may be given discretion as to the sentence that may be imposed provided it falls between a specified minimum and maximum. Where there are many options to choose from, Barak labels the discretion 'broad'. Where the options are few he labels it 'narrow'.[6]

Secondly, discretion may be guided in the sense that the matters which may or must be taken into account in its exercise may be specified.[7] Discretion has been characterized as strong or weak according to how much guidance is provided to the judge. Dworkin writes that 'strong' discretion occurs where the judge is 'simply not bound by standards set by the authority in question'.[8] If discretion is only guided by very open-textured standards, it may also be characterized at the strong end of the spectrum. For example, if a judge is required to make a choice having regard merely to what is fair, just, and reasonable in the circumstances, the judge has a strong discretion.

Where however the standards have been articulated in detail, the scope for the judge's choice is greatly circumscribed. The judge's choice may be confined to an exercise of judgment in the application of the standard. In such a case, the judge's discretion may be said to be 'weak'. One of the senses in which Dworkin uses weak discretion is 'that for some reason the standards an official must apply cannot be applied mechanically but demand the use of judgment'.[9]

It is impossible to pinpoint where weak discretion ends and strong discretion begins. It is a matter of degree. As Evans observes 'strong and weak discretion remain useful shorthands for the two ends of the discretionary decision making continuum.'[10]

4 Reasons for discretion

For a more complete understanding of discretion, it is also helpful to identify the reasons for the conferral of discretion and the consequences of its exercise on

[6] Barak (n 2 above), 8–9. [7] Ibid 18–19. [8] Dworkin (n 5 above), 32.

[9] Ibid 31. Dworkin gives the example of an order to a sergeant to take his five most experienced men on patrol where it is hard to determine which of the men have most experience. The second sense of 'weak discretion' that Dworkin identifies is authority to make a decision that cannot be reviewed: ibid 32. But this consequence of some types of discretion need not necessarily attach to all types of discretion. Consequences should depend on the reasons why the discretion was conferred: S. M. Waddams, 'Judicial Discretion' [2000] *Oxford U Commonwealth LJ* 59.

[10] S. Evans, 'Defending Discretionary Remedialism' [2001] 23 *Sydney L Rev* 463, 483.

subsequent cases. First, discretion may be a 'rule-building' discretion which, as Schneider states:

> arises where the rule-maker could devise tolerably effective rules, but concludes that better rules would be developed (or that the same rules could be developed more efficiently) if the decision-makers were allowed to develop rules for themselves as they go along.[11]

Secondly, it may be a 'rule-compromise' discretion which is conferred where the rule-makers 'cannot agree on rules or even guidelines, and they. . .then deliberately choose to pass responsibility to the decision-maker'.[12]

Both types are closely related. Choices are left to the courts but once they are made, rules are formed which must be followed in future cases unless there is a good reason for creating an exception or qualification to the rule. Thus, the scope of such discretions narrows over time and their strength is reduced.

These must be contrasted with discretion which is intended to be exercised afresh from case to case with the consequence that a decision in a prior case does not bind the court in a future case. Such a 'rule-failure' discretion, Schneider writes, 'is created where it is believed that cases will arise in circumstances so varied, so complex, and so unpredictable that satisfactory rules that will guide decision-makers to correct results in a sufficiently large number of cases cannot be written.'[13]

C Discretion as to Replicative Remedies

1 Introduction

The taxonomy proposed at the end of Chapter 5 divides remedies according to whether they are rights which replicate primary or secondary rights which existed before trial and hence belong in the 'replicative' category or are rights which bear little resemblance to prior substantive rights and hence belong in the 'transformative' category. Discretion in relation to remedies in the replicative category will now be examined. Discretion in relation to remedies in the transformative category will be examined in the next section. The central contention of this section is that a degree of discretion is not incompatible with a remedy being replicative in nature.

It is customary to distinguish between replicative remedies which originated at common law and those which originated in equity. Equitable remedies have come to be known as 'discretionary remedies'. Equitable replicative remedies are replicative remedies which the court may refuse because certain kinds of bars are found to operate. Many of these bars do not apply to remedies originating at common law and so it is appropriate to draw a distinction between remedies

[11] C. E. Schneider in K. Hawkins (ed.), *The Uses of Discretion* (Oxford: Clarendon Press, 1992), 64. [12] Ibid 64.
[13] Ibid 62.

based on their jurisdictional origin. However, the extent of this difference should not be overstated. Some bars, such as illegality and public policy, may be found to operate, under different names, in relation to common law remedies as well as equitable remedies.[14]

2 Discretion as to common law remedies

There is and has always been a degree of discretion with respect to the grant of common law remedies. Broad standards, such as reasonable care or reasonable foreseeability, have to be construed and applied at common law. Historically this discretion has not been given prominence. This may be because until the last century it was exercised predominantly by juries.[15] As jury trials have become rarer in civil litigation, this discretion has fallen to be exercised by judges.[16] It can no longer be ignored. It warrants closer study. Laycock examines the law governing the assessment of damages and concludes:

> [A] great deal of discretion is built into the measure of damages. . .[S]pecific performance cases are full of talk about conscience and discretion, overtly introducing the discretion that is inherent in the more flexible process of measuring damages. . .There are ways in which damage remedies are more flexible than equitable remedies. . .[17]

Burrows undertakes the same task and draws the same conclusion:

> this survey [of rules limiting awards of compensatory damages] shows that the statement often made that, in contrast to equitable remedies, common law remedies are non-discretionary and all or nothing seems misleading. . .[T]here is a large element of discretion in the rules and principles governing common law damages. Indeed, it is arguable that there is as much, and possibly more, discretion in relation to damages than there is in relation to, for example, the equitable remedies of specific performance and injunctions.[18]

There is clearly discretion to limit damages awards when applying the rules relating to causation, remoteness, and mitigation. These rules are open-textured because they embody standards of reasonableness.

Instances where discretion can lead to an outright refusal of common law remedies can also be found. The case of *White and Carter (Councils) Ltd v*

[14] See text to n 28 below and A. Burrows, 'We Do This at Common Law But That in Equity' (2002) 22 *OJLS* 1, 14–15.

[15] In contrast, the equity jurisdiction never made use of juries so decisions of this nature, namely as to the application of widely expressed standards, fell to be made by judges and attracted the label of 'discretion'.

[16] The decline of juries in relation to common law remedies is further discussed in Chapter 9.

[17] D. Laycock, 'The Triumph of Equity' (1993) 56(3) *Law and Contemporary Problems* 53, 72. Cooke J, writing extra-judicially, had earlier advocated that this discretion be expressly embraced: R. Cooke, 'Remoteness of Damage and Judicial Discretion' [1978] *CLJ* 288. See also J. Beatson, *The Use and Abuse of Unjust Enrichment* (Oxford: Clarendon Press, 1991), 250–1.

[18] A. Burrows, *Hochelaga Lecture 2001: Fusing Common Law and Equity: Remedies Restitution and Reform* (Asia Hong Kong: Sweet & Maxwell, 2002), 9. See also Burrows (n 14 above), 2, 10, 14.

McGregor[19] raised the possibility of a discretionary bar to the common law remedy of an award of an agreed sum. The appellants were advertising agents. They entered into a contract with an agent of the respondent whereby advertising signs were to be displayed on litter bins for a period of three years. The same day, the respondent repudiated the contract. The appellants did not accept the repudiation. They displayed the advertising for three years and sued to recover the agreed amount. The respondent argued that the appellants could only sue for damages and that they should have mitigated their loss by not performing the contract. The House of Lords held, by a majority of three to two, that the appellants were entitled to perform their side of the contract and to sue for the contract price.

Lord Hodson felt that to decide the case otherwise would in effect force the appellant to accept a variation of the contract on the grounds of unreasonableness and 'would make an action for debt a claim for a discretionary remedy'.[20] Lord Reid, whilst agreeing with other members of the majority as to the result, stated that the claimant would fail where he has 'no legitimate interest, financial or otherwise, in performing the contract, rather than claiming damages'.[21]

Lord Reid's qualification has been approved in subsequent cases.[22] Thus it seems that where an innocent party performs his side of the contract following breach without the contract-breaker's co-operation and seeks an award of an agreed sum then, as Lord Hodson observed, an open-textured or 'discretionary' bar becomes available. The defendant may raise the bar where the claimant has 'no legitimate interest' in obtaining that remedy or, what appears to be the same thing, where damages are an adequate remedy and the claimant ought 'in all reason' to accept the repudiation and sue for damages[23] or where damages are an adequate remedy and the claimant's action in performing the contract is 'wholly unreasonable'.[24] Where the bar operates, the claimant must rely on his or her right to damages which is qualified by a 'duty' to mitigate.

An award of an agreed sum may also be refused to the extent that it is a penalty.[25] A penalty is a sum expressed to be payable on the occurrence of a breach of the contract between the parties[26] which is a threat against, and

19 [1962] AC 413 (HL). 20 Ibid 445. 21 Ibid 431.

22 See the detailed discussion of the authorities in *Clea Shipping Corporation v Bulk Oil International Ltd (The Alaskan Trader)* [1984] 1 All ER 129 (Lloyd J); also *Stocznia Gdanska SA v Latvian Shipping Co* [1996] 2 Lloyd's Rep 132, 139 (CA) reversed on other grounds [1998] 1 WLR 574 (HL).

23 *Attica Sea Carriers v Ferrostaal (The Puerto Buitrago)* [1976] 1 Lloyd's Rep 250, 255–256 (CA) (Denning LJ).

24 *Gator Shipping Corp v Trans-Asiatic Oil Ltd SA (The Odenfeld)* [1978] 2 Lloyd's Rep 357, 374 (Kerr J).

25 *Jobson v Johnson* [1989] 1 WLR 1026, 1033, 1039–1040 and 1047 (CA). Compare *AMEV-UDC Finance Ltd v Austin* (1986) 162 CLR 170 (HCA).

26 But the doctrine is inapplicable if the right arises on the occurrence of another event: *Jervis v Harris* [1996] Ch 195, 206 (CA) (Millett LJ); contrast the contrary views of Deane J in *AMEV-UDC Finance Ltd v Austin* (1986) 162 CLR 170 (HCA).

punishment for, non-performance rather than a genuine pre-estimate of the loss likely to flow from such non-performance.[27] Determining whether a sum is or is not a genuine pre-estimate of loss involves an element of discretion as much as an application of a reasonableness standard.

Furthermore, as already stated, some equitable bars appear to have common law equivalents. The Law Commission observed, 'there are common law doctrines—such as those of illegality or public policy—which mirror in nature, if not in scope, the so-called "discretionary defences" in equity.'[28]

There is clearly a degree of discretion in the grant of remedies which originated in the common law jurisdiction, sometimes even in relation to the seemingly most non-discretionary remedy, the award of an agreed sum. This is the first reason why no attempt was made to divide remedies into 'discretionary' and 'non-discretionary' in constructing the taxonomy in Chapter 5.

3 Discretion as to equitable remedies

Discretion in relation to replicative remedies which originated in equity has been presented as an endemic and prominent feature of the equity jurisdiction. Two ways in which this discretion can be characterized will be identified and then a number of its features will be summarized.

(a) Characterized as discretion to grant or refuse the remedy

Discretion as to equitable replicative remedies may be taken to be a choice as to whether to grant or refuse an equitable remedy. As Jacob writes:

> The essence of a discretionary remedy is that, although the legal right to the claim or interest is established, yet the court retains the power, having regard to all the circumstances of the case, to refuse the remedy or to award it and if so upon specified terms.[29]

If so characterized, this discretion is weak. It is exercised according to well-settled although fairly broadly expressed rules. As Lord Romilly MR stated of such equitable discretion in *Haywood v Cope*:

> [T]he discretion of the court must be exercised according to fixed and settled rules; you cannot exercise a discretion by merely considering what, as between the parties, would be fair to be done; what one person may consider fair, another person may consider very

[27] *Dunlop Pneumatic Tyre Co Ltd v New Garage and Motor Co Ltd* [1915] AC 79, 86–87 (HL); see also *Phillips Hong Kong Ltd v A-G of Hong Kong* (1993) 61 Build LR 41 (PC). The doctrine was introduced into the common law by statute: F. H. Lawson, *Remedies of English Law* (2nd edn., London: Butterworth & Co, 1980), 42–3; Administration of Justice Act 1696 (UK) (8 & 9 Will. 3, c. 11); *Wall v Rederiaktiebolaget Luggude* [1915] 3 KB 66, 73.

[28] Law Commission *Aggravated, Exemplary and Restitutionary Damages* Report No 247 (London: The Stationery Office, 1997), [3.84].

[29] J. Jacob, *Fabric of English Civil Justice* (London: Stevens & Sons, 1987), 176. See also *Bristol City Council v Lovell* [1998] 1 WLR 446, 453 (HL).

unfair; you must have some settled rule and principle upon which to determine how that discretion is to be exercised.[30]

We have such fixed and settled rules in relation to equitable replicative remedies. These rules provide that certain equitable 'bars' may prevent certain equitable remedies from being granted. Burrows writes:

> [I]n contrast to damages, specific performance is not available for every breach of contract. Indeed, as in this chapter, specific performance is best approached negatively, that is by examining the numerous restrictions on its availability. Positively, it then follows that if the remedy is not barred by such restriction, a plaintiff who applies for it will succeed.[31]

It is submitted that the discretion in relation to equitable replicative remedies is not simply a discretion to grant or refuse the remedy, as the passage quoted from Jacob's lectures suggests. This appears to state the ambit of the court's choice too broadly. The discretion seems to reside in the 'fixed and settled rules' referred to by Lord Romilly MR which establish the bars to equitable remedies.

(b) Characterized as discretion as to whether a 'bar' to the remedy operates

Discretion as to equitable replicative remedies may be taken to be a choice as to whether certain 'bars' operate in the particular circumstances. If they do, the court is required to refuse the equitable replicative remedy.

These bars have been called discretionary considerations, standards, factors, maxims, matters, rules, and principles. They are broadly expressed and reflect the sensitivity of the courts to certain issues. They function as 'safety valves' allowing the court to individualize the availability of particular remedies.[32] In the case of specific performance, these bars include the need for court supervision, the need to maintain a personal relationship, a lack of readiness and willingness on the claimant's part to perform his side of the bargain, the unavailability of specific relief to the defendant (lack of mutuality), mistake, unfairness to or hardship on the defendant, disentitling conduct on the claimant's part (unclean hands), unreasonable delay (laches), futility of the order, impossibility of complying with the order, illegality, and the public interest. A number of these bars potentially apply to all equitable remedies. Such bars of general application will be referred to as the 'usual bars' to equitable remedies in the following chapters when it is necessary to refer to them in the context of particular remedies.[33]

It is relatively easy to determine which of these bars will be relevant in a given case and which will be irrelevant or of very little weight. However, it may be very

[30] (1858) 25 Beav 140, 151. See also *Lemare v Dixon* (1873) LR 6 HL 414, 423; *Doherty v Allman* (1878) 3 App Cas 709, 728 (HL); *R v Stafford Justices* [1940] 2 KB 33, 43 (HL).

[31] A. Burrows, *Remedies for Torts and Breaches of Contract* (2nd edn., London: Butterworths, 1994), 336. Repeated in substance in A. Burrows, 'Judicial Remedies' in P. B. H. Birks (ed.), *English Private Law Vol II* (Oxford: Oxford University Press, 2000), 864.

[32] The idea of a 'safety valve' discretion is taken from: Law Commission (n 28 above), 137.

[33] See Chapters 8 and 9.

difficult to determine whether the bars block the replicative remedy in a particular fact situation. This is the point at which the judge's discretion or choice plays its role. This is where the real discretion in relation to equitable replicative remedies resides.[34] The exercise of the judge's discretion involves ascribing weight to the relevant bars and the competing considerations[35] and balancing them against each other to reach a decision.[36] The weight given to the relevant equitable bar dictates whether the remedy should be refused because the judge cannot hold that the considerations weigh in the defendant's favour but grant the remedy anyway.

The discretion is narrow in the sense that it involves a choice between only two options: whether the bars operate to prevent the remedy being granted or not. Where the remedy is not barred, there is a further choice as to whether the *defendant's rights* should be effectuated in the same order, that is, whether the remedy should be granted on conditions. This will be examined separately below.[37]

If the court refuses an equitable replicative remedy, the substantive right which is not replicated generally continues to exist.[38] It does so in a similar way that a statute-barred debt continues to exist.[39] It is merely held to be unenforceable *in specie* in the particular circumstances.[40] It is inaccurate to label the underlying substantive right, whether legal or equitable, 'discretionary'. As Goode points out, the recognition of substantive equitable rights does not generally involve discretion.[41]

The discretion as to whether a bar to a remedy operates is not a rule-building or a rule-compromise discretion as defined by Schneider. The giving of particular weight to the considerations in a case does not bind lower courts to make the

[34] This is the scope of the 'discretionary space' referred to by Loughlan: P. Loughlan, 'No Right to a Remedy? An Analysis of Judicial Discretion in the Imposition of Equitable Remedies' (1989) 17 *Melbourne UL Rev* 131, 135. Contrast D. Jensen, 'The Rights and Wrongs of Discretionary Remedialism' [2003] *Singapore J of Legal Studies* 178, 193 who suggests that all judicial decisions have a precedent value and 'we should not suppose that there are certain types of legal questions, such as questions about the imposition of equitable remedies, which will be rule-free spaces forever.' However, this may not be consistent with some judicial remarks; for example, see text to n 42 below.

[35] The main competing consideration which must be outweighed for the bar to operate is that a claimant should enjoy his or her rights in specie as far as public policy will allow. Tilbury also identifies other considerations that may weigh in favour of the claimant: M. Tilbury, *Civil Remedies Vol 1 Principles of Civil Remedies* (North Ryde New South Wales: Butterworths, 1990), [6043].

[36] I. C. F. Spry, *The Principles of Equitable Remedies: Specific Performance, Injunctions, Rectification and Equitable Damages* (6th edn., Pyrmont New South Wales: Law Book Co, 2001), 4.

[37] See p 96 below. [38] See Chapter 8 p 127.

[39] As was seen in Chapter 4 p 59, there are non-discretionary bars at common law which prevent the grant of replicative common law remedies but do not extinguish the underlying substantive right. Such bars may operate in relation to statute-barred debts, contracts unenforceable for want of form, and rights under contracts with minors.

[40] But it may still be given indirect effect through the replication of a secondary right. See Chapter 10 p 165.

[41] R. Goode, 'Property and Unjust Enrichment' in A. Burrows (ed.), *Essays on the Law of Restitution* (Oxford: Clarendon Press, 1991), 222–3.

same choice in a future case. As Millett LJ stated in *Jaggard v Sawyer* in relation to exercises of discretion as to the withholding of an injunction and awarding damages in lieu under Lord Cairns' Act:

Reported cases are merely illustrations of circumstances in which particular judges have exercised their discretion in some cases by granting an injunction, and in others by awarding damages instead. Since they are all cases on the exercise of a discretion, none of them is a binding authority on how the discretion should be exercised. The most that any of them can demonstrate is that in similar circumstances it would not be wrong to exercise the discretion in the same way. But it does not follow that it would be wrong to exercise it differently.[42]

These are the indicia of a rule-failure discretion. In relation to this discretion as to the operation of bars, one may conclude, as Loughlan does, that 'there are not and cannot be rules in cases involving equitable relief'.[43] When viewed in this manner, statements such as Loughlan's do not contradict Lord Romilly's statement that any equitable discretion (to grant or refuse a remedy) must be exercised according to fixed and settled rules.[44] To reiterate, the discretion as to equitable replicative remedies does not displace rules, it is inherent in the rules which create the possible bars to such remedies.

The trial judge has no choice as to whether new bars may be introduced or existing ones ignored in the case before him. For example, in *FAI Insurances Ltd v Pioneer Concrete Services Ltd*[45] Young J held that 'unless there is established one of the equitable defences then general naughtiness or the desire of the court to censor the plaintiff's conduct, does not enter into the equation when one is considering whether the plaintiff should get relief'. However, at times an appellate court may make changes to what constitutes a bar just as it may update a common law rule to make it fit with current community standards.[46] This does not mean that the law in question should be labelled discretionary for all judge-made rules would then attract that label.

(c) Downplaying the term 'discretion' in relation to equitable remedies

Burrows writes:

[I]t is often said that, unlike damages, specific performance is a discretionary remedy. But it would be a mistake to imagine that this means that the law on specific performance is

[42] [1995] 1 WLR 269, 288 (CA). Contrast Jensen's view that courts ought to be bound by such choices made in prior cases; that is, 'if we really believe that like cases ought to be decided alike, then we ought to insist that every exercise of judicial discretion be taken to generate a reason for deciding the present case and future similar cases in a particular way': Jensen (n 34 above), 193.

[43] Loughlan (n 34 above), 135.

[44] Reproduced at text to n 30 above.

[45] (1988–9) 15 NSWLR 552, 554.

[46] The capacity to change equitable doctrines in this way was a recognized feature of equity. Equitable doctrines were 'established from time to time, altered, improved and refined from time to time': *Re Hallett's Estate* (1879) 13 Ch D 696, 710 (CA) (Sir George Jessel VC). But as at law, caution prevails. In *Re Diplock* [1948] Ch 465, 482 (CA) it was stated that the court will not invent a new equity jurisdiction merely because the 'justice' of the case before it requires it.

not clear and certain. In truth, the expression means no more than that, while there are no bars on damages,[47] which are therefore available as of right for breach of contract (or a tort), there are numerous, albeit clearly established, bars to specific performance. The same contrast can be made of all common law, as against equitable, remedies for breach of contract (and torts).[48]

Such suggestions that discretion in relation to equitable remedies ought to be downplayed may appear to be anathema to some equity lawyers. Although they may be welcomed by others. Lord Radcliffe stated that equity lawyers were 'sometimes both surprised and discomfited by the plenitude of jurisdiction and the imprecision of rules that are attributed to "equity" by their more enthusiastic colleagues.'[49]

Maitland suggested that the label 'discretionary' was overused in relation to the remedy of specific performance. He stated in his famous course of lectures on equity:

It used to be said, and from time to time this sort of thing is still repeated, that specific performance is a discretionary remedy, but I think that of late years this talk has lost its old meaning, and that the right to specific performance may now be regarded as a right which normally accrues to every contractor when a contract falling with certain recognised classes has been broken. The exceptions have been brought under heads.[50]

Similarly, Pomeroy concluded that the term 'discretionary' was 'misleading and inaccurate' when applied to specific performance and, seemingly, other equitable remedies.[51] Fry, the foremost authority on specific performance in his time, wrote that 'if the contract has been entered into by a competent party, and is unobjectionable in its nature and circumstances, specific performance is as much a matter of course, and therefore of right, as are damages.'[52] Kerr, the foremost authority on injunctions and Fry's contemporary, wrote: 'After the establishment of his legal right, and of the fact of its violation, a man is in general entitled as of course to a perpetual injunction to prevent the recurrence of the wrong, unless there be something special in the circumstances of the case'.[53]

[47] However Burrows' assertion that there are no bars on damages ought to be qualified for, as we have seen above, there are some defences to common law remedies which could be viewed as preforming the same function as the equitable 'bars'. Thus the limitation defence at law is similar to the laches (delay) bar in equity and the illegality defence at law is similar to the unclean hands bar in equity.

[48] A. Burrows, *Remedies for Torts and Breaches of Contract* (2nd edn., London: Butterworths, 1994), 336. Repeated in substance in A. Burrows, 'Judicial Remedies' in P. B. H. Birks (ed.), *English Private Law Vol II* (Oxford: Oxford University Press, 2000), 864.

[49] *Bridge v Campbell Discount Co Ltd* [1962] AC 600, 626 (HL).

[50] F. W. Maitland, *Equity: A Course of Lectures* (Cambridge: Cambridge University Press, 1936), 308.

[51] J. N. Pomeroy, *Equity Jurisprudence Vol III* (4th edn., San Francisco: Bancroft-Whitney Co, 1919), [1404].

[52] E. Fry, *A Treatise on the Specific Performance of Contracts* (3rd edn., London: Stevens, 1892), 19 (footnote omitted).

[53] W. W. Kerr, *On the Law and Practice of Injunctions* (3rd edn., London: Maxwell, 1888), 42. Footnote refers to *Imperial Gas Light & Coke Co v Broadbent* (1859) 7 HLC 600, 612.

In line with the tenor of these observations and in order not to place undue emphasis on the element of discretion involved, the replicative remedies that originated in equity will not be referred to as 'discretionary' remedies in this book. This is not to deny that there is an element of discretion in relation to such remedies; it is a matter of not giving it undue emphasis. This is the second reason why remedies were not categorized in Chapter 5 according to whether they are 'discretionary' or 'non-discretionary'.

Placing more emphasis on the discretionary element in the refusal of equitable remedies than it warrants may lead one to an erroneous conclusion that equity courts have traditionally exercised a broader and stronger discretion in relation to remedies than in fact they have or claimed to have.

It has been speculated that one reason why the element of discretion may have been overemphasized by some lawyers following the Judicature Act 1875 was to distinguish equity from the common law with the effect of preserving the Chancery bar's *de facto* monopoly over particular areas of practice.[54]

(d) 'Discretion' to impose conditions

When discretion in relation to equitable remedies is discussed, reference is often made to the discretion to 'mould' or 'fashion' an equitable remedy through the imposition of terms or conditions on the basis of the maxim that 'he who seeks equity must do equity'. However, the imposition of conditions in the grant of an equitable remedy can be viewed simply as an instance of the replication of the *defendant's* substantive rights against the *claimant* in the court's order. Strong authority for this proposition resides in the lucid statements of Wigram VC in *Hanson v Keating*:

> [The maxim that he who seeks equity must do equity] decides in the abstract that the court giving the plaintiff the relief to which he is entitled will do so only upon the terms of his submitting to give the defendant such corresponding rights (if any) as he also may be entitled to in respect of the subject matter of the suit; what these rights are must be determined aliunde by strict rules of law, not by any arbitrary determination of the court. The rule, in short, merely raises the question what those terms (if any) should be.
>
> . . .
>
> [A]s a general proposition, it may, I believe, be correctly stated, that the Plaintiff will never, in that character, be compelled to give a Defendant anything but what the Defendant might, as Plaintiff, enforce, provided a cause of suit arose.[55]

In the same vein, Hare writes in the preface to volume 11 of his reports:

> In the application of the common maxim, that those who have equity must do equity, the court confined its discretion within the plain and constitutional limit of imposing no terms on the suitor which could not be enforced in a suit instituted for the purpose, or which, apart from forms of proceeding, would not be the just result of such a suit; and

[54] S. Gardner, 'The Remedial Discretion in Proprietary Estoppel' (1999) 115 *LQR* 438, 465.
[55] (1844) 4 Ha 1, 5; 67 ER 537, 538–539.

disclaimed the arbitrary and dangerous, although not infrequently tempting power, of requiring him to submit to conditions which no legal or equitable principle could abstractly enjoin.[56]

Meagher, Gummow and Lehane take a similar view stressing that 'the limits of the maxim must be remembered. It does not empower a court of equity to impose on a plaintiff as a condition of relief any term which it considers reasonable. It can only impose terms which flow from the defendant's legal or equitable rights.'[57]

The court's discretion to impose conditions when it does not refuse an equitable remedy may be said to involve nothing more than the giving of direct effect to, or in other words the replication of, the defendant's rights which existed prior to the trial and did not cease to exist merely because a suit was brought against the defendant. It should not be taken to be a discretion to create remedies on a case-by-case basis which do not reflect substantive rights.[58] Such a leap would require independent justification.

D Remedial Discretion as to Transformative Remedies

1 Introduction

Transformative remedies are rights arising from certain judicial commands and statements which do not replicate a substantive right.[59] Their grant often, though not always, involves a degree of discretion. It may involve a choice as to whether to create the remedy and what content it should have, that is, what it should confer on the claimant and, correlatively, what it should require of the defendant. Discretion of this nature—which will be labelled 'remedial discretion'—needs to be examined more closely. There is a tendency to conflate this remedial discretion with (1) the discretion as to equitable replicative remedies described in the previous section; and (2) the creation of new rules of law through judicial activity. The purpose of this section is to distinguish remedial discretion from each of these.

2 Remedial discretion distinguished from discretion as to equitable replicative remedies

When refusing equitable replicative remedies and when exercising remedial discretion, the court makes two very different kinds of choice. In the case of the

[56] Hare, Volume 11 of Hare's Reports, XXV. Quoted in R. P. Meagher, J. D. Heydon and M. J. Leeming, *Meagher, Gummow and Lehane's Equity: Doctrines and Remedies* (4th edn., Sydney: Butterworths, 2002), [3-055]; 3rd edn., [311].

[57] Ibid [3-055]; 3rd edn., [311].

[58] But that does not mean that there are no instances where it was so used. The Australian High Court seems to have moved in that direction. See, for example, the judgment of the majority in *Bridgewater v Leahy* (1998) 194 CLR 457, 494 (HCA); *Giumelli v Giumelli* (1999) 161 ALR 473 (HCA); W. Gummow, 'Equity: Too Successful?' (2003) 77 *Australian LJ* 30.

[59] Particular transformative remedies are discussed in Chapter 13, including some which do not involve remedial discretion.

former, as we have seen, it has a choice to refuse to replicate an infringed substantive right of the claimant by refusing to restate it in an order or pronouncement. This is a choice *not to* order something. That something is clearly defined by the law relating to substantive rights.

In the case of remedial discretion, the court has a choice to create an entirely new remedy that does not replicate any of the claimant's substantive rights. This is a choice *to* order something. But that something is generally not defined by the substantive law. Further choices are required as to what is to be ordered. The creation of an entirely new right with new content requires a wide gamut of considerations to be taken into account. Hammond J, a proponent of remedial discretion, has written extra-curially that:

> This would involve in any given case a context specific evaluation of the potential modes of relief and the selection of that which is most appropriate having regard to a wide range of factors: the nature of the claim, social policy, economic efficiency, administrative techniques, the overall justice of the case, and any other relevant factors.[60]

He goes on discuss the following factors in more detail: the relative severity of the claimed remedies on the parties, economic efficiency, the 'weight' or moral value to be attached to the interest at stake, the effect of a given remedy on third parties or the public, the conduct of the parties, the difficulty of calculating loss, and the practicability of enforcement.[61] In effect, many of the policy choices that are entrenched in the law relating to substantive rights, particularly secondary rights, need to be reopened. The judge is required to reconsider these issues in each particular case. This aspect, as Jensen observes:

> appears to deny that a court's synthesis of grounds for a decision, on the basis of the relevant standards, can generate a rule that binds courts in relation to future similar cases. While a court is bound to apply the same legal standards as were articulated in previous cases, that court's assessment of the relevance and weight of those standards in relation to any one case justifies its decision *in that case only*.[62]

As a further example, we can take the Matrimonial Causes Act 1973 (UK). In dividing property upon the breakdown of a marriage, the court must arrive at a fair solution applying the criteria set out in section 25.[63] These criteria are wide ranging including the financial resources and needs which the parties have or are

[60] G. Hammond, 'Rethinking Remedies: The Changing Conception of the Relationship between Legal and Equitable Remedies' in J. Berryman (ed.), *Remedies: Issues and Perspectives* (Ontario: Carswell, 1991), 87, 88. See also P. Finn, 'Equitable Doctrine and Discretion in Remedies' in W. R. Cornish, R. C. Nolan, J. O'Sullivan and G. Virgo (eds), *Restitution: Past, Present and Future* (Oxford: Hart, 1998), 251, 273–4; D. Wright, *The Remedial Constructive Trust* (Sydney: Butterworths, 1998), Chapter 5 provides a non-exhaustive attempt to identify some such considerations in the case of a remedial constructive trust (see Chapter 14 p 214 below). Wright's attempt demonstrates how wide-ranging and widely expressed such considerations would need to be. For an analysis refer to Jensen (n 34 above), 202ff.

[61] Hammond (n 60 above), 103–5.

[62] Jensen (n 34 above) 184.

[63] *Cowan v Cowan* [2002] Fam 97, 118 (CA).

likely to have in the foreseeable future, the standard of living enjoyed by the family, and the contributions of the parties to the welfare of the family.

As can be seen from the above lists of relevant considerations, remedial discretion is much broader and stronger than discretion relating to equitable replicative remedies. The considerations which are to guide the judge in creating this type of transformative remedy are wide-ranging and very open-textured.

One cannot simply say that because courts exercise discretion to refuse equitable replicative remedies, it follows that they can or should be able to exercise remedial discretion. This is an inference that does not necessarily flow from the premise. The justifications for such a broader and stronger discretion must be presented. Remedial discretion raises concerns that will be touched upon in the next section.

3 Remedial discretion distinguished from judicial development of the law

Rotherham has written on the law relating to the non-consensual redistribution of property rights.[64] He observes that the courts have created many doctrines, such as those relating to express and constructive trusts, which operate with that effect.[65] He also discusses situations where courts redistribute property rights on a case-by-case basis.[66] Rotherham aims to provide 'a study of doctrines which allow for the acquisition of fully fledged rights of ownership or security without an owner's consent and the issues raised by such a redistribution of property rights.'[67] Unfortunately, he appears to assume that because courts at times create rules which function to redistribute property rights, they also have discretion to reallocate property rights on a case-by-case basis.[68] Consequently, he does not treat remedial discretion as a significant issue in relation to his subject matter. However, one must draw a distinction between the two activities he conflates. This distinction is obfuscated by Rotherham's unstable use of the term 'remedy'.[69] He applies it to certain non-consensually created substantive rights such as constructive and resulting trusts (calling these 'automatic remedies')[70] and also to rights arising from court orders.[71]

Here we must return to our earlier discussion of rules.[72] A choice made at an institutional level and enshrined in a rule may be said to be a choice made by

[64] C. Rotherham, *Proprietary Remedies in Context: A Study in the Judicial Redistribution of Property Rights* (Oxford: Hart, 2002).

[65] Ibid 7–10, 14, 19, 345.

[66] Ibid 24–30 referring to remedial constructive trusts in the USA and Canada.

[67] Ibid 1.

[68] He asserts that 'the idea of "proprietary remedies" implies that the courts, rather than simply enforcing existing rights, may award property rights as a remedy': ibid 2.

[69] P. B. H. Birks, 'Review of Proprietary Remedies in Context: A Study in the Judicial Redistribution of Property Rights' (2003) 119 *LQR* 156, 158.

[70] Rotherham (n 64 above), 29–30, 40.

[71] Ibid 24–30 see also n 68 above.

[72] See p 86.

'the law'. The resolution of disputes by reference to these institutionalized choices is the essence of the Rule of Law. Evans, a supporter of discretionary remedialism, writes that:

> [I]t does not take an extreme legal realist or sceptical post-modernist to recognise the mythic elements of the claim that it is the law that makes decisions about remedies, not judges. That myth, intimately connected with the declaratory theory of judicial decision-making is long exploded.[73]

This observation misses the point. The statement that certain choices are made 'by the law' rather than by judges does not contradict the proposition that judges make law. It is consistent with the proposition that judges can and do act as law-makers.[74] A proper understanding of the statement can be gained by drawing a distinction between two different right-generating activities, both of which could be considered to be different types of judicial law-making. This distinction is not clearly drawn by Rotherham or Evans. Unless we respect it, we are in danger of conflating remedial discretion with the judicial development of the law.

(a) Law-making at the institutional level (or 'rule-making')

First, judges may make law in the form of generally applicable rules which are intended to be followed in future cases.[75] This law-making is akin to the passing of a generally applicable Act of Parliament. Such rules constitute part of the common law and the choices they enshrine can be said to be made 'by the law' when the rules are applied in future cases. When a matter comes before a lower court judge who must follow an applicable rule, the judge is not permitted any choice as to the settled issue. The judge must follow the choice made in those circumstances 'by the law'. This upholds the ideal of like cases being treated alike. This state of affairs must be distinguished from that in which a choice as to an issue is left by the law to the trial judge.

(b) 'Law'-making at the instance-specific level (or 'remedy-making')

Secondly, judges may be said to make law, in a narrow sense, by creating jural relationships between particular individuals in the form of particular orders or pronouncements, that is, remedies. A remedy can be characterized as a 'law' laid down for particular persons in particular circumstances.[76] This 'law'-making is akin to the passing of a private Act of Parliament.

[73] Evans (n 10 above), 490 (footnote omitted).

[74] Lord Reid, 'The Judge as Law Maker' (1972) 12 *Journal of the Society of Public Teachers of Law* 22, 22; *Kleinwort Benson Ltd v Lincoln City Council* [1999] 2 AC 349, 358, 377–379 (HL).

[75] A. Mason, 'Legislative and Judicial Law-Making: Can We Locate an Identifiable Boundary?' (2003) 24 *Adelaide L Rev* 15.

[76] For realists, such as Frank, only this is the law. See Chapter 4 text to n 69.

Where a replicative remedy is granted, this 'law'-making[77] at the instance-specific level involves merely restating prior substantive rights. There is no noticeable alteration of the pre-existing jural relationship between the parties. The grant of the remedy simply involves giving effect to policy choices made at the institutional level, that is, 'by the law'. Here the law embodies the decisions about the availability and content of the remedy. The judge merely applies the law.

Where a transformative remedy is granted, this 'law'-making at the instance-specific level involves creating rights *de novo* or extinguishing existing rights. This usually involves making policy choices in the particular circumstances. If it does, this is where remedial discretion plays its role. The scope of these choices is the 'discretionary space' in relation to transformative remedies.[78] The choices that a transformative remedy which involved an exercise of remedial discretion embodies cannot be said to have been made 'by the law' in the sense described in the previous paragraph. The order gives effect to fresh policy choices made solely by the judge.[79]

Obviously the concerns surrounding institutional level judicial law-making and instance-specific judicial 'remedy-making' are different. The fact that the first occurs and is now accepted as unobjectionable does not, of itself, prove that the second should occur or be accepted if it does occur. There are important Rule of Law issues that must be considered.[80]

By not distinguishing the judicial development of the law from remedial discretion, we may end up ignoring the old dilemma of where the line between rules and case-by-case discretion should fall.[81] Rules promote equality before the law, predictability of decisions and have a hortatory effect. Case-by-case discretion on the other hand promotes flexible and case-sensitive dispute resolution. Where the line is to be drawn is an issue that every legal system must confront. These issues are beyond the scope of this book which goes no further than re-analysing the boundaries and structure of the law of remedies. But this re-analysis should assist both proponents and opponents of remedial discretion in the elucidation and discussion of these fundamental issues.

[77] It is best not to call the grant of a replicative remedy 'law'-making, although it can be characterized as such, but rather 'law-applying': J. Wróblewski (R. Bankowski and N. MacCormick (eds), *The Judicial Application of Law* (Dordrecht: Kluwer Academic Publishers, 1992), 318–19.

[78] Loughlan (n 34 above), 135.

[79] However, it must to be noted that not all transformative remedies involve remedial discretion. As will be seen, some transformative remedies are available as a matter of course: Chapter 13 p 206.

[80] For a summary of the issues at stake see P. B. H. Birks, 'Three Kinds of Objection to Discretionary Remedialism' (2000) 29 *Western Australian L Rev* 1, 8–17.

[81] Aristotle Politics Book III Chapter XI. P. Atiyah, 'From Principles to Pragmatism: Changes in the Function of the Judicial Process and the Law' (1979–80) 65 *Iowa L Rev* 1249.

E Conclusion

This chapter examined the role that discretion plays in relation to the categories of remedies that were suggested in the previous chapter. It further illustrated why replicative and transformative remedies were distinguished in Chapter 5. It also explained that, because of the potential operation of certain equitable bars, the category of replicative remedies has to be further sub-divided according to jurisdictional origin.

It was shown that it would be wrong to think that the discretion as to the grant of equitable remedies involves the creation of rights different from those which existed before trial. It is discretion merely as to whether the recognized bars prevent the replication of such substantive rights in the particular case. This kind of discretion does not turn a replicative remedy into a transformative remedy.

In contrast, the remedial discretion usually associated with transformative remedies is discretion to create a remedy which bears little resemblance to the claimant's substantive rights. Having a different function, it is broader and stronger than the discretion exercised in relation to equitable replicative remedies. It is also erroneous to conflate it with the judicial development of legal rules.

7

Replicating Primary Rights: Common Law Remedies

A Introduction

Chapters 7 to 13 illustrate and further explain the concepts and taxonomy developed in the previous chapters. They put the theory established in the first part into practice. The purpose of these chapters is not to set out in detail the law relating to all remedies or to provide a textbook on remedies. It is to demonstrate the scope of a law of remedies founded on a stable concept, to illustrate the content of each category identified in Chapter 5 and to show in outline which remedies replicate which kinds of substantive rights and, conversely, which substantive rights are replicated in which remedies. The material has been kept as brief as possible, at the risk of some superficiality, because the primary focus of this work is not the content of the law of remedies itself but rather the scope and organization of the subject. Furthermore, detailed discussion of the origin or content of particular substantive rights lies outside the scope of a work on remedies as defined in Chapter 4. Of course, some discussion of substantive rights which are said to be replicated in particular remedies is required to prove that replication is indeed occurring. One arrives at this proof by comparing the remedy with which the claimant leaves the court and the substantive right which the claimant had before coming to court. An examination of the nature of the substantive right being replicated also shows how the remedy fits into the taxonomy developed in Chapter 5. Consequently some discussion of substantive rights is unavoidable; however, they are not discussed as, and always clearly distinguished from, remedies.

We begin with remedies that replicate primary rights. We will see that for a primary right to be replicated in a court order it must satisfy three criteria.[1] First, it must be infringed or in danger of being infringed. If it correlates with a positive duty, its infringement may be actual, threatened, or continuing. If it correlates with a negative duty, its infringement may be threatened or continuing. Second, the right in question must not be extinguished by its infringement. Third, there must be no policy reasons which militate against the replication of the right.

[1] As will be seen in Chapter 10, the role of secondary rights is to supplant or reinforce those primary rights that cannot or should not be replicated.

This chapter will focus on remedies originating at common law. Particular remedies will be examined in the context of leading cases to illustrate why they belong in their assigned category. Three issues will be explored in relation to each remedy: the nature of the remedy; the nature of the substantive right that it replicates; and the means of executing the remedy.

B Replication of Primary Rights

The replication of a right usually involves ordering the person who is under the corresponding duty to do what he or she is required to do or abstain from doing what he or she is required not to do.[2] For example, if *X* is under a duty to convey Whiteacre to *Y* then the replication of *Y*'s primary right to the conveyance means ordering *X* to convey Whiteacre to *Y*, that is, ordering *X* to do what *X* ought all along to have done.

1 Primary rights capable of replication

The rights that the courts will give effect to through replication in court orders are limited. Replication will be entertained by a court only where there is an actual or apprehended breach of a positive duty, or there is an apprehended or continuing[3] breach of a negative duty.

Some rights are sought to be protected before they are infringed. For example, injunctions are often sought to prevent apprehended breaches of negative duties. Although a negative duty is not directly enforceable after a breach (in the sense that it is impossible for the court to compel its performance retrospectively), before its breach (or during a continuing breach) the court can make an order replicating the duty and attaching additional sanctions in the case of its breach (or a continuation of its breach). This is the area of *preventive* remedies which seek to protect rights by preventing future breaches of duty. These can be distinguished from *corrective* remedies which attempt to effectuate rights by aiming to redress their past infringements.

2 Primary rights not capable of replication

A right that has ceased to exist cannot be replicated in a court order.[4] A right generally does not cease to exist on infringement. But it may cease to exist where its subject matter is destroyed. For instance, a right in relation to a chattel will cease to exist if the chattel is destroyed, a right to bodily integrity will cease to exist

[2] The exception is where a declaration is made. The court does not order but merely states what is required of the defendant.

[3] A continuing breach is simply a past, present, and apprehended (i.e. future) breach that will eventuate unless something is done to prevent it. '[A] continuing trespass. . .is in law a series of trespasses from time to time': *Goodson v Richardson* (1874) 9 Ch App 221, 224 (CA).

[4] But it can be recreated by a transformative remedy, for example, an order granting relief from the forfeiture of a lease: see Chapter 13 p 212.

if a person is killed, a contractual right will cease to exist if the contract is terminated for breach.

Similarly a past infringement of a right that correlates with a negative duty cannot be redressed simply by ordering the infringer not to breach the duty. Requiring the person owing the duty to abstain from doing what he or she has already done would be a fruitless exercise. The past cannot be undone. The law can only regulate future conduct.[5]

3 Primary rights not replicated for policy reasons (bars)

This brings us to a third category, primary rights that can sensibly be replicated but as a matter of policy are not replicated because the legal system chooses to give them effect in an indirect way, that is, by means of secondary rights. Whether a court is bound to, or even permitted to, replicate a right that correlates with a potentially directly enforceable duty depends on policy factors. Not all rights that are capable of being replicated are given effect in this direct way in court orders. For example, a court may refuse to give direct effect to a right to personal services because this could be tantamount to slavery or because it would be impossible to monitor and ensure adequate performance.[6] A court could not bring about the painting of a masterpiece if the artist staunchly refused to paint one.

C Replication at Common Law and in Equity

As described earlier,[7] the courts have traditionally taken different approaches to the award of remedies in their common law and equity jurisdictions. In the case of remedies awarded in the common law jurisdiction, judges consider themselves bound to confer the remedy sought by the claimant where a cause of action has been proved and the defendant fails to make out a defence. In such circumstances, the claimant is said to have a 'right' to the remedy.[8]

In the case of remedies awarded in equity, the approach appears to be different, at least as a matter of form. Judges do not consider themselves bound to make the order sought by the claimant merely because a cause of action has been proved by the claimant. The claimant is not considered to have a right to the remedy at this stage. Judges are said to be required to take certain considerations into account and exercise a 'discretion' as to whether or not to grant the remedy.[9] Prior to a favourable decision, the claimant is said merely to have an 'equity' to seek relief. Meagher, Gummow and Lehane write: 'The term ['equity'] also refers to the circumstances of a particular case which the party concerned asserts call for the intervention of a court of equity; thus a plaintiff cannot seek the

[5] A. Kocourek, *Jural Relations* (2nd edn., Indianapolis: Bobbs-Merrill, 1928), 3.
[6] Chapter 8 p 140. [7] Chapter 5 p 81.
[8] One may query against whom such a jural relation may be asserted and how it may be enforced.
[9] Chapter 6 p 91.

assistance of a court of equity in aid of his legal rights if he does not have an "equity".'[10]

This difference of approach is primarily historical and is all too easily exaggerated. Although in some jurisdictions, notably Australia, there has been a recent tendency to inflate the element of discretion, in England the discretion underlying equitable remedies has operated in so settled a fashion that the discretionary approach of equity could quite readily be translated into the rule-based approach of common law.[11] It is to be hoped that as the rules of law and equity are further fused over time, the approaches will become more uniform and the historical origin of remedies will lose its importance.[12] Its apparent importance will also wane if we cease to under-emphasize discretion in relation to common law remedies and to over-emphasize it in relation to equitable remedies. Perhaps we will be able to move on from a definition of equitable remedies based on jurisdictional origin to a definition based on another feature, namely, that they are remedies which are merely subject to a greater range of open-textured bars because of a need for a 'safety-valve' on their availability, primarily because of their more drastic enforcement mechanisms.[13]

Particular common law remedies that replicate primary rights will now be briefly examined. Equitable remedies that replicate primary rights are the subject matter of the next chapter.

D Award of Sum Due Under a Contract

1 Form of the order

An award of a sum due under a contract[14] may be expressed in the following form:

IT IS ORDERED that the defendant:

1. pay the claimant the sum of £. . .[15]

or, in the case of an award of a sum due under a contract which requires assessment by the court, say, an award of a reasonable price for services rendered

[10] R. P. Meagher, J. D. Heydon and M. J. Leeming, *Meagher, Gummow and Lehane's Equity: Doctrines and Remedies* (4th edn., Sydney: Butterworths, 2002), [4-135]; 3rd edn., [426].

[11] Chapter 6 p 94.

[12] A. Burrows, 'We Do This at Common Law But That in Equity' (2002) 22 *OJLS* 1.

[13] Chapter 5 p 81.

[14] The generic label 'award of money due under a contract' is used here because the more specific 'award of an agreed sum' does not cover a group of awards which replicate primary rights to the payment of amounts which are not ascertained at the time of the contract, and hence not 'agreed sums'; e.g. the award made in *Jervis v Harris* [1996] Ch 195 (CA). The generic label chosen here does not inadvertently cover awards of damages as they are not, strictly speaking, 'due under the contract'. As Fry LJ stated in *Birmingham and District Land Co v London and North Western Railway Co* (1886) 34 Ch D 261, 276: 'A breach of contract gives rise, or may give rise, to a right to damages, but those damages are not the subject of the contract. They arise from the breach of the contract, and therefore they are in no sense the subject of the contract itself. When a man contracts that he will do a thing, it can hardly be taken as implying a contract as to what will arise if he does not do the thing.'

[15] This is the core provision of Forms such as No 45 Judgment after trial before judge without jury, No 46 Judgment after trial before judge with jury, No 44 Part 24 (summary)

under a contract:

To the Defendant
The claimant obtained judgment against you on................ for an amount to be decided by the court.

[Master][District judge]........ has decided the amount and ordered that you should pay £........ [including interest to date of judgment] and £........ for costs [costs to be assessed].

You must pay to the claimant a total of £........[16]

The judgment may be obtained by default where the defendant fails to enter an appearance or a defence:

To the Defendant
You have not replied to the claim form.

It is therefore ordered that you must pay the claimant £........ for debt [and interest to date of judgment] and £........ for costs [less £........ which you have already paid]

You must pay to the claimant a total of £........[17]

A judgment may be entered in a foreign currency, in which case the order would state:

It is ordered that the defendant pay the claimant (*state the sum in the foreign currency*) or the Sterling equivalent at the time of payment.[18]

A judgment for the payment of money must be for payment to a person and cannot be merely to a bank account.[19]

judgment for claimant. Forms No 45 and No 46 are cited as examples of general forms of a trial judgment: CPR Part 40 PD(B) [14.1.1]. CPR Part 4 PD Table 2 lists these pre-CPR High Court forms as forms which may continue to be used under the new rules: CPR Part 4 PD [1.3]. For other examples of court orders discussed in this book the reader is referred to *Atkin's Encyclopaedia of Court Forms in Civil Proceedings* (2nd edn., London: Butterworths) and A. R. Ingpen (et al) *Seton's Forms of Judgments and Orders in the High Court of Justice and Court of Appeal: Having Special Reference to the Chancery Division* (7th edn., London: Stevens, 1912).

[16] N34HC Judgment for claimant (after amount decided by court HC) and N34 Judgment for claimant (after amount decided by court CC). The forms further provide optional paragraphs which can be inserted where the defendant is allowed to pay the debt by instalments. CPR Part 4 PD Table 1 lists these forms as new 'N' forms which may be used in the High Court and the county courts: CPR Part 4 PD [1.3].

[17] Form N30 Judgment for claimant (default HC) and (default CC). These forms are used where a default judgment is given: CPR Rule 12.2. There are other variants of these forms which are substantially similar and are used where the claimant accepts an offer for payment made by the defendant: CPR Part 14 PD [4.2] or there is a determination or re-determination by the court of the rate of payment following a request by the defendant for time to make the payment: CPR Part 14 PD [10.4] and Rule 14.3. Again, the various forms provide paragraphs which can be inserted where the defendant is allowed to pay the debt by instalments.

[18] CPR Part 40 PD [10].

[19] *In Leeds Banking Co* (1866) 1 Ch App 150.

2 Nature of the remedy

An award of a sum due under a contract is the most commonly sought remedy in respect of contracts.[20] This is because the main duty of at least one party to the overwhelming majority of contracts is the duty to pay. It is present in the case of contracts of sale,[21] lease, hire, employment, and for other services. Contracts of loan and insurance place *both* parties under duties to pay. But, as Burrows observes, the remedy is often and 'rather uncomfortably' relegated to discussions of damages in standard contract texts.[22] Sometimes it is omitted altogether. For example, a leading equity text states: 'The only remedy which the common law afforded for breach of contract was an award of damages. In equity, however, the due performance of the contract itself was in many cases enforced upon the ground of inadequacy of the damages recoverable for breach.'[23] This is incorrect. For the vast majority of contracts, due performance of the contract itself was enforced at common law by means of an action in debt culminating in an award of an agreed sum.

(a) Function of the remedy

The remedy embodied in an award of a sum due under a contract is always a corrective remedy. This is because the award gives effect to an accrued right to payment which has not been satisfied. The claimant cannot obtain the remedy before the right to payment has accrued, that is, before the payment is due.[24]

(b) Effect on substantive rights

The judicial remedy is the claimant's new officially declared right to be paid the awarded sum. The judicial remedy—arising from the order of the court—replicates and replaces the claimant's substantive right under the contract. The debt due under the judgment becomes 'the sole debt between the parties. . .[T]he original debt is gone, *transit in rem judicatam*, a fresh debt is created with different consequences.'[25] Thus the debt or, as it is sometimes put, the claimant's cause of action based on the right to the payment under the contract is said to merge with

[20] See Chapter 5 n 14.

[21] For example, Sale of Goods Act 1979 (UK) s 49.

[22] A. Burrows, *Remedies for Torts and Breach of Contract* (2nd edn., London: Butterworths, 1994), 315. Burrows cites '*Cheshire, Fifoot & Furmston's Law of Contract* (12th edn., 1991), 616–18; *Anson's Law of Contract* (26th edn., 1984), 467–8, 491 and Treitel *Law of Contract* 883–90.'

[23] J. McGhee, *Snell's Equity* (30th. edn., London: Sweet & Maxwell, 2000), [40-01].

[24] J. Beatson, *Anson's Law of Contract* (28th edn., Oxford: Oxford University Press, 2002), 630. However, where there is an anticipatory breach, the claimant can accept the repudiation and seek damages: *Hochster v De la Tour* (1853) 2 E & B 678; 118 ER 922. The claimant may also be able to seek specific performance or damages in lieu: *Hasham v Zenab* [1960] AC 316 (PC). For the latter see Chapter 12 p 212.

[25] *Re European Central Railway Co* (1876) 4 Ch D 33, 37–38 (CA).

the remedy.[26] 'All [the defendant's] liability is merged therefore in the judgment,—the old debt disappears and the judgment is left in its place.'[27] The judgment generates a new duty on the defendant and extinguishes the old one. '[I]t has always been the rule at common law that a debt or damages is extinguished in a remedy of a higher nature.'[28] A judgment or order is a remedy of a higher nature than rights under a simple contract or a contract embodied in a deed.

(c) *Advantages of the remedy*

An award of a sum due under a contract has a number of advantages over an award of damages. First, an award of an agreed sum is not reduced because of a failure to mitigate loss.[29] Secondly, in the case of an award of an agreed sum, difficult questions relating to the assessment of damages, such as questions of causation and remoteness, are avoided.[30] The advantages were summed up by Lord Millett in *Jervis v Harris*:

> The plaintiff who claims payment of a debt need not prove anything beyond the occurrence of the event or condition on the occurrence of which the debt became due. He need prove no loss; the rules as to remoteness of damage and mitigation of loss are irrelevant; and unless the event on which the payment is due is a breach of some other contractual obligation owed by the one party to the other the law on penalties does not apply to the agreed sum. It is not necessary that the amount of the debt should be ascertained at the date of the contract; it is sufficient if it is ascertainable when payment is due.[31]

Although the same benefits could be secured by the award of specific performance,[32] it is usually preferable to seek the common law remedy because, due to its origin, it is subject to a smaller range of bars than a decree of specific performance.

3 Nature of the substantive right replicated

An award of a sum due under a contract replicates a personal right to a payment due under a contract. That is, it restates and replaces the prior substantive right arising from consent. Two sub-forms of the award can be distinguished: one

[26] *King v Hoare* (1844) 13 M & W 494, 504; *Florence v Jenings* (1857) 2 CB (NS) 454; *Kendall v Hamilton* (1879) 4 AC 504, 526 and 542 (HL); *Ex parte Fewings* (1884) 25 Ch D 338, 349, 353 and 355 (CA); *Thoday v Thoday* [1964] P 181, 197–198 (CA); *Republic of India v India Steamship Co Ltd* [1993] AC 410, 417 (HL).

[27] *Re Hodgson Beckett v Ramsdale* (1885) 31 Ch D 177, 188–189 (CA) (Bowen LJ).

[28] *Re King & Beesley* [1895] 1 QB 189, 193 (Kennedy J).

[29] *Anglo-African Shipping Co of New York Inc v Mortner* [1962] 1 Lloyd's Rep 81, 84 (Megaw J). Contrast Treitel's view that the mitigation rules should apply 'where at the time of repudiation the claimant has not yet done all that is required of him to make that action available': G. H. Treitel *The Law of Contract* (10th edn., London: Sweet & Maxwell, 1999), 947. See also the discussion of *McGregor's case* in Chapter 6 p 90.

[30] *The Odenfeld* [1978] 2 Lloyd's Rep 357, 374–375 (Kerr J).

[31] [1996] Ch 195, 202–203 (CA).

[32] *Beswick v Beswick* [1968] AC 58 (HL).

which replicates a consensual right to the payment of a specified or agreed sum and another which replicates a consensual right to the payment of an unspecified sum.

(a) Right to the payment of an agreed sum

First, the award may replicate a right to a payment of an agreed sum, in which case the judgment may be called an award of an agreed sum. As Burrows states:

> The award of an agreed sum is a remedy which protects the promisee's expectations by enforcing the defendant's contractual promise to pay a sum of money. . .The remedy can be regarded as a hybrid, being like damages in that it is common law and monetary but like specific performance in that its function is to compel performance of a positive contractual obligation.[33]

For example, such an award may replicate a right to the payment of a purchase price, agreed remuneration, liquidated 'damages',[34] or a sum payable on an event other than breach.[35] An award of an agreed sum which replicates the right to an agreed price or remuneration is the most common type of award of a sum due under a contract. The case of *Carlill v Carbolic Smoke Ball Company*[36] provides a famous illustration of such an award. The claimant caught the flu despite using the defendant's Carbolic Smoke Ball. She claimed the 'reward' of £100 which the defendants had promised to pay in such an event. The Court of Appeal upheld the first instance judgment where Hawkins J had given the remedy by ruling that 'the plaintiff is entitled to recover the 100l. I therefore direct a verdict to be entered for the plaintiff for 100l., and judgment accordingly with costs.'

It must be stressed that an award of an agreed sum never gives effect to a secondary right, that is, a right arising from a wrong. The right to liquidated 'damages' (or, applying a more accurate label, 'liquidated compensation'[37]) is no exception because it arises from consent. As Tettenborn states 'A promise to pay £1000 in the event of a breach of contract is analytically a primary obligation, like any other debt'.[38] It is merely triggered by, or accrues, on the breach of another contractual obligation. Although in *Photo Production Ltd v Securicor Transport Ltd*[39] Lord Diplock considered liquidated compensation clauses to

[33] A. Burrows, *Remedies for Torts and Breach of Contract* (2nd edn., London: Butterworths, 1994), 315. By a positive obligation, Burrows means an obligation to do an act: 335.

[34] Being a sum of money which the parties have agreed on which represents a genuine pre-estimate of the loss consequent upon a particular breach: *Dunlop Pneumatic Tyre Co Ltd v New Garage and Motor Co Ltd* [1915] AC 79 (HL).

[35] *Exports Credits Guarantee Department v Universal Oil Products Co* [1983] 2 All ER 205, 223 (HL).

[36] [1893] 1 QB 256.

[37] If one takes a payment of 'damages' to mean a payment of money made *in substitution for* the performance of a primary duty then the term should not be applied to a payment of money made in actual performance of a primary duty.

[38] A. Tettenborn, *An Introduction to the Law of Obligations* (London: Butterworths, 1994), 211.

[39] [1980] AC 827, 850 (HL).

confer secondary rights, in this work such rights are treated as primary because of their consensual origin. This is consistent with the earlier position of Bowen LJ in *Birmingham and District Land Co v London and North Western Railway Co* who distinguished a right to damages from a consensually created right to compensation:

> [A] right to damages. . .is not a right to indemnity as such. It is the converse of such a right. A right to indemnity as such is given by the original bargain between the parties. The right to damages is given in consequence of the breach of the original contract between the parties. It is an incident which the law attaches to the breach of a contract, and is not a provision of the contract itself.[40]

Bowen LJ's remarks as to the nature of an indemnity apply with equal force to a liquidated compensation clause. Such a clause is a provision of the contract itself. It evidences a right given by the original bargain between the parties.

(b) Right to the payment of an unspecified sum

An award of a sum due under a contract may replicate a right to the payment of the reasonable value of goods or services provided under a contract which does not specify the price, in which case the judgment may be called a *quantum valebat* or *quantum meruit* award respectively.[41] Similarly, it may replicate a right to a payment of a sum which is not ascertainable at the time the contract is made.[42] This may include a right to a payment under an indemnity clause.[43]

In these cases, the award must liquidate or quantify the payment to which the claimant is entitled.[44] That is, the judge must set an appropriate sum for the payment that the defendant is bound to make. In doing so, the judge applies the standard of reasonableness in the case of *quantum valebat* or *quantum meruit* awards or the terms of the particular clause in the case of an indemnity.

[40] (1886) 34 Ch D 261, 274–275. See also Fry LJ's remarks at 276.

[41] An unliquidated contractual right to payment is said to arise where a workman is engaged on the basis that he will be paid for the work done but no price is fixed: *Lakeman v Mountstephen* (1874) LR 7 HL 17; or where there is an agreement to purchase goods but the price is not fixed: Sale of Goods Act 1979 (UK) s 8(2).

[42] A claim by a lessor for the costs of repair which he was entitled to under the lease was held to be a debt claim even though the sum was not ascertained when the contract was made: *Jervis v Harris* [1996] Ch 195 (CA). See also *Amantilla Ltd v Telefusion plc* (1987) 9 Con LR 139, 144–145.

[43] Some cases suggest that an indemnity is a primary right to the payment of compensation: *Caledonia North Sea Limited (Respondents) v British Telecommunications Plc (Appellants) (Scotland) and Others* [2002] 1 Lloyd's Rep 553, 572 (HL); see also *Transthene Packaging Co Ltd v Royal Insurance (UK) Ltd* [1996] LRLR 32, 41. Contrast *Firma C-Trade SA v Newcastle P & I Assn* [1991] 2 AC 1, 35 (HL) where Lord Goff stated that, 'I accept that, at common law, a contract of indemnity gives rise to an action for unliquidated damages, arising from the failure of the indemnifier to prevent the indemnified person from suffering damage. . .'; see also The '*Italia Express*' [1992] 2 Lloyd's Rep 281, 285; *Sprung v Royal Insurance (UK) Ltd* [1997] CLC 70; *Callaghan v Dominion Insurance Co Ltd* [1997] 2 Lloyd's Rep 540.

[44] See Chapter 5 p 79.

4 Enforcement of the remedy

The sum awarded must be paid by the defendant within 14 days of the date of the order unless a different date is specified.[45] Thus the order cannot be said to be breached, or the remedy infringed, until the expiry of that time.

An award of a sum due under a contract is a remedy enforceable by:[46] the seizure and sale of the defendant's goods (a warrant of execution or writ of fieri facias)[47]; a charging order on the defendant's land, securities or funds in court[48] which can be followed by an order for the sale of the property; a third party debt order (formerly known as a garnishee order)[49]; the appointment of a receiver[50]; and in the county court, an attachment of earnings order.[51] An award of a sum due under a contract is not generally enforceable by committal.[52]

E Award of Restitution for Unjust Enrichment at the Expense of Another

It is in the area of unjust enrichment that scholars have had the greatest difficulty in drawing a distinction between substantive rights and remedies. The unstable concept of a remedy seems to have clouded approaches. As was shown in Chapter 3, many books on remedies focus on substantive rights arising from unjust enrichment. Under the guise of 'restitutionary remedies', they duplicate the work of books which purport to discuss such rights. As Burrows points out: 'there is relatively little to say [about remedies]...in relation to restitution for unjust enrichment by subtraction that has not already been said in discussing the cause of action of unjust enrichment.'[53]

It cannot be otherwise. When a remedy replicates a substantive right, the main focus should be on the nature and scope of the substantive right in question and bars or defences to its replication. Discourse in terms of 'remedy' unnecessarily diverts attention from the nature of the subject matter under investigation. The subject matter in cases of unjust enrichment is predominantly substantive rights.[54]

[45] CPR Rule 40.11. [46] CPR Part 70 PD [1.1].

[47] CPR Sch 1 RSC Orders 46 and 47 and CCR Order 26. Enforcement is carried out by bailiffs in the case of county court judgments and by the sheriff in the case of High Court judgments.

[48] CPR Part 73. [49] CPR Part 72. [50] CPR Part 69. [51] CCR Order 27.

[52] CPR Part 70 PD [1.2]. See also CPR Sch 1 RSC Order 45 r 5 and CCR Order 28. The availability of imprisonment for debt was severely restricted by the Debtors Acts 1869 and 1878 (UK).

[53] A. Burrows, 'Judicial Remedies' in P. B. H. Birks (ed.), *English Private Law Vol II* (Oxford: Oxford University Press, 2000), 816.

[54] P. B. H. Birks and C. Mitchell, 'Unjust Enrichment' in P. B. H. Birks (ed.), *English Private Law Vol II* (Oxford: Oxford University Press, 2000), 591–3; P. B. H. Birks, *Unjust Enrichment* (Oxford: Oxford University Press, 2003).

If the law in this area is uncertain or undeveloped, it is generally the substantive right and the event which brings it into being that are hazy and require further debate and definition, not the remedy.[55] The remedy is only a judicial restatement of the right. If the substantive right that has arisen in a given situation can be precisely defined, the question of what replicative remedy may potentially be awarded is clear. The only remaining issue is whether it is barred in the particular circumstances.

1 Form of the order

An award of restitution for unjust enrichment takes the same form as an award of a sum due under a contract:

IT IS ORDERED THAT the defendant:

1. pay the claimant the sum of £........[56]

The other forms of order discussed in relation to awards of a sum due under a contract are equally applicable to awards of restitution for unjust enrichment.

2 Nature of the remedy

An award of restitution for unjust enrichment is always a corrective remedy. It is the most common remedy in relation to rights arising from unjust enrichment. This is because most rights which arise from unjust enrichment are personal rights to the payment of money.

Traditionally, awards of restitution for unjust enrichment have been labelled according to the forms of action by which they were sought. These included money had and received, money paid to the defendant's use, *quantum meruit*, and *quantum valebat*. This terminology is anachronistic and undescriptive. Burrows writes that '[a]s a matter of principle, rather than history, there is no good reason why there should be several different remedies to effect the same restitution'.[57] The generic phrase 'an award of restitution for unjust enrichment at the expense of another' (or simply an award of 'restitution for unjust enrichment') will be preferred here. It is taken to encompass all the awards that could be sought by these forms of action. It should be recalled that one of the sources of instability of the term remedy is that it is used as a synonym for form or cause of action.[58]

[55] Estoppel provides a good case study of a situation where the right is poorly defined and much of the debate is conducted in the language of remedies: S. Gardner, 'The Remedial Discretion in Proprietary Estoppel' (1999) 115 *LQR* 438; J. Edelman, 'Remedial Certainty or Remedial Discretion in Estoppel after Giumelli' (1999) 15 *JCL* 159. See Chapter 8 p 132.

[56] Form No 45 Judgment after trial before judge without jury.

[57] A. Burrows, *The Law of Restitution* (London: Butterworths, 1993), 29. See also P. B. H. Birks, *Introduction to the Law of Restitution* (Oxford: Clarendon Press, 1985), 78.

[58] See Chapter 2 p 11.

3 Nature of the substantive right replicated

An award of restitution for unjust enrichment is similar to an award of a sum due under a contract in that it also replicates a personal right to the payment of money. The right may be liquidated or unliquidated,[59] that is, it may be a right to the payment of a specified sum or an unspecified sum. However, in the case of this remedy, the right that is effectuated is one arising from unjust enrichment rather than consent.

For example, *Baker v Courage & Co*[60] involved a primary right to restitution arising from unjust enrichment. Mr Baker, the claimant, leased a pub in London. He purchased the freehold reversion from the owner. £1,000 pounds of the purchase price for the reversion was not paid immediately but secured by a mortgage. In 1896, the defendants, a brewing company, agreed to purchase the claimant's interests in the property. The defendants lent £1,000 to the claimant to discharge the mortgage. The claimant also owed other monies to the defendants. When the balance due to the claimant was calculated, these other debts were set off against the purchase price but the £1,000 which had been lent to the claimant to discharge the mortgage was not taken into account. The claimant was paid £9,000. He was only entitled to £8,000. On the day of completion he deposited the £9,000 with the defendants at interest. He progressively drew out money. In 1909, when only £1,000 remained on deposit, the defendants discovered their mistake and refused to pay that sum to the claimant. The claimant sued for its recovery. The defendants attempted to set off the mistaken payment and also counter-claimed for its recovery. The claimant argued that the set-off and counter-claim were barred by the Statute of Limitations. One of the defendants' arguments was that the statute did not commence to run until the cause of action accrued and that it did not do so until the defendants gave notice of the discovery and demanded repayment of the money.

Hamilton J held that the cause of action arose independently of the notification of a discovery or demand for repayment. His Honour stated: 'it does not appear to me that notice of the mistake was necessary to raise a duty in Mr. Baker to pay the overpayment back.'[61] The claimant succeeded. This case illustrates that the primary right for the return of the mistaken payment arises immediately on the happening of the unjust enrichment. It is this substantive right which is replicated in an award of restitution for unjust enrichment.

4 Enforcement of the remedy

An award of restitution for unjust enrichment is enforceable in the same manner as an award of a sum due under a contract.

[59] *Pavey & Matthews Pty Ltd v Paul* (1987) 162 CLR 221 (HCA).

[60] [1910] 1 KB 56; *Agip (Africa) Ltd v Jackson* [1990] Ch 265, 282 (first instance); *Kleinwort Benson Ltd v Lincoln City Council* [1999] 2 AC 349 (HL).

[61] *Baker v Courage & Co* [1910] 1 KB 56, 65.

F Order for the Recovery of Land

1 Form of the order

The core provision of an order for the recovery of land may be expressed in the following form where the claimant is seeking recovery of land from trespassers, first in the case of an interim possession order:

On the........ of........ 20........ the court considered an application for an interim possession order

The court ordered that all person(s) in occupation of............... must vacate the premises within 24 hours of service of this order...[62]

and, in the case of the final order:

(enter name of judge) ordered that the applicant do recover possession of the land mentioned in the originating application and interim possession order in this matter, namely *(description of the premises)*[63]

It is particularly noteworthy that this form of order is not addressed to a particular defendant but instead is binding on all persons in the world at large.

However, where the claimant is seeking recovery of possession from a known defendant who initially entered into possession lawfully, the order will usually be directed to the defendant (and also provide for the payment of damages and costs):

...**the court orders that**:

1. the defendant give the claimant the possession of............... on or before................ 20........[64]

The order may be suspended, allowing the defendant to rectify a breach of a lease or rental agreement. In this case, it takes the following form:

To the defendant(s)

1. The court has ordered that **unless** you make the payments as set out in paragraph 3 you must give the claimant possession of............... on........[65]

[62] Form N134 Interim possession order: CPR Part 4 PD Table 3. Table 3 lists this and other pre-CPR county court forms as forms which may continue to be used under the new rules: CPR Part 4 PD [1.3].

[63] Form N136 Possession order (under Ord 24 Part I CCR): CPR Part 4 PD Table 3.

[64] Form N26 Order for possession. There are other variants of this forms which are substantially similar: N26 Order for possession (accelerated possession procedure) (assured shorthold tenancy); N31 Order for possession (mortgaged premises) (suspended): CPR Part 4 PD Table 1. See also N27 Order for possession on forfeiture (for rent arrears); N27(2) Order for possession on forfeiture (for rent arrears)(suspended): CPR Part 4 PD Table 3.

[65] Form N28 Order for possession (rented premises) (suspended): CPR Part 4 PD Table 1.

The remedy may also be given in the form of a summary judgment:

> . . .the Court having found that the defendant has no real prospect of successfully defending the claim *or* [issue of (*define the issue*)] and that there is no other reason why the claim *or* [issue of (*define the issue*)] should be disposed of at a trial
>
> **IT IS ORDERED** that the defendant:
>
> 1. give the defendant possession of the land described in the [claim form][particulars of claim] as (*description of land*).[66]

An order for the recovery of land is the second most commonly sought remedy after an award of an agreed sum.[67] Presumably the vast majority of actions for the recovery of land are brought against defaulting tenants and mortgagors.

2 Nature of the remedy

The remedy embodied in an order for the recovery of land may operate as a corrective remedy, that is, one which is intended to put an end to a continuing breach of duty. In *McPhail v Persons Unknown*,[68] the remedy was given to facilitate the eviction of squatters from houses which they had occupied. It ended a continuing trespass.

The remedy may also be utilized as a preventive remedy. The case of *University of Essex v Djemal*[69] concerned student sit-in protests on the campus of a university. The university obtained and executed an order for possession of the part of its premises occupied by the protesting students. The students then occupied a different part of the premises, level 6 of the administration building. The university sought a second possession order covering its entire premises, that is, 'that they do recover possession of the premises at the University of Essex, Wivenhoe Park, Colchester in the County of Essex'.[70] The students vacated level 6 before the hearing of the summons but threatened to take similar sit-in action in the future. The judge at first instance restricted his order to the particular part of the premises which had been actually occupied by the students. The university successfully appealed. The Court of Appeal held that the order should have been made in the wide terms in which it was sought. Buckley LJ stated that:

> The jurisdiction in question is a jurisdiction directed to protecting the right of the owner of property to the possession of the whole of his property, uninterfered with by unauthorised adverse possession. In my judgment the jurisdiction to make a possession

[66] No 44 Part 24 judgment for claimant (summary): CPR Part 4 PD Table 2.

[67] In the year 2000, there were 239,957 claims for the possession of land issued in the county courts and 814 claims for the recovery of land/property issued in the Queen's Bench Division of the High Court: Lord Chancellor's Department *Judicial Statistics England and Wales for the Year 2000* (Norwich: The Stationery Office 2001), 39.

[68] [1973] Ch 447 (CA).

[69] [1980] 1 WLR 1301 (CA).

[70] Ibid 1305.

order extends to the whole of the owner's property in respect of which his right of occupation has been interfered with, but the extent of the field of operation of any order for possession which the court may think fit to make will no doubt depend upon the circumstances of the particular case.

In the present case there was, when the matter was before the judge, a threat to take what is described as "further direct action," which presumably meant similar action to the action which had already been taken, action which might be taken in respect of any part of the university property. In those circumstances it would, in my judgment, have been open to the judge to have made an order extending to the whole of the university property, or he might have made an order extending to particular parts, such as the administrative offices, of the university property. In my judgment he was in error in thinking that he was bound, by the terms of R.S.C., Ord. 113, to restrict his order to that particular part of the university property of which the students were then in actual adverse possession.[71]

Thus, the order was made with the aim of preventing threatened breaches of the university's right to possession of its land. This was a preventive remedy.[72] If the students had returned to protest, a writ of possession could be immediately served on the sheriff requiring him to eject them.[73]

3 Nature of the substantive right replicated

(a) The claimant's substantive right

An order for the recovery of land, formerly known as ejectment, was said to give direct effect to title to land, in particular, to the immediate right to recover possession of land.[74]

According to Honoré, the 'right to possess' has two aspects: a claim that others should not interfere with one's possession and a claim to be put into possession.[75] These two aspects, or rights, were effectuated through different remedies: an injunction and damages in the case of the former and an order for the recovery of land in the case of the latter.[76] Thus it is said that '[t]respass to land is an

[71] Ibid 1304.

[72] However, in *Environment Secretary v Drury* [2004] 1 WLR 1906, 1913 (CA) it was held that an owner will not be entitled to a possession order as a preventive remedy unless persons are already in wrongful occupation of another area of his land. Wilson J stressed at 1913 that 'the inclusion in a possession order of an area of land owned by the claimant which has not yet been occupied by the defendants should be exceptional.'

[73] In effect, this decision extended the remedy to cover interference with possession (the traditional preserve of trespassory protection and hence injunctions) rather than just recovery of possession.

[74] *University of Essex v Djemal* [1980] 1 WLR 1301, 1304 (CA) (Buckley J); *Manchester Airport Plc v Dutton* [2000] QB 133, 139 (CA) (Chadwick LJ (dissenting)).

[75] T. Honoré, 'Ownership' in A. G. Guest (ed.), *Oxford Essays in Jurisprudence* (Oxford: Oxford University Press, 1961), 113.

[76] However, this distinction begun to break down when an order for the recovery of land became usable as a preventive remedy to prevent threatened interference with possession: *University of Essex v Djemal* [1980] 1 WLR 1301 (CA). But see also *Environment Secretary v Drury* [2004] 1 WLR 1906, 1917–1918 (CA).

entirely separate cause of action with entirely different consequences. Trespass is based on interference with land in the possession of the claimant. . ., whereas ejectment is the recovery of land through the strength of the claimant's title.'[77]

The substantive right that is replicated in an order for the recovery of land is a right exigible against anyone, other than someone with stronger title, who is on the land in question. The availability of the order for the recovery of land dictates that the substantive right which is replicated must be characterized as a proprietary right. As stated in Chapter 4, the availability of the remedy gives rise to the substantive right.

The above analysis is somewhat clouded by the decision of the Court of Appeal in *Manchester Airport Plc v Dutton*.[78] Laws and Kennedy LJJ held that a licensee company who had never been in possession of the land in question could obtain an order for the recovery of land because, according to the majority, it would have been entitled to such an order had it been in possession. The majority decision has been criticized.[79] Chadwick LJ dissented holding that the remedy could only be obtained by a person who had a right to be in exclusive occupation which did not include a mere licensee. It is respectfully suggested that the minority position ought to be preferred.

The majority decision provides a classic example of the difficulties caused by the loose use of a term which denotes a number of concepts. A Hohfeldian analysis brings the problem to the fore. The claimant's 'right' to occupy land under a mere licence was a right in the sense of a 'privilege' (or liberty) which annulled the duty to stay off that would otherwise be owed by it to the owner. In the *Dutton* case, this concept of a right in the sense of a privilege was confused with the concept of a right in the sense of a 'claim', that is, a right which correlates with a duty. Consequently, the majority of the court gave a remedy which ordinarily replicates a right in the nature of a claim when all the claimant had before coming to court was a right in the nature of a privilege.

(b) The nature of the right's replication

An order which simply provides that the claimant do recover possession of the land is the strongest example of an order which replicates an owner's right to possession. An owner has a primary right exigible against the world at large to the possession of his land. The order in the form referred to simply restates that very right in an official and authoritative manner. The owner is not required to establish a wrong, that is, a breach of duty.

[77] B. McGuire et al, *Tolley's Claims to the Possession of Land* (Croydon: Tolley, 2001), Introduction /2.

[78] [2000] QB 133 (CA). Distinguished in *Countryside Residential (North Thames) Ltd v T (A Child)* (2001) 81 P & CR 2 (CA) where it was held that a licence to access was not sufficient to obtain the order, the claimant must have a licence to occupy.

[79] The decision has been described as 'striking': C. Harpum et al, *Megarry and Wade—The Law of Real Property* (6th edn., London: Sweet & Maxwell, 2000), 1445. See also W. Swadling, 'Opening the Numerous Clausus' (2000) 116 *LQR* 354.

The order which provides that the named defendant give possession to the claimant also replicates the owner's *primary* right to the possession of his land. However, it does not replicate that right in its entirely but merely one instantiation of it, that is, one of the numerous rights that the claimant may be said to have against individuals in the world at large.[80] This is still replication because the order does not confer a right on the claimant that is different from one he or she had before the order was made. Prior to the making of the order, the defendant was under a duty, due to the claimant's ownership, to give possession to the claimant. After the making of the order the defendant is also under a duty, arising from the order, to give possession to the claimant. There is no transformation, either of this particular instantiation of the claimant's right nor of the claimant's right against the world at large which continues to subsist unimpeded against other individuals not named in the order.

The above analysis which maintains that orders for the recovery of land directly effectuate rights *in rem* ought to be contrasted with the suggestion of Grantham and Rickett that a separate right *in personam* is created between the owner and the person in possession on the interference with the owner's right *in rem*. They write that 'the doctrinal nature of a right *in rem* is such that any interference with the asset in which the right inheres must and can be sanctioned only by the creation of a new right *in personam* in the claimant as against the particular individual who has so interfered'.[81] If this were correct then an order for the recovery of land would belong in the category of remedies which replicate secondary rights. But this view is problematic. It cannot take account of the order for the recovery of land in its simplest form, namely, that 'the claimant do recover possession of the land'.

Grantham and Rickett's position is based on the premise that 'the right *in rem* is inert and can be made to bear directly on the particular defendant only through the imposition of a further personal obligation'.[82] However, the form of the order for the recovery of land which operates against the world at large falsifies that premise. It shows that the right *in rem* is not always inert but in fact is sometimes given direct effect — replicated — in a court order. In this instance, the form which the remedy takes provides us with a clearer understanding of the substantive law and aptly demonstrates the utility of reproducing examples of court orders in a book on remedies.

4 Enforcement of the remedy

An order for the recovery of land is a remedy which is executable by the claimant himself or by an officer of the court. In the latter case, the warrant or writ of

[80] C. R. Noyes, *The Institution of Property* (New York: Longmans, Green & Co, 1936), 341.

[81] R. B. Grantham and C. E. F. Rickett, 'Property Rights as a Legally Significant Event' [2003] *CLJ* 717, 728. See also 729–34, 740.

[82] Ibid 733.

possession[83] commands the bailiff or sheriff to enter the land and cause the claimant to have possession of it. The writ is directed to the sheriff and states that: 'YOU ARE NOW COMMANDED: (1) to enter the land detailed in Schedule 1 and cause the claimant (*name*) to have possession of it'.[84]

The remedy is enforceable against non-parties who are found on the land,[85] however they can apply to have the order set aside. As Lord Denning stated in the *McPhail* case:

> The plaintiff could at once issue a writ of possession which was executed against the premises themselves. The sheriff's officers turned out everyone who was there. If there was some one else there, in addition to the defendant, he too would be turned out unless he applied to come in and defend.[86]

If the evicted occupants of the land wrongfully retake possession, a warrant or writ of restitution may be issued.[87] The writ is again directed to the sheriff and states that 'YOU ARE NOW COMMANDED: (1) to enter the land detailed in Schedule 1 and cause the claimant (*name*) to have restitution of the land'.[88] Where the order for the recovery of land requires the defendant to give possession to the claimant on a particular day, the order is also enforceable by punishment for contempt.[89]

[83] CPR Sch 1 RSC Order 45 r 3, CCR Order 24 r 6 and Order 26 r 17.

[84] Forms No 66 and 66a: CPR Part 4 PD Table 2. For the warrants of possession used in the county court see Forms N49 and N52: CPR Part 4 PD Table 3.

[85] *R v Wandsworth County Court ex parte Wandsworth LBC* [1975] 1 WLR 1314.

[86] *McPhail v Persons Unknown* [1973] Ch 447 (CA) 458.

[87] CPR Sch 1 CCR Order 26 r 17(4).

[88] Form No 68: CPR Part 4 PD Table 2. For the warrants of restitution used in the county court see Forms N50 and N51: CPR Part 4 PD Table 3. The latter forms do not use the term 'restitution' but state that the district judge and bailiffs must 'restore possession'.

[89] CPR Sch 1 RSC Order 45 r 3(1), CCR Order 26 r 18. For a discussion of punishment for contempt see Chapter 8 p 133ff.

8

Replicating Primary Rights: Equitable Remedies

A Introduction

This chapter deals with remedies that originated in equity. As previously explained, courts have historically approached the granting of these remedies from a different perspective. Although an actual or threatened infringement of a substantive right might be proved, one of a number of bars may prevent the equitable order being made. These broadly defined bars to replication reflect the sensitivity of the courts to certain issues. The courts consider these issues in each case before making an order coercing the defendant, under the threat of contempt proceedings, to do or abstain from doing the very thing required by the primary duty to which he or she is subject. The bars themselves are not the subject matter of this chapter. They are mentioned only in passing. The focus is on the remedies themselves.

In this chapter, as in the last, three issues will be examined in relation to each remedy: the nature of the remedy; the nature of the substantive right that it replicates; and the means of executing the remedy.

B Injunction Replicating a Primary Right

Almost any right correlating with a duty, arising from any event, may be potentially replicated in an injunction. At its broadest, an injunction is simply an authoritative official restatement of a duty owed by the defendant. Although, as a matter of convention certain remedies replicating particular rights are not labelled 'injunctions'. In *CSR Ltd v Cigna Insurance Australia Ltd* Dawson, Toohey, Gaudron, McHugh, Gummow, and Kirby JJ stated that 'it should be borne in mind that the term "injunction" in the parlance of equity has no fixed definition and that it is legal usage which decides which court orders are to be identified as injunctions'.[1] For example, a remedy

[1] (1997) 189 CLR 345, 390 (HCA). See also *Cardile v LED Builders Pty Ltd* (1999) 198 CLR 380 (HCA).

replicating a positive contractual right is traditionally referred to as 'a decree of specific performance'.[2] This remedy will be discussed separately below;[3] however, it could be characterized as a species of injunction for, as Tettenborn observes:

> [t]here is no reason in logic to distinguish a mandatory injunction, which orders a person to do a positive act, from an order of specific performance, which orders him positively to perform his contract; the difference merely reflects a long mental separation of contractual and other obligations.[4]

Similarly, an order for the execution of a trust could also be characterized as a species of injunction. Again it is normally treated as a separate remedy. The same could be said of an order for the return of a specific chattel or an order for the restoration of a fund. But the High Court of Australia has stressed that the latter are not injunctions as ordinarily understood.[5]

1 Form of the order

The core provision of an injunction takes the following form:

The Court ordered that [name and address of defendant]
is forbidden (whether by himself/herself or by instructing or encouraging any other person)[6] [terms of what the defendant must not do]
This order shall remain in force until (the........ of........ at........ o'clock unless before then it is revoked by) further order of the court.
And it is ordered that [name of defendant]
shall [the terms of any orders requiring acts to be done] on or before [time (and place) as ordered][7]

The order must be expressed in the clearest terms. '[A] person should have to look at and look only at the order to see what it was that he was enjoined from

[2] But Meagher, Gummow and Lehane note that specific performance in the 'proper' sense dealt with a fairly narrow range of rights (namely, rights to the execution of instruments) whereas most of the orders now commonly treated as decrees of specific performance are actually mandatory injunctions analogous to specific performance: R. P. Meagher, J. D. Heydon and M. J. Leeming, *Meagher, Gummow and Lehane's Equity: Doctrines and Remedies* (4th edn., Sydney: Butterworths, 2002), [20-015]; 3rd edn., [2003]. See p 141 below.

[3] Although specific performance is very frequently discussed before injunctions, it is submitted that being capable of characterization as a specialized kind of mandatory injunction it is better discussed after injunctions. The general should be discussed before the particular unless there is a good reason for proceeding otherwise.

[4] A. Tettenborn, *An Introduction to the Law of Obligations* (London: Butterworths, 1984), 223.

[5] *Cardile v LED Builders Pty Ltd* (1999) 198 CLR 380, 396 (HCA).

[6] In the case of a company the words in brackets are replaced with '(whether by its servants, agents, officers or otherwise)'.

[7] Form N16 Injunction order: CPR Part 4 PD Table 3. See also Form N138 Injunction order (Protection from Harassment Act 1997); *Atkin's Court Forms* (2nd edn., 2001 Issue), Vol 22(1) [23].

doing'.[8] Maitland gives the following examples of prohibitory injunctions, that is, injunctions which require the defendant to abstain from doing an act:

Let an injunction be awarded against the defendants the Mayor, Alderman and Burgess of Leeds to restrain the said defendants, their servants, agents and workmen from causing or permitting the sewage of the borough of Leeds or any part thereof to flow or pass through the main sewer or any other outfall into the river Aire unless until the same shall be sufficiently purified and deodorized so as not to be or create a nuisance or become injurious to the public health.

Let the defendant E be restrained from infringing the plaintiff's trade marks registered under the Trade Marks Registration Act 1875, or either of them, and from selling or offering for sale any tea in, or from otherwise using, wrappers having imprinted thereon any imitation or colourable imitation of the plaintiff's trade marks or either of them.

Let an injunction be awarded to restrain the defendant from using or permitting to be used the premises called X or any part thereof for the purpose of balloon ascents, fireworks, dancing, music, or other sports or entertainments, whereby a nuisance may be occasioned to the annoyance or injury of any inmates of the asylum in the pleadings mentioned.[9]

An injunction may be mandatory, that is, it may require the defendant to perform a positive act. For example, it may require trustees to transfer property to beneficiaries as in *Re Sandeman's Will Trusts*[10] where the order was made in the following terms:

the defendant trustees subject to. . .[the mortgage over the trust assets] being paid off or provision made for the payment thereof pay and transfer to the two plaintiffs their moiety of the testator's residuary personal estate including their moiety of the 3167 preferred ordinary and 702 ordinary shares in D. Sandeman & Son and J. Calrow & Son, Ltd.

Relevantly for mandatory injunctions, a practice direction to the Civil Procedure Rules states that '[a]n order which requires an act to be done (other than a judgment or order for the payment of an amount of money) must specify the time within which the act should be done' and that '[t]he consequences of failure to do an act within the time specified may be set out in the order'.[11]

For an injunction to be enforceable by punishment for contempt, it must have a penal notice stating: 'If you the within-named [ ] do not comply with this order you may be held to be in contempt of court and imprisoned or fined, or [in the case of a company or corporation] your assets may be seized.'[12]

[8] *Re a Bankrupt* (1965) 109 SJ 334, 334 (CA) (Lord Upjohn).

[9] F. W. Maitland, *Equity: A Course of Lectures* (Cambridge: Cambridge University Press, 1936), 318–19.

[10] [1937] 1 All ER 368, 372.

[11] CPR Part 40 PD [8].

[12] CPR Part 40 PD [9.1].

2 Nature of the remedy

A prohibitory injunction replicates a negative primary right, that is, a right which correlates with a duty to forbear from doing an act. A mandatory injunction replicates a positive primary right, that is, a right which correlates with a duty on the other party to do an act.

(a) Duration of operation

An injunction, like any other judgment or order, 'takes effect from the day when it is given or made, or such later date as the court may specify'.[13] A court may suspend the operation of an injunction in some circumstances seemingly on the grounds of hardship or certain conduct on the claimant's part.[14] However, such suspensions are often controversial as in *Woollerton and Wilson Ltd v R Costain Ltd*[15] where an injunction restraining a trespass was suspended until the completion of the defendant's building works because of the claimant's unmeritorious conduct in seeking to maximize its financial gain. However, in *Charrington v Simons Co Ltd*[16] a suspension of a mandatory injunction for three years was said to have exceeded the judge's discretion and was quashed. The court reserved its opinion on the correctness of the *Woollerton case* and noted that neither counsel thought it was correct.[17]

An injunction may be final or interim. A final injunction is of perpetual duration, hence it is also called a perpetual injunction. An interim injunction is awarded before trial and lasts at most to the date of the trial. Its purpose is to preserve the *status quo* pending a trial or until a specified date.[18]

(b) Function of the remedy

A prohibitory injunction always functions as a preventive remedy. '[A]n injunction is not a remedy for a past breach, but is a means for preventing further breaches'.[19] It is usually sought to prevent the continuance of an infringement of a right.[20] A prohibitory injunction may also be sought to prevent a threatened infringement from occurring. In such a case it is called a *quia timet* ('because

[13] CPR Rule 40.7(1).

[14] *Pride of Derby and Derbyshire Angling Association Ltd v British Celanese Ltd* [1953] Ch 149—an injunction was suspended for two years.

[15] [1970] 1 WLR 411.

[16] [1970] 1 WLR 598, 603 (CA).

[17] The *Woollerton* case was also doubted in *John Trenberth Ltd v National Westminster Bank Ltd* (1979) 39 P & CR 104.

[18] *The Siskina* [1979] AC 210, 256 (HL). Traditionally, a distinction was drawn between an interlocutory injunction the purposes of which was to preserve the status quo until trial and an interim injunction the purpose of which was to preserve the status quo until a specified date, usually the hearing of an application for an interlocutory injunction. However, both types are now referred to as interim injunctions in CPR Part 25.

[19] *Carlton Illustrators v Coleman & Co Ltd* [1911] 1 KB 771, 782.

[20] *Dicker v Popham Radford & Co* (1890) 63 LT 379; *Martin v Price* [1894] 1 Ch 276 (CA).

he fears') injunction. In *Redland Bricks Ltd v Morris*,[21] Lord Upjohn defined a *quia timet* action as 'an action for an injunction to prevent an apprehended legal wrong, though none has occurred at present'.

The mere existence of a substantive right does not necessarily create an entitlement to judicial intervention. *X* should not be able to successfully sue *Y*, a random stranger who has shown no desire to go anywhere near *X*'s land, and obtain an injunction prohibiting *Y* from entering *X*'s land. This is so even though *X* has a clear right that *Y* not enter the land without his consent. It would be inefficient for such random actions to be countenanced by the law. As Lord Dunedin said, 'no one can obtain a quia timet order by merely saying "Timeo[22]"; he must aver and prove that what is going on is calculated to infringe his rights.'[23] The claimant must show that there is imminent danger of such an infringement and that it is likely to cause substantial damage if it occurs.[24]

Of course, ordering the defendant to cease doing an act cannot redress a past breach of the defendant's obligation not to do that act. For example, merely ordering the defendant not to enter the claimant's land does not redress past trespasses. Consequently, a prohibitory injunction is usually granted along with a corrective remedy such as an award of damages which usually replicates a secondary right arising from the breach of the primary right.

In contrast to a prohibitory injunction, a mandatory injunction usually functions as a corrective remedy. It aims to redress a past infringement of a primary right by compelling the doing of the act that will realize that right.

(c) Advantages of the remedy

The most important advantage of an injunction is that the claimant obtains an order requiring the defendant to do or abstain from doing the very thing that the substantive duty requires the defendant to do. The claimant does not need to make do with an approximate money substitute. His or her rights cannot be said to be compulsorily acquired by the defendant through a payment.[25] It has been observed that giving damages instead of specific relief may be tantamount to 'enabling the rich man to buy the poor man's property without his consent, for that is really what it comes to.'[26]

[21] [1970] AC 652, 664 (HL). However, the injunction considered in this case was sought to prevent further landslides due to excavations that had already been carried out. It was not a *quia timet* injunction to prevent a wrong but rather a mandatory injunction to undo a wrong that had already been committed: see A. Burrows, *Remedies for Torts and Breach of Contract* (2nd edn., London: Butterworths, 1994), 390.

[22] 'I fear, I am afraid.'

[23] *Attorney General of Canada v Ritchie Contracting and Supply Co* [1919] AC 999, 1005 (PC).

[24] *Fletcher v Bealey* (1885) 28 Ch D 688; *Hooper v Rogers* [1975] Ch 43 (CA); Burrows (n 21 above), 421.

[25] *Woollerton and Wilson Ltd v R Costain Ltd* [1970] 1 WLR 411, 413 (Stamp LJ).

[26] *Krehl v Burrell* (1878) 7 Ch D 551, 554 (Jessel MR) affd (1879) 11 Ch D 146 (CA).

Secondly, damages are often difficult to quantify and there is a risk that the claimant may be under-compensated by a monetary award which is often a mere approximation of the loss suffered. Thirdly, a claimant who has obtained an injunction need not be concerned with the risk of the defendant's bankruptcy or insolvency. This is a significant concern for a claimant who merely holds an award of damages. Fourthly, the decree is backed by a strong enforcement mechanism. A defendant who fails to comply with the order may be punished for contempt of court. Fifthly, an injunction obviates the need for multiple suits to be brought in relation to a continuing wrong.[27]

If the claimant does wish to settle for a sum of money, the remedy gives him or her a strong post-judgment bargaining position allowing him or her to get a better financial result than if only damages had been awarded. The high cost of complying with the injunction may cause the defendant to offer a sum of money to the claimant to forgo the awarded remedy. The sum may far exceed the actual loss suffered by the claimant.[28]

(d) Effect on substantive rights

By analogy with a decree of specific performance,[29] a substantive right replicated in an injunction continues to exist and does not become merged in the order. The right that arises from the making of the order (that is, the remedy) also continues to exist until the injunction is discharged. The parties are usually free to negotiate away the underlying substantive right but the effect of a subsequent agreement on the remedy is not completely clear.

The traditional view is that the claimant may waive a breach of an injunction. Lord Diplock stated that 'no sufficient public interest is served by punishing the offender if the only person for whose benefit the order was made chooses not to insist on its enforcement'.[30] But the Rule of Law and respect for the courts are undermined if court orders are allowed to be ignored. Buxton J is reported to have held that '[o]nce a court order applied the applicant could not give permission for the other party to act in breach of it. . .[A] court order was not open to negotiation. . .[T]he correct course was to return to the court.'[31] There is a range of views and a prudent defendant would apply to the court for a discharge of the injunction before acting on an agreement with a claimant to act contrary to it.[32]

[27] *Doherty v Allman* (1878) 3 App Cas 709 (HL).

[28] B. Thompson, 'Injunction Negotiations: An Economic, Moral and Legal Analysis' (1975) 27 *Stan LR* 1563.

[29] See 7 p 137.

[30] *Attorney General v Times Newspapers Ltd* [1974] AC 273, 308 (HL).

[31] *R v Commissioners of Inland Revenue, ex parte Kingston Smith* (1996) The Times, August 15, 514.

[32] See also C. J. Miller, *Contempt of Court* (3rd edn., Oxford: Oxford University Press, 2000), [2.18] where after surveying the authorities the author concludes that 'there are circumstances (for example, cases of open contumacy) in which the interest of the public transcends that of the parties immediately concerned'.

Where an injunction is refused, the substantive legal right which the court refused to replicate continues to exist.[33] Although, as Lord Nicholls stated in *Attorney General v Blake*,[34] the refusal has 'the effect in practice of sanctioning the indefinite continuance of a wrong'. In *Jaggard v Sawyer*,[35] Millett LJ observed that, 'Thereafter the defendant may have no right to act in the manner complained of, but he cannot be prevented from doing so. . .[T]he practical consequence of withholding injunctive relief is to authorise the continuation of an unlawful state of affairs.' However, even then the claimant may not be entirely without recourse. He or she is left to any further legal rights that he may have, such as his or her secondary rights to damages at law.[36]

3 Nature of the substantive right replicated

The courts have frequently stressed that an injunction replicates a pre-existing 'right'.[37] The statement of Sir George Baker P in *Paton v Trustees of British Pregnancy Advisory Service* sums up the position:

> In considering the law the first and basic principle is that there must be a legal right enforceable in law or in equity before the applicant can obtain an injunction from the court to restrain an infringement of that right. That has long been the law.[38]

For example, in *Day v Brownrigg*[39] the claimant failed to obtain an injunction because he was unable to point to a substantive right. The defendant bought a house called 'Aston Villa' and renamed it 'Aston Lodge'. The claimant's neighbouring house was called 'Aston Lodge'. The claimant alleged damage and sought an injunction to stop the defendant from continuing to use the new name. The Court of Appeal held that there was no legal right to the exclusive

[33] This is the logical position where law and equity are administered in different courts. Thus in *Wood v Scarth* specific performance of an agreement for a lease was refused in the Court of Chancery (1855) 2 K & J 33 but the common law court held that there was an enforceable agreement (1858) 1 F & F 293. The position is not so clear in relation to purely equitable rights.

[34] [2001] 1 AC 268, 281 (HL). [35] [1995] 1 WLR 269, 288 (CA).

[36] *Goodson v Richardson* (1874) 9 Ch App 221, 223 (CA). For example, in *Patel v Ali* [1984] Ch 283 specific performance of the primary right was refused because of hardship but the secondary right to damages was given effect. See also *Shaw v Applegate* [1977] 1 WLR 970 (CA).

[37] *North London Railway Co v Great Northern Railway Co* (1883) 11 QBD 30, 40 (CA); *The Siskina* [1979] AC 210 (HL); *ABC v Lenah Game Meats Pty Ltd* (2001) 185 ALR 1 (HCA); Meagher et al (n 2 above), [21-035]; 3rd edn., [2107]. Sometimes it is said that injunctions are granted in the absence of a 'right' in order to restrain judicial proceedings in another court or in the aid of judicial proceedings: L. A. Sheridan, *Injunctions and Similar Orders* (Chichester: Barry Rose, 1999), 126–7. Such orders will not be considered here as they are outside of the concept of a remedy as defined in Chapter 4 because they do not either temporarily or permanently settle the main dispute between the parties. However, in so far as they place a defendant under a duty which did not exist before, they are clearly transformative. They are also frequently controversial. Meagher et al state that the decision in *Re Oriental Credit Ltd* [1988] Ch 204 where a party was restrained from leaving the country in order to be examined by liquidators was 'astonishing' and 'in defiance of both principle and the House of Lords' (n 2 above), [21-070]; 3rd edn., [2113].

[38] [1979] QB 276, 278. [39] (1878) 10 Ch D 294.

use of a name of a house. Accordingly the grant of an injunction by the trial judge was overruled.

(a) Negative primary right (prohibitory injunction)

Maitland was referring to prohibitory injunctions when he said the following: 'Let us see what an injunction is. It is an order made by the Court forbidding a person or class of persons from doing a certain act, or acts of a certain class, upon pain of going to prison for an indefinite time as contemnors of the Court.'[40]

(i) Common law rights

(a) Replication of negative contractual rights Lord Cairns LC stated:

> If parties, for valuable consideration, with their eyes open, contract that a particular thing shall not be done, all that a Court of Equity has to do is to say, by way of injunction, that which the parties have already said by way of covenant, that the thing shall not be done; and in such case the injunction does nothing more than give the sanction of the process of the Court to that which already is the contract between the parties. It is not then a question of the balance of convenience or inconvenience, or of the amount of damage or of injury — it is the specific performance, by the Court, of that negative bargain which the parties have made, with their eyes open, between themselves.[41]

Of course the usual bars to equitable remedies potentially apply to the grant of an injunction which replicates a negative contractual obligation. These include the adequacy of damages,[42] acquiescence,[43] inequitable conduct or 'unclean hands',[44] delay,[45] and triviality of the infringement.[46] If a bar to replication is given sufficient weight in the particular circumstances then the order will be refused.

In the often cited case of *Lumley v Wagner*[47] the court granted a prohibitory injunction which replicated the claimant's right not to have the defendant sing at another London theatre for three months. This situation was close to one where the grant of an injunction would, in effect, amount to specific performance. In such cases the courts appear to have become more sensitive to the dangers of compelling the performance of personal services and now the same bars are considered to be potentially applicable in such a situation as in relation to the grant of specific performance.[48]

[40] Maitland (n 9 above), 318.
[41] *Doherty v Allman* (1878) 3 App Cas 709, 719–720 (HL). Compare *Cardile v LED Builders Pty Ltd* (1999) 198 CLR 380, 396 (HCA).
[42] *London and Blackhall Rly Co v Cross* (1886) 31 Ch D 354, 369 (CA).
[43] *Shaw v Applegate* [1977] 1 WLR 970 (CA).
[44] *Telegraph Despatch and Intelligence Co v McLean* (1873) 8 Ch App 658 (CA).
[45] *Archibold v Scully* (1861) 9 HL Cases 360.
[46] *Armstrong v Sheppard and Short Ltd* [1959] 1 QB 384, 396.
[47] (1852) 1 De GM & G 604, 42 ER 687.
[48] *Page One Records v Britton* [1968] 1 WLR 157.

(b) Replication of negative non-contractual legal rights Prohibitory injunctions which replicate negative duties not arising from an agreement often give effect to personal and proprietary rights protected by the law of tort. As Maitland points out, '[a] very large part of the whole province of Tort is a proper field for the injunction.'[49] Such injunctions are most usually sought to give effect to real property rights such as the right to enjoy quiet possession of one's land. For example, in *Kennaway v Thompson*[50] the defendant powerboat club was restrained from carrying on activities which caused a nuisance and hence interfered with the claimant's enjoyment of her land.

Such an injunction is available as a matter of course, unless one of the usual bars to equitable remedies, described above, is found to operate.[51] However, the court may refuse the remedy and give an award of damages in substitution for it where the injury to the claimant's rights is small, capable of being estimated in money, can be adequately compensated by a small money payment, and where the case is one in which it would be oppressive to grant an injunction.[52]

(ii) Equitable rights

Equitable rights are rights that were not recognized in common law courts. These rights, which are recognized only in the exclusive equity jurisdiction, are often replicated in court orders. Negative duties of trustees are often replicated in prohibitory injunctions. For example, the primary duty of trustees not to distribute funds inconsistently with the trust[53] or the primary duty of trustees not to sell property in breach of trust[54] have been effectuated in prohibitory injunctions. The usual bars, except the adequacy of damages, appear to apply.[55]

(iii) Statutory rights

Rights which are created by statute may also be replicated in an injunction in an appropriate case. In *Attorney General v Sharp*[56] the defendant's statutory duty not to operate buses without a licence was replicated in a prohibitory injunction. However, where a private individual is seeking to enforce a public right, issues of standing to sue are of foremost importance. Generally, the claimant must show either that a private right of his or hers has also been infringed or that he or she has suffered special damage because of the infringement of the public right.[57] But of

[49] Maitland (n 9 above), 325.

[50] [1981] QB 88 (CA). See Chapter 5 text to n 57 for the wording of the order.

[51] W. W. Kerr, *On the Law and Practice of Injunctions* (J. M. Paterson (ed.), 6th edn., London: Sweet & Maxwell, 1927), 30.

[52] *Shelfer v City of London Electric Lighting Co* [1895] 1 Ch 287, 322–323 (CA); applied in *Jaggard v Sawyer* [1995] 1 WLR 269 (CA). Awards of damages in addition to and in substitution for an injunction are discussed in Chapter 12 p 199 and Chapter 13 p 212.

[53] *Fox v Fox* (1870) LR 11 Eq 142.

[54] *Dance v Goldingham* (1873) LR 8 Ch App 902 (CA).

[55] *Heavener v Loomes* (1924) 34 CLR 306, 326 (HCA).

[56] [1931] 2 Ch 121 (CA).

[57] *Meade v London Borough of Haringey* [1979] 1 WLR 637 (CA).

course not all statutory rights are public rights. Most intellectual property rights are founded on statute. Injunctions are frequently granted to restrain infringements of such private rights.[58]

(b) Positive primary non-contractual right (mandatory injunction)

This category does not include decrees of specific performance which are essentially mandatory injunctions replicating primary contractual rights.[59] It also does not include mandatory injunctions which replicate secondary rights and function to undo wrongs (sometimes called 'restorative injunctions').[60] Thus it covers the remaining cases where primary rights, not being contractual rights, are replicated in court orders.

(i) Common law rights

The case of *Gravesham Borough Council v British Railways Board*[61] provides an example of a situation where a claimant sought a mandatory injunction which would give direct effect to a non-contractual positive primary right. In this case, it was a right correlating with a common law duty to operate a ferry. The injunction was refused because a reduction in the number of services was found not to have breached the duty to operate the ferry. However, Slade J appeared to accept that in exceptional circumstances a mandatory injunction could be available in such a case.

(ii) Equitable rights

Positive equitable rights are often replicated in court orders. Normally this is done as a matter of course, subject to the usual equitable bars. A few examples of such rights will be given here. The first is the right of a beneficiary who is entitled to a distribution of trust property. In an extreme case, this right may arise from a direction by the beneficiary under the rule in *Saunders v Vautier*.[62] The rule provides that an adult beneficiary, of sound mind and entitled to the entire beneficial interest under the trust, may have the trust property transferred at his or her direction.

In *Re Sandeman's Will Trusts*,[63] the defendant trustees held half the testator's shares on trust for the plaintiffs. The claimant beneficiaries demanded to have legal title to the shares transferred to them. Clauson J held that 'it is quite plain that the plaintiffs' rights must be given effect to; and they must have their half of the shares in question transferred to them. In my view, that is the order, and the only order which I can make.' The form of the order made was reproduced above.[64]

[58] *Carlton Illustrators v Coleman & Co Ltd* [1911] 1 KB 771.
[59] Specific performance is discussed at p 134ff.
[60] Mandatory injunctions which replicate secondary rights, or which are transformative in nature, are dealt with in Chapter 11 p 189ff.
[61] [1978] Ch 379.
[62] (1841) 4 Beav 115; affirmed (1841) Cr & Ph 240.
[63] [1937] 1 All ER 368, 372.
[64] See text to n 10 above.

A similar order may be made following the accounting process where a shortfall in the trust fund is found.[65] Where the beneficiaries are entitled to the entire beneficial interest, the beneficiaries' right to the distribution of the trust property is replicated in this order.[66] But where beneficiaries are not yet so entitled, other primary rights that form part of the trust relationship may be replicated at this stage. For example, the trustee may be ordered to restore the trust fund,[67] either by a payment of money or by the purchase of replacement property. As Elliott concludes:

> [the orders that may be made against a trustee at the conclusion of an accounting] either enforce primary duties the trustee incurred when he undertook the trust, such as the duty to distribute the fund, or the duty to segregate and protect the fund, or else they enforce the primary duty he incurred when he was removed from office to transfer the fund to the new trustee.[68]

Elliott also notes that such orders are 'not granted in order to enforce secondary duties to make good the breach of trust as a damages award is.'[69] The duties are primary as the trustee's duties to distribute the fund or the duty to segregate and protect the fund arise by virtue of the trustee's position and not due to any wrong committed by the trustee.

Some directions to trustees,[70] being orders that trustees perform one or more of their primary duties, also belong in this class of orders. For example, in *Re Tillott*[71] the court made an order directing a trustee to sign and deliver to the claimant an authority enabling the claimant to obtain information about the trust property from a third party. The remedy replicated the trustee's primary duty 'to give his *cestui que trust* proper information as to the investment of the trust estate'.[72]

Although equitable remedies which replicate the primary duties of trustees have received no attention at all in general works on remedies, it is suggested

65 See text to n 165 below.

66 *Target Holdings Ltd v Redferns* [1996] 1 AC 421, 435 (HL).

67 Ibid 434; *Hillsdown Plc v Pensions Ombudsman* [1997] 1 All ER 862, 897. Though, according to the High Court of Australia, such an order should not be labelled an 'injunction': *Cardile v LED Builders Pty Limited* (1999) 198 CLR 380, 396 (HCA).

68 S. Elliott, 'Compensation Claims Against Trustees' (DPhil Thesis Oxford University 2002), 140.

69 In contrast, Chambers suggests that some such rights are secondary, apparently, because they effect compensation: R. Chambers, 'Liability' in P. B. H. Birks and A. Pretto (eds), *Breach of Trust* (Oxford: Hart, 2002), 8–10, 16–17. It may be that Chambers is forced to take this view because he has fallen into the error identified in Chapter 5 of treating direct enforcement and compensation or restitution as mutually exclusive categories. For example, he states at 8: 'It is important to note that, in many cases, the order to pay will effect compensation or restitution rather than direct enforcement.'

70 But not all directions fall in this category as some do not replicate existing rights (for example, they may merely authorise the trustees to make a certain investment that they could not otherwise make) and hence must be classed as transformative. See Chapter 13 pp 214 and 216 and Chapter 13 text to n 84.

71 [1892] 1 Ch 86. *Buttle v Saunders* [1950] 2 All ER 193.

72 Ibid 88 (Chitty J).

that, in order not to paint an incomplete and hence misleading picture of the law relating to the direct enforcement of primary rights, they ought to be characterized as mandatory injunctions, or at least as closely analogous remedies, and discussed alongside other such orders.

This brings us to a difficult question raised by equitable doctrines such as estoppel. Say the claimant improves the defendant's land in reliance on the defendant's promise of a gift. The claimant will be able to obtain an order against the defendant requiring a conveyance of the land.[73] Does the order requiring a conveyance made by the court in such proprietary estoppel cases *replicate* a substantive right? It seems clear that it does. Lord Denning MR spoke in such terms in *Crabb v Arun District Council* when he said, '[t]he new rights and interests, so created by estoppel, in or over land, will be protected by the courts'.[74] Lord Scarman said that the proprietary estoppel action concerned 'an infringement of an equitable right possessed by the plaintiff'.[75] Of course the replication of such a substantive right can be refused because a bar to an equitable remedy operates.

In ascertaining the content of this substantive right, as it has arisen in the particular case, the courts are guided by 'the minimum equity to do justice to the plaintiff'.[76] In this area, and in newly emergent areas such as the Australian doctrine of promissory estoppel,[77] the substantive law ought to be taken to be in a process of settling down.[78] As it does so, it should be possible to say with more certainty when primary rights arise from events such as induced detrimental reliance, what the content of such primary rights is,[79] and when and what secondary rights arise from their infringement. This would be consistent with the work of commentators such as Spence who argue that equitable estoppel is underpinned by a moral duty to ensure the reliability of induced assumptions which gives rise to primary obligations to prevent harm and secondary obligations to compensate if harm occurs.[80]

Alternatively, one may take the view that the law in this area is concerned with remedial discretion, not rights, and that it will never be possible to say in estoppel

[73] *Dillwyn v Llewelyn* (1862) 4 De F & J 517.

[74] [1976] Ch 179, 187 (CA) (Lord Denning MR).

[75] Ibid 199.

[76] Ibid 198 (Scarman LJ); *Gillett v Holt* [2001] Ch 210 (CA); *Jennings v Rice* [2002] EWCA Civ 159 (CA).

[77] *Waltons Stores (Interstate) Ltd v Maher* (1988) 164 CLR 387 (HCA).

[78] A large part of the discretion in this area may be a 'rule-building' or 'rule-compromise' discretion: Chapter 6 p 87. Gardner suggests that the English law in this area is becoming less discretionary and more rule-based: S. Gardner, 'The Remedial Discretion in Proprietary Estoppel' (1999) 115 *LQR* 438, 461ff. Contrast *Giumelli v Giumelli* (1999) 161 ALR 473 (HCA). See also P. B. H. Birks, 'Three Kinds of Objection to Discretionary Remedialism' (2000) 29 *Western Australian L Rev* 1, 7.

[79] At this moment of the law's development, the content of rights arising from estoppel is still relatively unclear: Gardner (n 78 above). However, decisions such as *Jennings v Rice* [2002] EWCA Civ 159 (CA) are giving a clearer indication of what such rights require of the defendant.

[80] M. Spence, *Protecting Reliance: The Emergent Doctrine of Equitable Estoppel* (Oxford: Hart, 1999), 2.

cases that a person comes under a duty to do a particular act before an order of the court is made.[81] If this view is correct then awards made in estoppel cases will have to be characterized as transformative remedies.

(iii) Statutory rights

Positive statutory rights may be enforced by mandatory injunctions. For example, it has been held that a mandatory injunction could be granted replicating a local authority's positive duty to provide accommodation for the homeless[82] or to maintain houses.[83]

4 Enforcement of the remedy

If the defendant breaches an injunction,[84] he or she is in contempt of court.[85] The defendant may be punished, usually on the motion of the claimant,[86] by an order for committal of the defendant to prison,[87] by a fine,[88] or by a writ of sequestration against the defendant's property.[89] The latter directs and authorizes named reputable persons (sequestrators) to take and keep possession of the contemnor's property until the contempt is purged. It is used where the defendant is out of jurisdiction or where the defendant is a body corporate. In the case of a company, the order can be further enforced by a writ of sequestration against the property of a director or any other officer or an order for committal against such an officer.[90]

Committal must be for a fixed time up to a maximum of two years in prison if ordered by a superior court.[91] The defendant may obtain early release by purging his or her contempt or showing readiness to do so.[92] Third parties

[81] That is, that the discretion to determine the 'minimum equity' is a strong, broad, 'rule-failure' discretion: Chapter 6 p 87.

[82] *De Falco v Crawley Borough Council* [1980] QB 460 (CA).

[83] *Parker v Camden London Borough Council* [1986] Ch 162 (CA).

[84] The breach of injunction must be established beyond reasonable doubt: *Re Bramblevale Ltd* [1970] Ch 128. The court may refuse to punish the defendant on a number of grounds: Meagher et al (n 2 above), [20–270]; 3rd edn., [2054].

[85] For a more detailed discussion of enforcement by punishment for contempt see Miller (n 32 above), Chapter 14.

[86] The court may also act of its own motion: *R v Commissioners of Inland Revenue, ex parte Kingston Smith* (1996) The Times, August 15.

[87] But enforcement by committal is only possible where it is permitted by the Debtors Acts 1869 and 1878 (UK): CPR Sch 1 RSC Order 45 r 5(1)(b)(iii) and Order 52 also CCR Order 29 r 1; *Mander v Falke* [1891] 3 Ch 488; Sheridan (n 37 above), 254–79.

[88] *Heatons Transport (St Helens) Ltd v Transport and General Workers Union* [1973] AC 15, 109 (HL); *Mullen v Hackney London Borough Council* [1997] 1 WLR 1103 (CA).

[89] CPR Sch 1 RSC Order 45 r 5; *Inland Revenue Commissioners v Hoogstraten* [1985] QB 1077; Sheridan (n 37 above), 23–7.

[90] *Phonographic Performance Ltd v Amusement Caterers (Peckham) Ltd* [1964] Ch 195.

[91] Contempt of Court Act 1981 (UK) ss 14(1), 14(4A).

[92] CPR Sch 1 RSC Order 52 r 8.

can be punished for contempt where, with knowledge of the injunction, they assist in its breach or act so as to prejudice the administration of justice.[93]

Injunctions are not always enforced by punishment for contempt. Sometimes they may be executed by direct recourse to the defendant's assets or by a substituted act of a third party. Where the defendant must give possession of land to the claimant, this may be achieved by means of a warrant or writ of possession which directs the bailiff or sheriff to enter the land and cause the claimant to have possession of it.[94] In the case where the defendant must deliver goods, this may be achieved by means of a warrant or writ of specific delivery which directs the bailiff or sheriff to cause the goods to be delivered to the claimant.[95] Where the defendant must do another act, 'the Court may direct that the act required to be done may, so far as practicable, be done by the party by whom the order or judgment was obtained or some other person appointed by the Court, at the cost of the disobedient party'.[96] In all these cases, the remedy could also be enforced by punishment for contempt.[97]

Orders to pay money may be enforced in the same manner as an award of an agreed sum.[98] In relation to orders directing trustees to pay money, it must be noted that where a trustee or a person acting in a fiduciary capacity has breached an order to pay a sum in his or her possession or under his or her control then potentially the order may be enforced by imprisonment for up to one year.[99]

C Decree of Specific Performance of a Contract

1 Form of the order

The core provision of a decree of specific performance takes the following form:

> THIS COURT orders that the agreement dated [ ] referred to in the Particulars of Claim be specifically performed and carried into execution.[100]

The rules of court require that such an order must specify the time within which the act should be done (unless it is for the payment of money) and the consequences of failing to comply with the order.[101]

[93] *Attorney General v Times Newspapers Ltd* [1991] 2 All ER 98; Sheridan (n 37 above), 281–90.

[94] See Chapter 7 p 119.

[95] See Chapter 9 p 157.

[96] CPR Sch 1 RSC Order 45 r 8; *Parker v Camden London Borough Council* [1986] Ch 162 (CA). See also Supreme Court Act 1971 (UK) s 31 which empowers the High Court to order the execution of an instrument by a nominated person where the defendant refuses to comply with an order to do so.

[97] CPR Sch 1 RSC Order 45 r 5.

[98] Chapter 7 p 112.

[99] Debtors Act 1869 (UK) s 4(3).

[100] *Atkin's Court Forms* (2nd edn., 2001 Issue), Vol 37 [87]–[108].

[101] CPR Part 40 PD [8].

An example of a decree of specific performance awarded to a vendor which embodies a remedy requiring a defendant purchaser to perform an agreement for the purchase of land provides:

THIS COURT orders that the agreement dated [ ] mentioned in the particulars of the claim be specifically performed and carried into execution.

AND IT IS ORDERED that interest be computed at the rate of........ per cent per annum on the sum of £........ (the residue of the purchase money for the property mentioned in the agreement) from........ 20........, when the purchase ought to have been completed according to the terms of the said agreement to the day to be fixed hereinafter directed.

AND IT IS ORDERED that the following accounts be taken. . .[*This paragraph is reproduced in the Common Account section below*[102]]

AND IT IS ORDERED that what shall be found due on the said account of rents and profits be deducted from the said purchase money and interest and costs as aforesaid, and the balance certified by the district judge. And it appearing that the defendant has accepted the claimant's title to the said property IT IS ORDERED that the claimant be at liberty to prepare and execute a conveyance to the defendant (as to be delivered to the defendant as hereinafter provided) such conveyance to be settled by the court in case the parties differ.

And upon the claimant at a time and place to be appointed by the court after the said conveyance shall have been so executed as aforesaid delivering to the defendant the said conveyance together with all deeds and writings in his possession or power relating solely to the property and giving an acknowledgement and undertaking for production of deeds relating to other properties as provided by s. 64 of the Law of Property Act 1925.

IT IS ORDERED that the defendant do at the same time and place pay to the claimant the amount of the said certified balance.[103]

As with an injunction, a decree of specific performance must include a penal notice to be enforceable by punishment for contempt.[104]

2 Nature of the remedy

(a) *Function of the remedy*

A decree of specific performance gives rise to a remedy which is either corrective or preventive. The case of *Dougan v Ley*[105] provides an example of the remedy functioning in a corrective manner. The defendant contracted to sell a taxi-cab and licence to the claimant but later refused to perform the contract. The claimant successfully sued for a decree of specific performance of the defendant's duty to transfer the chattel and the special rights attaching to it.

[102] See text to n 161 below.

[103] Form N302 Judgment in action for specific performance (vendor, title accepted). CPR Part 4 PD Table 3 lists this pre-CPR county court form as a form which may continue to be used under the new rules: CPR Part 4 PD [1.3]. For a reported example see *Cooper v Morgan* [1909] 1 Ch 261.

[104] CPR Part 40 PD [9.1].

[105] (1946) 71 CLR 142 (HCA).

As Fry points out, when operating as a corrective remedy, specific performance cannot achieve exactly the same position as due performance because of the inherent time delay. It is often necessary to combine it with an award of damages[106] so as to do complete justice:

To say, as above is said, that the courts enforce actual execution according to the stipulations and terms of the contract is not quite exact: for the Court rarely, if ever, interferes until the time for performance has passed and default been made: consequently the performance enforced by the court is almost always behind time as compared with due performance voluntarily yielded.[107]

The remedy may also function in a preventive manner. Specific performance is available to prevent a threatened breach of contract rather than to correct a breach that has already occurred. In *Hasham v Zenab* it was held that '[a]ll that is required is to show circumstances which will justify intervention by a court of equity.'[108] This may be stating the principle too broadly. Burrows observes that it is an actual or anticipatory breach of contract that in practice makes it equitable for the court to grant specific performance. He also adds that theoretically a threat to break a contract not amounting to an anticipatory breach could also suffice.[109]

In *Turner v Bladin* the High Court of Australia held that:

Proceedings for specific performance of a contract which is of such a kind that it can be specifically enforced can be commenced as soon as one party threatens to refuse to perform the contract or any part thereof or actually refuses to perform any promise for which the time of performance has arrived.[110]

Jones and Goodhart observe that this suggests that an action for specific performance brought before either an actual or threatened breach of contract will fail. But they note that there is no authority which expressly states that this proposition is correct.[111] Spry adds a further explanation of the conditions required for the grant of specific performance as a preventive remedy:

There must be more than a theoretical or remote possibility of a breach, but otherwise a greater or lesser possibility that there will be a failure to perform may be found to be sufficient in the general circumstances; and in particular the degree of probability of a

[106] Since the enactment of Lord Cairns' Act in 1858, the courts have power, in their equity jurisdiction, to grant damages either in combination with specific performance or in substitution for it: Supreme Court Act 1981 (UK) ss 49, 50.

[107] E. Fry (G. R. Northcote ed.), *A Treatise on the Specific Performance of Contracts* (6th edn., London: Stevens, 1921), 3.

[108] [1960] AC 316, 329 (PC) (Lord Tucker). It should be noted that in this case there was an anticipatory breach of contract. In *Marks v Lilley* [1959] 1 WLR 749, the other leading case in this area, there was an actual breach of a non-essential term, namely a failure to complete on time where time was not of the essence.

[109] Burrows (n 21 above), 335.

[110] (1951) 82 CLR 463, 472 (HCA).

[111] G. Jones and W. Goodhart, *Specific Performance* (2nd edn., London: Butterworths, 1996), 237.

future breach that must be shown before the court will intervene depends on the extent of hardship that the plaintiff may suffer if the breach occurs and on any other matters that bear on the justice or injustice of granting relief immediately.[112]

Burrows writes that a decree of specific performance cannot be made at an interlocutory stage, instead an interlocutory mandatory injunction must be sought.[113]

(b) Advantages of the remedy

The advantages of a decree of specific performance are many. First, the claimant obtains an order requiring the defendant to do the very thing that the substantive duty requires the defendant to do. The claimant is not saddled with a money substitute which may not be sufficient to alleviate the claimant's grievance. Damages may under-compensate the claimant.

Secondly, in contrast to an award of damages, the claimant who seeks specific performance need not have adjusted his position to mitigate his or her loss. Thirdly, the decree is backed by a strong enforcement mechanism. A defendant who fails to comply with the order may be punished for contempt of court. Fourthly, the decree may offer advantages in the event of the defendant's bankruptcy or insolvency.[114] Fifthly, the remedy may put the claimant in a very strong post-judgment bargaining position.

Sixthly, where specific performance of an obligation to pay money is obtained, additional benefits over an award of an agreed sum or damages include that it avoids a multiplicity of suits where the payments are to be made in instalments[115] and that it allows the vendor to divest him or herself of the property he or she is selling and any burdensome obligations that may attach to it.[116] Finally, it can also overcome restrictions imposed by privity of contract, allowing a contract for the benefit of a third party to be enforced.[117]

(c) Effect on substantive rights

Contractual rights continue to exist after the remedy is given. As Sir Wilfrid Greene MR stated in *Austins of East Ham Ltd v Macey*:

> An order for specific performance does not get rid of the contract. The contract is not merged in the order, but it is treated, and always has been treated by the court of equity, as still subsisting.[118]

[112] I. C. F. Spry, *The Principles of Equitable Remedies: Specific Performance, Injunctions, Rectification and Equitable Damages* (6th edn., Pyrmont New South Wales: Law Book Co, 2001), 78.

[113] Burrows (n 21 above), 336.

[114] *Lysaght v Edwards* (1876) 2 Ch D 499; *Re Wait* [1927] 1 Ch 606 (CA).

[115] *Beswick v Beswick* [1968] AC 58, 88–9 (HL).

[116] *Dougan v Ley* (1946) 71 CLR 142, 150 (HCA).

[117] *Beswick v Beswick* [1968] AC 58 (HL) and *Coulls v Bagot's Executor and Trustee Co* (1967) 119 CLR 460 (HCA) but this advantage is now less important in England because of *Alfred McAlpine Construction Ltd v Panatown Ltd* [2001] 1 AC 518 (HL) and the Contracts (Rights of Third Parties) Act 1999 (UK).

[118] [1941] Ch 338, 341 (CA).

However, the making of the order gives rise to new rights.[119] These new rights take precedence. 'It is the provisions of the order and not of the contract which regulate how the contract is to be carried out.'[120] If the claimant or the defendant fails to comply with the order, the innocent party may apply for it to be discharged.[121] But it is no longer open to the innocent party to accept the repudiation and treat the contract as terminated. The leave of the court must be obtained.[122]

3 Nature of the substantive right replicated

The remedy arising from a decree of specific performance is simply an authoritative official restatement of a duty owed by the defendant under a contract.[123] Maitland writes:

> In granting a decree of specific performance — or a judgment for specific performance — the court in effect says to the defendant, You must perform specifically the contract into which you entered — that is to say you must do the very thing that you promised to do on pain of going to prison as a contemner of this Court.[124]

Much has already been said about specific performance when illustrating points made in earlier chapters.[125] To recapitulate, a decree of specific performance gives direct effect to a positive primary contractual right.

The decree of specific performance is equitable in origin and hence subject to certain bars. Apart from the usual bars to replication already mentioned in relation to injunctions, certain other bars may be relevant. Some bars to the remedy of specific performance, such as the lack of 'mutuality', potentially apply to the replication of any kind of contractual rights. The court may refuse a decree of specific performance where such an order would not be made if sought by the defendant against the claimant. For example, in *Flight v Bolland*[126] a minor was refused specific performance because it would not be decreed against the minor. The court is concerned not to leave the defendant who has performed his or her side of the bargain under the threat of contempt

[119] W. N. Hohfeld, 'Relations Between Equity and Law' (1913) 11 *Michigan LR* 537, 551.

[120] *Singh v Nazeer* [1979] Ch 474, 480 (Megarry V-C).

[121] *Austins of East Ham Ltd v Macey* [1941] Ch 338 (CA); *Johnson v Agnew* [1980] AC 367, 399 (HL).

[122] *Halkett v Earl of Dudley* [1907] 1 Ch 590, 601; *Sunbird Plaza Pty Ltd v Maloney* (1988) 166 CLR 245, 260 (HCA); contrast Meagher et al. (n 2 above), [20-265]; 3rd edn., [2053].

[123] In England only a right arising from an agreement backed by consideration (thus excluding deeds) may be replicated in a decree of specific performance: *Jeffreys v Jeffreys* (1841) Cr & Ph 138; 41 ER 443. In Australia, specific performance may be available if promissory estoppel can be established: *Waltons Stores (Interstate) Ltd v Maher* (1988) 164 CLR 387 (HCA). Furthermore, unlike in England, specific performance is also available in Australia to enforce rights which are not contractual but exist because of the doctrine of part performance: *Regent v Millet* (1976) 133 CLR 679 (HCA).

[124] Maitland (n 6 above), 301.

[125] Especially Chapter 5 p 70ff.

[126] (1828) 4 Russ 298; 38 ER 817.

proceedings, with only a remedy in damages if the claimant does not uphold his or her side of the bargain.

The relevance of particular bars may depend on the nature of the acts that the defendant's contractual duty requires. The acts may be conveniently divided into three categories. The defendant may be required to (a) transfer assets (land, goods or choses in action), (b) provide services, or (c) pay money. Duties requiring each of these categories of acts may be replicated in a decree of specific performance. As will be seen, different bars come to the fore in relation to each of these categories. One of the benefits of describing this remedy by providing examples of the substantive rights which it replicates is that this helpful framework for discussing bars to specific performance is revealed. However, in-depth discussions of the substantive rights and the operation of relevant bars are left to specialist works.

(a) Right to the transfer of an asset

A contract of purchase always confers a right correlating with a contractual duty to a transfer of land, goods or choses in action. This right to a transfer may be replicated in a decree of specific performance, provided that the court does not consider that an award of damages or an agreed sum would be an adequate remedy. As Lord Selborne stated, 'The Court gives specific performance instead of damages only when it can by that means do more perfect and complete justice.'[127]

A duty to convey land is specifically enforced because each lot of land is unique and hence damages are thought to provide an inadequate remedy.[128] Duties to transfer personalty such as shares or goods[129] are not specifically enforceable if the subject matter is available in the market.[130] Clearly an award of damages is adequate if the claimant can buy the subject matter elsewhere.[131] However, damages will not be adequate if the subject matter is unique such as an antique jar[132] or is difficult to obtain such as a taxi licence in a heavily regulated market.[133]

(b) Right to the provision of a service

A right correlating with a duty to provide a service may be replicated in a decree of specific performance. Here the courts are sensitive to a number of matters.

[127] *Wilson v Northampton & Banburry Junction Railway Co* (1874) 9 Ch App 279, 284 (CA).

[128] *Adderly v Dixon* (1824) 1 Sim & St 607, 610; 57 ER 239, 240; *Dougan v Ley* (1946) 71 CLR 142, 150 (HCA) (Dixon J). But, at least in Canada, this not invariably so: *Semelhago v Paramadavam* (1996) 136 DLR (4th) 1.

[129] Sale of Goods Act 1979 (UK) s 52 gives the court power to specifically enforce a contract to deliver specific or ascertained goods. The principles on which a decision is made are the same as where the statute does not apply: Burrows (n 21 above), 338. Strictly speaking, when classified according to origin, such orders belong with other statutory remedies below.

[130] *Duncuft v Albrecht* (1841) 12 Sim 189; 56 ER 1104.

[131] *Re Schwacher* (1907) 98 LT 127, 128.

[132] *Falke v Gray* (1859) 4 Drew 651; 62 ER 250.

[133] *Dougan v Ley* (1946) 71 CLR 142 (HCA).

First, due to the serious consequences that could flow from non-compliance, it must be clear and certain what the contractual duty requires the defendant to do before the remedy will be given.[134] Thus replication of a duty to construct 'a railway station' where the design and materials were not specified in the contract was refused.[135]

Secondly, if a duty to provide a service is to be carried out over a significant period of time, the need for continual supervision may weigh against the grant of the remedy. This is because the enforcement of such a decree would be complex and burdensome for the court. Thus the duty to maintain a resident porter in constant attendance was not specifically enforced in one case.[136] But whether the bar is triggered depends on the circumstances of the particular case. Thus a similar duty to employ a resident porter was replicated in another case.[137]

A distinction has been drawn between duties which require a result to be achieved and those which require the carrying on of an activity.[138] Specific performance is less likely to be granted in the latter case because of the need for greater supervision and more likelihood of repeated applications to court. Thus a duty to 'open for retail trade during the usual hours of business' was not specifically enforced.[139]

Generally, a duty to perform personal services will not be replicated in a decree of specific performance.[140] This seems to give effect to two principal policy objections. First, enforcement of such a decree could require constant supervision. Secondly, it could be tantamount to slavery if persons were obliged to perform services under the threat of being jailed for contempt. However, the policy against specific performance of contracts for personal services, although strong, is not absolute.[141] For example, specific performance of such a contract was ordered where both the employee and the employer wanted to perform the contract but the employer had been coerced by a union to repudiate it.[142] But it must be noted that section 236 of the Trade Union and Labour Relations (Consolidation) Act 1992 (UK) provides that an employee cannot be compelled to do any work or attend at any place

[134] Lord Hoffman observed in *Co-operative Insurance Society Ltd v Argyll Stores (Holdings) Ltd* [1998] AC 1, 15 (HL) that a contractual obligation may not be sufficiently precise to be specifically enforced even though it is not void for uncertainty and might be relied upon in support of a claim for damages.

[135] *Wilson v Northampton & Banburry Junction Railway Co* (1874) 9 Ch App 279 (CA).

[136] *Ryan v Mutual Tontine Westminster Chambers Association* [1893] 1 Ch 116 (CA).

[137] *Posner v Scott-Lewis* [1987] Ch 25. Similarly a right to the performance of building work was replicated in *Wolverhampton Crop v Emmons* [1901] 1 KB 515, 525 as it was sufficiently certain what was required to be done.

[138] *Co-operative Insurance Society Ltd v Argyll Stores (Holdings) Ltd* [1998] AC 1 (HL).

[139] Ibid.

[140] *Maiden v Maiden* (1908) 7 CLR 727 (HCA).

[141] Megarry J described it as 'a strong reluctance rather than a rule': *Giles v Morris* [1972] 1 All ER 960, 969.

[142] *Hill v CA Parsons & Co Ltd* [1972] Ch 305; *Posner v Scott-Lewis* [1987] Ch 25.

for the doing of any work by way of an order for specific performance or an injunction.

(c) Right to the payment of money

A right to the payment of money may be specifically enforced in some circumstances.[143] This is an unusual remedy for the infringement of such a right as in most situations a common law award of an agreed sum or an award of damages would be an adequate remedy. Similarly, specific performance of a loan contract will not be ordered, except in an exceptional case.[144]

Often a vendor may sue for specific performance of a purchaser's obligation to pay the price.[145] Where damages would be an inadequate remedy for the purchaser, they are deemed to be inadequate for the seller, entitling the seller to a decree of specific performance which replicates the purchaser's duty to pay the price and accept title. Another example of a decree of specific performance which replicated a duty to pay money is provided by *McIntosh v Dalwood (No 4)*[146] where a claimant entitled to an indemnity obtained specific performance of an obligation to pay a third party. The advantage was that the claimant did not have to pay the debt himself 'and perhaps to ruin himself in doing so'.[147] If specific performance were not available, he would have had to pay and only then could he have sued the provider of the indemnity to recover the amount which he had paid.

An award of an money due under a contract cannot function as a preventive remedy, that is, it cannot be obtained before the right to payment arises. Whereas, as we have seen, a decree of specific performance can be obtained in such circumstances.

(d) Two senses of 'specific performance'

Sometimes cases and texts refer to a distinction between two senses of specific performance.[148] The first kind, specific performance 'proper', is said to apply to duties that require the execution of an instrument[149] or another act 'in law' which will confer rights on the claimant. An example is a duty requiring the execution

[143] *Beswick v Beswick* [1968] AC 58 (HL).

[144] *Rogers v Challis* (1859) 27 Beav 175; *Loan Investment Corp of Australia v Bonner* [1970] NZLR 724, 735 (PC).

[145] *Odessa Tramways Co v Mendel* (1878) 8 Ch D 235; *Turner v Bladin* (1951) 82 CLR 463, 473 (HCA); *Johnson v Agnew* [1980] AC 367 (HL).

[146] (1930) 30 SR (NSW) 415 (NSWSC). Street CJ adopted Fry's views: *Fry on Specific Performance* (6th edn., London: Stevens, 1921), 731.

[147] Ibid 418.

[148] *Wolverhampton and Walsall Ry Co v London and NW Ry Co* (1873) LR 16 Eq 433, 439; *JC Williamson Ltd v Lukey and Mulholland* (1931) 45 CLR 282, 297 (HCA).

[149] Where the right to be replicated correlates with a duty on the defendant to execute a document, specific performance of that duty to execute will be generally ordered even though the document may require personal services or it may establish a personal relationship: *Giles v Morris* [1972] 1 All ER 960, 969.

of a conveyance of land which, when performed, will confer ownership on the claimant. The second kind, also referred to as a mandatory injunction analogous to specific performance, applies to duties that require the doing of an act which will not create a new right in the other party. Their performance will only extinguish a right. An example is a duty to provide a service, such as to paint a house which, when performed, will extinguish the claimant's contractual right to have his or her house painted.[150] Views differ as to whether there is any significance left in the distinction.[151] It seems that, as Spry and Tilbury observe,[152] the relevant principles in both situations are the same although their application may vary in these two contexts.

4 Enforcement of the remedy

Specific performance is a remedy enforceable in the same manner as an injunction.[153] However, due to the complexity of the process, enforcement of an order for the specific performance of a contract for the sale of land requires a number of applications to court and takes place in a number of stages.[154]

D Order for the Execution of a Trust and Order for a Common Account

An order for the execution of a trust is an order that replicates the trustee's duties to perform the trust.[155] A common account is an order that replicates one particular primary duty. As Chambers states: 'The common account is, as the name suggests, the most common form of account. It is available, without any allegation of wrongdoing, to enforce the trustees' primary duty to provide information to the beneficiaries.'[156]

At the outset it is necessary to distinguish a common account from both an account on the basis of wilful default and an account of profits. Orders for accounts on the basis of wilful default and orders for the account of profits replicate rights arising from wrongs, that is, secondary rights. They are therefore dealt with in Chapter 12.

[150] *Puddephatt v Leith* [1916] 1 Ch 200 provides an example of an order which replicated a contractual right but was labelled a 'mandatory injunction'. The injunction was granted to enforce an agreement by the mortgagee of shares to vote in accordance with the wishes of the mortgagor.

[151] *Australian Hardwoods Pty Ltd v Commissioner for Railways* [1961] 1 WLR 425, 433–436 (PC). Cf Meagher et al (n 2 above), [20-015] and [20-060]; 3rd edn., [2003] and [2012] who maintain that it has an important role to play.

[152] Spry (n 112 above) 52; M. J. Tilbury, *Civil Remedies Vol 1 Principles of Civil Remedies* (Sydney: Butterworths, 1990), [6003].

[153] See p 133 above.

[154] Jones and Goodhart (n 111 above), 249–58.

[155] See p 145.

[156] Chambers (n 69 above), 17.

1 Form of the order

(a) Order for execution of a trust[157]

The core provision of an order for the execution of a trust takes the following form:

IT IS ORDERED that the trusts of the [Settlement made .... 20 .... between .... and ....] be performed and carried into execution.[158]

The wording is very similar to an order for the specific performance of a contract.[159] It is essentially an order for the specific enforcement or performance of a trust. It may be sought by the beneficiaries or the creditors of the trust.

(b) Order for a common account

An order for a common account, as made against a trustee, provides that the court orders:

An account of the money come to the hands of the Defendants or either of them or to the hands of any person or persons by the order or for the use of the Defendants or either of them in respect of the interest dividends rents or income of the property for the time being comprised in or subject to the trusts of the [Settlement] or in respect of the sale or disposal of any parts thereof which have been sold or disposed of.[160]

The following is an order for a common account made alongside a decree of specific performance:

AND IT IS ORDERED that the following accounts be taken that is to say

1. An Account of what is due to the claimant for the balance of the said purchase price and interest.
2. An Account of the rents and profits of the said property received by the claimant or by any other person or persons by the order or for the use of the claimant since (*i.e. date for completion*) 20................ And it is ordered that the claimant's costs are summarily assessed at £................

. . .AND IT IS ORDERED that what shall be found due on the said account of rents and profits be deducted from the said purchase money and interest and costs as aforesaid, and the balance certified by the district judge.[161]

[157] The order for the administration of a deceased estate, though a closely related remedy, will not be considered here.
[158] *Atkin's Court Forms* (2nd edn., 2000 Issue), Vol 41 [118]; also [119] and [249]. For orders in relation to the administration of deceased estates see Form N298 Order for administration; Form PF10CH Judgment in beneficiaries' administration action; Form PF11CH Judgment in creditors' administration action; see also Form 307 District judge's order (accounts and inquiries) for the form in which the results of such accounts and inquiries are set out.
[159] S. Elliott and C. Mitchell, 'Remedies for Dishonest Assistance' (2004) 67 *MLR* 16, 25.
[160] *Atkin's Court Forms* (2nd edn., 2000 Issue), Vol 41 [118].
[161] See text to n 103 above.

2 Nature of the remedy

A court ordered account is taken before a master or district judge if the proceedings are in the High Court and a district judge if they are in a county court.[162] The process may involve *surcharge* or *falsification* by the beneficiaries. Austin J explained these rather unusual terms with clarity in *Glazier v Australian Men's Health (No 2)*:

> A surcharge is the showing of an omission for which credit ought to have been given. A falsification is the showing of a charge which has been wrongly inserted, the falsifying party alleging that money shown in the account as paid was either not paid or improperly paid.[163]

Thus, a beneficiary can surcharge the account where a trustee has received trust funds or property and has not made an entry in the receipts side of the account.[164] Naturally, this will result in an entry being made on the receipts side of the account. A beneficiary can falsify the account where the trustee makes an unauthorized disbursement or investment. This will result in the deletion of an entry on the disbursements side. To prevent a windfall to the beneficiary, any entry corresponding to the unauthorized investment on the receipts side of the account will also be deleted.

If the receipts and disbursements do not balance, an ancillary remedy will be given by the court directing the accounting party to honour the account by making up the shortfall. Such orders have already been considered above.[165]

(a) Function of the remedy

An order for the execution of a trust or a common account may be corrective. Beneficiaries may seek this order where the trustees have not performed their primary duties. It may also be preventive. Beneficiaries, or the trustees themselves,[166] may seek the order where there is a likelihood that the trustees' duties may be breached. The court also has power to grant an order directing a party to prepare and file accounts relating to the dispute as an interim remedy.[167]

(b) Advantages of the remedy

It is preferable to seek an order for the execution of a trust or a common account (together with a consequential order) rather than equitable compensation[168] for

[162] CPR Part 40 PD [9]; CPR Part 40 PD sets out rules relating to the account taking process.

[163] [2001] NSWSC 6 [38]. See also Lord Millett, 'Equity's Place in the Law of Commerce' (1998) 114 *LQR* 214, 225–6.

[164] In the case of an order for an account on the basis of wilful default (but not in the case of a common account) the trustee must account not only for *what has in fact been received but what ought to have been received.* See Chapter 11 p 183.

[165] See text to n 65 above.

[166] Trustees may wish obtain an order for the execution of a trust where what their duties require of them is unclear and hence they need the court's guidance. For example, *Minors v Battison* (1876) 1 App Cas 428 (HL).

[167] CPR Rule 25.1(1)(n).

[168] See Chapter 11 p 179.

a number of reasons. No issues of estimation of loss, causation or remoteness can arise. As Lord Millett wrote extra-curially:

> [upon a common account an] unauthorised investment will then be treated as having been bought with his own money and on the trustees behalf. He will be required to account to the trust estate for the full amount of the disbursement — *not* the amount of the loss. That is what is meant by saying that the trustee is liable to restore the trust property; and why common law rules of damage and remoteness are out of place.[169]

Another advantage of seeking an account is that the claimant will not be required to give particulars of the entries that the claimant will be disputing, whereas if the claimant were alleging a breach of trust, such particulars would have to be provided.[170]

(c) Effect on substantive rights

An order for the execution of a trust does not extinguish the trustees' duties. They continue to exist even in cases where the trustees are ordered to transfer the trust property to the court.[171] However, the trustees' powers are suspended.[172] *A fortiori*, an order for a common account does not extinguish the pre-existing duty of the trustees to render an account.

3 Nature of the substantive right replicated

The order for the execution of a trust replicates the positive primary rights of the beneficiaries to the performance of the trust.[173] As Lord Browne-Wilkinson stated in *Target Holdings Ltd v Redferns*, 'The basic right of a beneficiary is to have the trust duly administered in accordance with the provisions of the trust instrument, if any, and the general law.'[174] An order for the execution of a trust used to be available as a matter of course until the judicature reforms of the late nineteenth century. These reforms made it necessary to show that there were issues that could not be properly resolved except by means of a general administration rather than by the newer remedies of a common account and an account on the basis of wilful default.[175] This is enshrined in the Civil Procedure Rules which provide that 'The court will only make an administration order [*which includes an order for the execution of a trust*] if it considers that the issues between the parties cannot properly be resolved in any other way.'[176]

The order for a common account is more focussed than an order for the execution of a trust because it gives effect to one primary right, namely, the

169 Millett (n 163 above), 226.
170 *Re Wells* [1962] 1 WLR 874 (CA).
171 *Thompson v Tomkins* (1862) 2 Dr & Sm 8, 24, 62; 62 ER 524; *Berhardt v Glasworthy* [1929] 1 Ch 549.
172 *Minors v Battison* (1876) 1 App Cas 428, 438 (HL).
173 Elliott and Mitchell (n 159 above), 23.
174 [1996] 1 AC 421, 434 (HL).
175 *Re Blake* (1885) 29 Ch D 913, 918, 919 (CA).
176 CPR Part 64 PD [3.1].

beneficiaries' right to have an account rendered, or more broadly, the trustee's duty to provide information to the beneficiaries.[177] As Harman J held in *Attorney General v Coke*:

> [I]t has always been the law that persons in a fiduciary position are bound to account to those for whom they are fiduciary, and that extends beyond pure trust claims to such matters as agents who hold property which is the property of their principals and who have long been held liable to account.[178]

Accountable parties, that is, those who owe a duty to account, include executors, partners upon the dissolution of a partnership, mortgagees in possession, and solicitors in relation to their trust funds or other trustees. The duty of the accountable party is essentially one to render an account which sets out receipts and disbursements. Where there is a duty to account, the persons owed that duty, especially beneficiaries of a trust, are entitled to the remedy of account as a matter of course,[179] unless one of the usual bars to equitable remedies applies. The ancillary remedy requiring the accounting party to make up any shortfall also gives effect to a primary right, not a secondary right.[180] Such an order is in its nature 'one for replacement of trust funds, and not for damages'.[181]

4 Enforcement of the remedy

An order for an execution of a trust or a common account can be enforced in the same manner as an injunction. But it is unnecessary to go this far in most circumstances. Where there is a failure to render an account, the court can presume everything most unfavourable to the defendant that is consistent with the established facts.[182] This provides a strong incentive for the defendant to comply.

E Rectification 'Order'

A rectification 'order' or decree is a remedy which may be granted where a document does not correctly record the agreed terms of a contract because of a mistake made in the document's preparation.[183]

[177] *Re Dartnall* [1895] 1 Ch 474 (CA); Chambers (n 69 above), 7 and p 131 above.
[178] [1988] Ch 414, 420. [179] *Re Wells* [1962] 1 WLR 874 (CA).
[180] Elliott and Mitchell (n 159 above), 28 point out that a claim seeking substitutive performance of a trustee's duty to apply the property in accordance with the trust (e.g. by payment of a monetary substitute for property that should have been held by the trustee) is not based on wrongful misconduct.
[181] *British America Elevator Co v Bank of British North America* [1919] AC 658, 666 (PC) (Haldane LC). [182] *Gray v Haig* (1855) 20 Beav 219, 52 ER 587.
[183] *Frederick E Rose (London) Ltd v William H Pim Jnr & Co Ltd* [1953] 2 QB 450, 461 (CA).

1 Form of the order

An example of an order for rectification provides:

IT IS ORDERED that the agreement dated. . . . . .19/20. . .in the pleadings mentioned be rectified by substituting in clause. . .thereof the words (*insert appropriate wording*) for the words (*insert appropriate wording*)[184]

2 Nature of the remedy

(a) Function of the remedy

An order for rectification serves a preventive function. It may prevent a future infringement of the claimant's contractual right by a defendant who intends to act in accordance with the incorrectly recorded terms of the contract rather than the actually agreed terms. It may also serve a corrective function in that it may bring about compliance with the actually agreed terms by authoritatively demonstrating to the defendant that, by acting on the erroneous document, he has infringed the claimant's rights. However, if the defendant does not or is unlikely to comply with his authoritatively restated obligations, the claimant can obtain an ancillary enforceable order such as specific performance or an award of damages.

(b) Effect on substantive rights

The rectification 'order' reflects the parties' substantive rights which have not been correctly stated in writing, it does not alter their content. As James V-C stressed in *McKenzie v Coulson*, 'Courts of Equity do not rectify contracts; they may and do rectify instruments purporting to have been made in pursuance of the terms of contracts.'[185] Thus the order does not create a right with new content.[186] The remedy is replicative, not transformative. It is akin to a declaration of right.[187]

The order does no more than restate, in appropriate written form, the substantive right of the parties. For example, in *Johnson v Bragge* Cozens-Hardy J granted an order for rectification of a deed which provided how the deed ought to be read:

I shall declare that the deed of August 5, 1865, was, in the particulars hereinafter specified, executed under mistake, and that the deed ought to be rectified *by reading the same as if* in the recital, after the words "under the will of his maternal grandfather John Walmesley," there had been added the words "and of the settlement made by his parents

[184] *Atkin's Court Forms* (2nd edn., 1999 Issue), Vol 24(2) Form 46. Based on the order made in *Olley v Fisher* (1886) 34 Ch D 367. See also *Atkin's Court Forms* (2nd edn., 2000 Issue), Vol 18 [386].

[185] (1869) LR 8 Eq 368, 375.

[186] But Lawson classes it as a constitutive remedy: F. H. Lawson, *Remedies of English Law* (2nd edn., London: Butterworth & Co, 1980), 246.

[187] Of course, it may be necessary to enforce the declared right by an ancillary remedy if the defendant does not perform the contract as rectified.

dated the 9th of December, 1864, respectively"; and I shall order a copy of this declaration to be indorsed on the settlement.[188]

The order thus merely provides the words that authoritatively evidence the substantive rights of the claimant, which rights have been shown to already exist.

The remedy is subject to the usual bars such as laches or acquiescence.[189] It will also be barred where a bona fide third party for value without notice acquires an interest under the document.[190]

3 Nature of the substantive right replicated

Most consensual rights which are incorrectly recorded in a document may be replicated in a rectification order. Thus, the remedy has been granted in relation to leases, insurance policies, bills of exchange, trust deeds, and wills.

4 Enforcement

'After rectification the written agreement. . .is to be read as if it had been originally drawn in its rectified form.'[191] Thus once the rectification order is made, there is no need to enforce the order. However, the order may be made along with another enforceable order such as a decree of specific performance[192] or, as reproduced above, an order that the rectified document be indorsed with a copy of the order document.

F 'Order' for Rescission

1 Form of the order

An example of an order for the rescission of a sale and setting aside of a conveyance (purchaser's action) provides:

THE COURT DECLARES that the sale by the Defendant to the Claimant of the property known as (*address*) was induced by the [fraudulent misrepresentation] of the Defendant and ought to be rescinded and set aside and that the conveyance dated .... 20........ and made between (*name the parties*) for effecting the said sale is void

AND IT IS ORDERED THAT:

(1) The agreement for the said sale dated the .... 20........ and made between (*name the parties*) be delivered up to the Claimant to be cancelled[193]

(2) . . .

[188] [1901] 1 Ch 28, 37. Emphasis added.

[189] *Beale v Kyte* [1907] 1 Ch 564.

[190] *Smith v Jones* [1954] 1 WLR 1089.

[191] *Craddock Bros v Hunt* [1923] 2 Ch 136, 151 (CA).

[192] *Olley v Fisher* (1886) 34 Ch D 367.

[193] *Atkin's Court Forms* (2nd edn., 2000 Issue), Vol 18 [416]. Based on *Edwards v M'Leay* (1818) 2 Swan 287 and *Hart v Swaine* (1877) 7 Ch D 42.

An example of an order setting aside a sale on the ground of undue influence (vendor's action) provides:

THE COURT DECLARES that an agreement dated........ 20........ and made between (1) X. Y. deceased and (2) the Defendant for the sale of the property therein described ought to be set aside on the ground that it was obtained from the said X. Y. when he was of an advanced age and without advice and by the exercise of undue influence on the part of the Defendant over the said X. Y. his patient

IT IS ORDERED THAT:

(1) The said [agreement *or* sale] be set aside accordingly;
(2) The Defendant do reconvey the said property to the Claimants or to whom they may direct freed and discharged of and from all charges and incumbrances made or created by the Defendant or any person or persons claiming through or under him, such reconveyance to be settled by the Court in case the parties differ. . .[194]

In *Horsler v Zorro* Megarry J suggested why the orders are phrased so as to state that the contract 'ought to be rescinded':

the process of rescission is essentially the act of the party rescinding, and not of the court. Of course, if matters are disputed, the dispute may have to be determined by the court, and until the decision is given it will not be known whether or not there has been a proper and effectual rescission: but that does not mean that there is no rescission until the court speaks. . .Of course, applications to the court are often made because consequential relief is sought, whether as part of the restitutio in integrum or otherwise; and although the older forms of order were sometimes expressed as being an order that the contract "be rescinded" (see *Seton's Judgments and Orders*, 7th ed. (1912), pp. 347, 2218), I think the more modern, and preferable, practice is to make a declaration that the contract "ought to be rescinded"; see *Atkin's Court Forms*, 2nd ed. (1972), vol. 18, pp. 301, 302. Indeed, I would have thought that at least in some cases a declaration that the contract had been rescinded on such-and-such a date might be better still.[195]

This view of rescission as an act of a party rather than the court will now be further explained.

2 Nature of the remedy

Rescission of a contract according to rules which originated at common law has traditionally operated from the claimant's exercise of his or her power to rescind. The court's order merely declared and confirmed that the claimant had validly exercised his or her power and hence had rescinded.

Rescission in equity, that is, rescission of a contract voidable according to rules which originated in equity, was sometimes said to be effected by the court's order. That is, it was thought to operate as a transformative remedy—a remedy which extinguishes prior substantive rights and creates new rights which do not replicate

[194] Ibid [418]. Based on *Dent v Bennett* (1839) 4 My & Cr 269.

[195] [1975] Ch 302, 310.

the content of any pre-existing rights.[196] This model may be characterized as recission by court order.

However, the current trend of English and Australian authorities suggests that rescission in equity may now operate in at least a number of cases in the same way as rescission at law. In such cases, it is an act of the party, and not the court order, which extinguishes the substantive rights and sometimes creates new rights.[197] The High Court of Australia held in *Alati v Kruger*:

> It is not that equity asserts a power by its decree to avoid a contract which the defrauded party himself has no right to disaffirm, and to revest property the title to which the party cannot affect. Rescission for misrepresentation is always the act of the party himself: *Reese River Silver Mining Co Ltd v Smith* (1869) LR 4 HL 64 at p 73. The function of the court in which proceedings for rescission are taken is to adjudicate upon the validity of a purported disaffirmance as an act avoiding the transaction *ab initio*, and, if it is valid, to give effect to it and make appropriate consequential orders. . .[198]

Thus the court order in such situations merely declares the legal relations that existed before it was made.

O'Sullivan reviews the relevant authorities and concludes that rescission in equity is, like rescission at law, effected by an election to disaffirm in certain cases.[199] He writes that:

> Disaffirming triggers equitable rights and obligations reversing the effects of the transaction; for instance, by revesting equitable title to the property transferred. This has become the dominant account of equitable rescission in England today, at least in the cases of fraud and misrepresentation.[200]

3 Nature of the substantive right replicated

Where the recission by election model applies, an election to disaffirm terminates contractual rights and, sometimes, gives rise to consequential rights that undo the consequences of the transaction. In *Alati v Kruger* it was held that:

> Of course a rescission which the common law court would not accept as valid cannot of its own force revest the legal title to property which has passed, but if a court of equity would treat it as effectual the equitable title to such property revests upon the rescission.[201]

Such consequential rights may require property to be re-transferred or money to be repaid. They are primary rights because they do not arise from wrongs.

[196] This view appears to be taken in Meagher et al (n 2 above), [24-085]; 3rd edn., [2416]. Compare D. O'Sullivan, 'The Evolving Structure of Equitable Rescission with Particular Reference to Rescission for Fraud and Breach of Fiduciary Duty' (DPhil Thesis Oxford University 2001), 240.

[197] *Daly v Sydney Stock Exchange Ltd* (1985) 160 CLR 371, 387–389 (HCA); *Lonrho v Fayed (No 2)* [1992] 1 WLR 1, 11–12; *Twinsectra Ltd v Yardley* [1999] Lloyd's Rep 438, 461–462 (CA).

[198] (1955) 94 CLR 216, 224 (HCA).

[199] O'Sullivan (n 196 above), 215.

[200] Ibid 221. Misrepresentation Act 1967 (UK) s 2(2) supports this model referring to a contract that 'has been rescinded'.

[201] (1955) 94 CLR 216, 224 (HCA).

If the rescission by election model applies, then when a court makes a rescission order, the court confirms that the rescission by election has been effective to extinguish rights and replicates any substantive consequential rights that have been found to have arisen from the making of that election. The remedy is therefore a replicative one. If the recission by court order model applies, the remedy which is granted belongs in the transformative category.

4 Enforcement

There will be no need to enforce the rescission 'order' or decree if the contract is executory, that is, still unperformed. If the contract is executed, that is, performed by one or both parties, then an enforceable order which replicates any consequential rights to the return of property may be necessary. Such an ancillary order could be characterized as a mandatory injunction which replicates a primary right.

9

Replicating Primary Rights: Statutory Remedies

A Introduction

Statutes may confer power on courts to grant remedies that otherwise could not have been granted either at common law or in equity. Sometimes such remedies are replicative.[1] Here, we will deal with the two most important statutory (or statute-based) remedies in private law: orders for the recovery of goods and declarations of primary rights. Both of these remedies replicate primary rights. As will be seen in Chapter 12, very similar remedies also replicate secondary rights.

The remedies considered in this chapter, though statutory, have roots in equity and the approach that the courts take to granting them has been influenced by their pedigree in that a significant degree of 'discretion' is traditionally said to be exercised in granting them. Again, three issues will be examined in relation to each remedy: the nature of the remedy; the nature of the substantive right that it replicates; and the means of executing the remedy.

B Order for the Recovery of Goods (or their Value)

The court's power to make an order for the recovery of goods or their value is conferred by the Torts (Interference with Goods) Act 1977 (UK). Section 3 provides that where a wrongful interference with goods is proved the court has a discretion to make an order for the delivery of the goods and for the payment of consequential damages[2] (this will be referred to as 'an order for delivery up of goods') or the claimant may require an order for delivery of the goods which gives the defendant[3] the option of paying the value of the goods and for the payment of

[1] Transformative statutory remedies are discussed in Chapter 13.

[2] Consequential loss includes a hire charge where a profit earning chattel is converted: *Hillesden Securities Ltd v Ryjack Ltd* [1983] 1 WLR 959.

[3] For historical reasons why the defendant was given this option see F. W. Maitland, *The Forms of Action at Common Law* (Cambridge: Cambridge University Press, 1962), 62.

consequential damages (this will be referred to as 'an order in alternative form') or simply an order for the payment of damages. In this section, we are only concerned with the first two orders and, in the case of the second, only in so far as it replicates the primary right to possession. In so far as it replicates a secondary right, the order will be examined in Chapter 12.

A closer examination of these orders gives interesting insights. The characterization of a remedy as a right arising from a judicial command allows us to see that the order in alternative form that the defendant deliver the goods or pay damages by reference to their value, together with, in either case, the payment of any consequential damages, actually gives the claimant a combination of three remedies. The order embodies two inconsistent remedies which the defendant is allowed to choose between and a third which is consistent with either of the first two. The right to the delivery of the goods is one remedy, the right to the payment of their value is the second, and the right to consequential damages is the third. Each of the three remedies replicates a separate primary or secondary right.

1 Form of the order

The core provision of an order for delivery up or of an order in alternative form may assume the following form:

To the Defendant
The court has decided that the claimant recover from you the following goods of the claimant wrongly kept by you, namely:................................ of the value of £........ [and also the sum of £........ for damages for the detention of the goods,] and £........ for costs.

District Judge [master]........ ordered
[that you return the goods to the claimant or that you pay £........, their value, to reach the claimant by........][4]

[that you return the goods to the claimant by.................] And also that you pay (£........ damage) and £........ for costs to reach the claimant by. . .[5]

or in the case of hired goods:

District Judge........ **has ordered** that the claimant do recover against the defendant the following goods of the claimant wrongly detained by the claimant, namely: of the value of £........ [and also the sum of £........ for arrears of hire rent,] and £........ for costs.

District Judge................ **has ordered** that the defendant do return the goods to the claimant, or do pay the sum of £........, their value, to reach the claimant by. . .[6]

[4] This paragraph is not included where the order is for the specific recovery of goods.
[5] Form N32 Judgment for return of goods: CPR Part 4 PD Table 1. See also *Atkin's Court Forms* Vol 39 [267–269].
[6] Form N32 Judgment for delivery of goods: CPR Part 4 PD Table 1.

Where the order is in alternative form, the defendant usually exercises his or her option by either paying the value or actually returning the goods to the claimant but in some circumstances a communication of the choice to return the goods to the claimant is enough. It has been held that a defendant who chooses to satisfy such an order by a return of bulky goods must communicate to the claimant that he or she regards the property in the goods as being in the claimant and that the claimant can have them collected.[7]

Minutes of an order for delivery up of steel without giving the defendant the option of paying its value are reproduced in the law report of a leading case as follows:

> Order that defendants permit plaintiffs to take their steel not before 10 a.m. on March 18, 1980.[8]

2 Nature of the remedy

(a) Function of the remedy

The order for delivery up of goods may function as a corrective or preventive remedy.[9] It seems that the order in alternative form may function as a corrective remedy only.

(b) Advantages of the remedy

The advantages of these remedies are similar to the advantages of injunctions, the main one being that the defendant's duty is given direct effect which may lead to the claimant's recovery of his or her goods *in specie*.

(c) Effect on substantive rights

These remedies do not extinguish the defendant's property rights in the goods. Where an order for the recovery of goods or their value is made, the claimant continues to remain the owner of the goods until the judgment is satisfied, whether by payment of their value or their return.[10] This, of course, is advantageous in the event of the defendant's insolvency.

3 Nature of the substantive right replicated

An order for delivery up of goods gives direct effect to the claimant's right to recover possession of the goods. This right is also sometimes called the right to

[7] *Metals & Ropes Co Ltd v Tattersall* [1966] 1 WLR 1500. This was a case in relation to the remedy for detinue but the same principle would apply to the statutory remedy.

[8] *Perry (Howard E) & Co Ltd v British Railways Board* [1980] 1 WLR 1375, 1386.

[9] Torts (Interference with Goods) Act 1977 (UK) s 4(1) empowers the court to make interlocutory orders for delivery up of goods; CPR Rule 25.1(1)(e).

[10] *Ellis v John Stenning & Son Ltd* [1932] 2 Ch 81 (CA); Torts (Interference with Goods) Act 1977 (UK) s 5(1).

immediate possession. An order for the recovery of goods or their value replicates *both* this primary right to recover possession of the goods and the secondary right to the payment of their value that arises from the torts of conversion, trespass, or negligence. The rest of this section is only concerned with the primary right. The secondary right is discussed in Chapter 12.

The claimant's right to possession may stem from ownership or a lesser proprietary interest in the goods. The claimant has no right to possession of goods where the defendant has a superior right to possession because of a hire agreement or a possessory lien.

As was pointed out in relation to the right to possess land,[11] the right to possession has two aspects: the first is a right to enjoyment of actual possession (this correlates with a negative duty on others not interfere with the possession) and the second is a right to recover possession (this correlates with a positive duty on another to give up possession). These rights are primary in that they are part of the claimant's property in the goods. These rights to possession do not arise from a wrong.[12]

Historically, the right to enjoy actual possession of goods was protected by the tort of trespass to goods. The right to the recover possession of goods was protected by the torts of detinue and conversion. But there was no machinery in the nature of a vindicatio or any action analogous to ejectment to *directly* claim these rights. There still is no such machinery.

The tort of detinue occurred where a defendant was in possession of the claimant's goods and refused to deliver them up on demand,[13] that is, where the claimant's right to recover possession of the goods was infringed. Detinue has been abolished[14] but the judgments that could be made if it was proved were made available as orders in relation to 'wrongful interference with goods' which includes the torts of conversion, trespass to goods, negligence, or any other tort so far as it results in damage to goods or to an interest in goods.

Due to the statutory reforms, these torts or, moving to modern terminology, 'wrongs' now protect both the right to recover possession and the right to enjoy possession, and the court has power to replicate these primary rights in its order upon one of these wrongs being proved. These wrongs act as triggers empowering the court to make an order which may replicate the primary right to possession which does not itself arise from the wrong. Of course, these wrongs also give rise to secondary rights to damages. Thus in an action for wrongful interference with goods, the claimant comes to court with both primary and secondary rights. The court may replicate either or both of these types of rights in its order.

[11] See Chapter 7 p 117.

[12] See R. B. Grantham and C. E. F. Rickett, 'Property Rights as a Legally Significant Event' [2003] *CLJ* 717 for a contrary view. Discussed in Chapter 7 p 119 above.

[13] *General and Finance Facilities Ltd v Cook Cars (Romford) Ltd* [1963] 1 WLR 644, 650–651 (CA) (Diplock LJ).

[14] Torts (Interference with Goods) Act 1977 (UK) s 2(1).

If the claimant seeks an order in alternative form, the court must grant it if the cause of action is established. This order replicates both the primary right to recover possession and the secondary right to the payment of the value of the goods (and the secondary right to the payment of consequential damages). Such an order can be said to be available as a matter of course.

If the claimant seeks recovery of goods without giving the defendant the option to pay, that is, an order for delivery up of goods, the remedy will replicate only the primary right to recover possession (and the secondary right to the payment of consequential damages). It will only be granted in the court's discretion. It has been held that the power 'ought not to be exercised when the chattel is an ordinary article of commerce and of no special value or interest, and not alleged to be of any special value to the plaintiff, and where damages would fully compensate.'[15] In *Perry (Howard E) & Co Ltd v British Railways Board*,[16] a defendant was ordered to deliver up 500 tons of steel belonging to the claimant where it was not readily available in the market and damages would not adequately compensate the claimant for disruption to its business. Robert Megarry VC also noted that an order for delivery up can take the form of 'an order requiring a defendant to allow the plaintiff to collect for himself goods which the defendant is unable or unwilling to deliver to him in the sense of collecting and transporting them'.[17]

4 Enforcement of the remedy

An order for delivery up of goods which does not give an option of paying their value may be enforced by a writ or warrant of specific delivery, an order for committal, or a writ of sequestration.[18] If the defendant does not comply with an order for delivery up of goods, the court can order that he or she pay their value instead.[19]

However, even committal to prison may not lead to goods being delivered up as *Enfield LBC v Mahoney*[20] illustrates. The defendant refused to comply with an order to deliver up a lead cross of historical value, said to be the Glastonbury Cross made in the days of King Arthur. He was sentenced for two years for contempt of court but released early as it was found that he had been punished enough and further imprisonment would not make him comply with the order.

An order in alternative form may be enforced by a writ or warrant of delivery to recover the goods or their assessed value[21] or, in some cases, by a writ of sequestration.[22] Under a writ or warrant of delivery the sheriff or bailiff is ordered to cause the claimant's goods to be delivered to the claimant or, if those goods are

15 *Whiteley Ltd v Hilt* [1918] 2 KB 808, 819 (CA) (Swinfen Eady MR). These comments were made in relation to remedies for detinue but they are equally applicable to the current statutory remedy.

16 [1980] 1 WLR 1375, 1382.

17 Ibid 1385.

18 CPR Sch 1 RSC Order 45 r 4(1), CCR Order 26 r 16, 18.

19 Torts (Interference with Goods) Act 1977 (UK) s 3(4).

20 [1983] 1 WLR 749 (CA).

21 CPR Sch 1 RSC Order 45 r 4, CCR Order 24 r 16.

22 CPR Sch 1 RSC Order 45 r 4(2)(c).

unable to be obtained, to seize in execution the goods, chattels and other property of the defendant and raise the assessed value of the claimant's goods.[23] Alternatively, at the enforcement stage, the claimant can apply for a writ or warrant of specific delivery to recover the goods themselves.[24] This writ may be enforced by punishment for contempt.

C Declaration of Primary Right

A declaration is a non-enforceable[25] (or 'non-coercive'[26]) authoritative restatement of a substantive right. The leading work on declarations states that 'A declaratory judgment is a formal statement by a court pronouncing upon the existence or non-existence of a legal state of affairs.'[27] It is the remedy with the widest ambit, potentially available in any situation where a right is infringed or threatened. The remedy may declare whether a party has a particular status, who has title to goods or land, or how a contract should be construed. It can effectuate all rights whether founded on statute or judge-made law. Although declarations were not unknown to equity, the declaration as we know it today is characterized as 'neither a legal nor an equitable remedy, but statutory.'[28]

1 Form of the judgment

The core provision of a declaratory judgment simply states:

THE COURT DECLARES (set out what is declared)

or

IT IS DECLARED THAT (set out what is declared).[29]

Examples of the remedy include:

DECLARED that the organ presently situate in the Mission Church or Chapel of Ease known as St Paul's Church (*address*) is the property of the Plaintiff[30]

[23] See Form No 65 Writ of delivery: CPR Part 4 PD Table 2; Forms No 48 Warrant of delivery: CPR Part 4 PD Table 3.
[24] CPR Sch 1 RSC Order 45 r 4(2), CCR Order 24 r 16(2). See Form No 64 Writ of delivery: CPR Part 4 PD Table 2; Forms No 46 Warrant of delivery: CPR Part 4 PD Table 3.
[25] It is non-enforceable in the sense that a claimant cannot seek enforcement of it without a further application to court and the defendant is not in contempt for contravening it. But see p 164 below.
[26] See Chapter 5 n 135 for an explanation of why the term 'non-enforceable' has been preferred here.
[27] Lord Woolf and J. Woolf *The Declaratory Judgment* (London: Sweet & Maxwell, 2002), [1.02].
[28] *Tito v Waddell (No 2)* [1977] Ch 106, 259 (Megarry VC) following *Chapman v Michaelson* [1909] 1 Ch 238 (CA). See discussion in Woolf (n 27 above), [4.021]–[4.029].
[29] *Atkin's Court Forms* (2nd edn., 1996 Issue) Vol 18 Form 4 to Form 98.
[30] Ibid Form 20.

The Court having adjudged that the Defendant has on........ 19........ repudiated the contract made on........ 19........ between the Plaintiff and the Defendant IT IS HEREBY DECLARED that the said contract has been terminated and that the Plaintiff is since........ 19........ no longer bound under any terms of the said contract[31]

DECLARED that the Defendants have infringed the Plaintiff's copyright in the work entitled "........" by their publication in the........ newspaper dated........ 19........ of an article entitled " .... "[32]

DECLARED that the Plaintiff is entitled to a lien on the said property in respect of the [balance of the] said purchase money with interest thereon at the rate of........ per cent per annum from the........ 19........ until payment and also for the Plaintiff's costs of this action[33]

2 Nature of the remedy

(a) Function of the remedy

Where there has been no actual or threatened infringement of a right, a declaration can be refused as serving no purpose.[34] The courts will not generally grant a declaration that is merely advisory,[35] of no practical utility, or deals with a hypothetical dispute.[36] But a dispute as to future rights is not necessarily hypothetical.[37] Thus a declaration may serve a preventive function in that it may prevent a future infringement of an existing or future right by the defendant or the claimant. It may also serve a corrective function in that it may authoritatively demonstrate to the defendant that he or she is infringing the claimant's rights. Most defendants will then comply with their legal obligations without it being necessary to threaten them with a further enforceable order.

Interim declarations are possible.[38]

(b) Advantages of the remedy

A declaration is a speedy, and hence inexpensive, remedy.[39] A declaration is more widely available than other remedies. It allows 'negative relief' to be obtained, that is, the court may declare the absence of a duty or the absence of a breach of duty.[40]

[31] Ibid Form 32. [32] Ibid Form 35. [33] Ibid Form 85. See also Vol 37 [105], [106].

[34] *Mellstrom v Garner* [1970] 1 WLR 603 (CA). But it does not have to be refused as pleading and proof of an actual or threatened infringement are not required. However, it is submitted that where no actual or threatened infringement of a right is possible or even slightly probable, at present or in the future, then the declaration is purposeless or hypothetical and should be refused.

[35] Advisory opinions were politically abused, for example, by Charles I who obtained an opinion that ship-money could be levied without Parliament's consent. See Woolf (n 27 above), [4.004].

[36] *Re Clay* [1919] 1 Ch 66 (CA).

[37] *Commonwealth v Sterling Nicholas Duty Free Pty Ltd* (1972) 126 CLR 297 (HCA) 305; *The Trustees of the Church Property of the Diocese of Newcastle v Ebbeck* (1960) 104 CLR 394, 400–401 (HCA).

[38] CPR Rule 25.1.

[39] Woolf (n 27 above), [1.09].

[40] *Guaranty Trust Co of New York v Hannay & Co* [1915] 2 KB 536 (CA).

It also allows future rather than subsisting rights to be adjudicated. A claimant seeking a declaration may also appear less aggressive or belligerent than if he or she were seeking an enforceable remedy. This may help to maintain a workable relationship between the parties.[41]

As there is no need to plead and prove an actual or impending infringement of a substantive right for the existence or non-existence of the right to be put in issue, a declaration allows questions such as whether a right of way exists over land to be tried directly without the need for trespass or assault to be threatened or carried out.[42] This serves to uphold the public's respect for the law. Similarly, it gives the parties to a contract an avenue for determining their obligations without either party assuming the risk of repudiating the contract to make the issue justiciable.[43] The dispute can be resolved before a claim arises.

(c) Effect on substantive rights

A declaration does not extinguish prior rights but does make the matters declared *res judicata* thereby preventing subsequent litigation between the parties in relation to the same matters.[44]

3 Nature of the substantive right replicated

Declarations replicate substantive rights. In *Gouriet v Union of Post Office Workers*[45] Lord Diplock stressed that the remedy is a 'declaration of rights' and continued:

> The only kinds of rights with which courts of justice are concerned are legal rights; and a court of civil jurisdiction is concerned with legal rights only when the aid of the court is invoked by one party claiming a right against another party, to protect or enforce the right or to provide a remedy against that other party for infringement of it, or is invoked by either party to settle a dispute between them as to the existence or nature of the right claimed. So for the court to have jurisdiction to declare any legal right it must be one which is claimed by one of the parties as enforceable against an adverse party to the litigation, either as a subsisting right or as one which may come into existence in the future conditionally on the happening of an event.
>
> The early controversies as to whether a party applying for declaratory relief must have a subsisting cause of action or a right to some other relief as well can now be forgotten. It is clearly established that he need not. Relief in the form of a declaration of right is generally superfluous for a plaintiff who has a subsisting cause of action. It is when an infringement

[41] E. R. Sunderland, 'A Modern Evolution in Remedial Rights—The Declaratory Judgment' (1917) 16 *Michigan LR* 69, 76.
[42] F. H. Lawson, *Remedies of English Law* (2nd edn., London: Butterworth & Co, 1980), 237.
[43] Woolf (n 27 above), [1.12]; *David Jones Ltd v Leventhal* (1927) 40 CLR 357 (HCA).
[44] Woolf (n 27 above), [1.07]. A. W. Scott and W. A. Seavey, *Restatement of the Law of Judgments* (St Paul: American Law Institute Publishers, 1942), 344.
[45] [1978] AC 435, 501 (HL).

of the plaintiff's rights in the future is threatened or when, unaccompanied by threats, there is a dispute between parties as to what their respective rights will be if something happens in the future, that the jurisdiction to make declarations of right can be most usefully invoked. But the jurisdiction of the court is not to declare the law generally or to give advisory opinions; it is confined to declaring contested legal rights, subsisting or future, of the parties represented in the litigation before it and not those of anyone else.[46]

As Lord Diplock stated, there is no need for the claimant to assert a cause of action, that is, a set of facts which give rise to a right and an actual or threatened infringement of that right.[47] In *Guaranty Trust Co of New York v Hannay & Co*[48] a declaration was made that the defendant had no right to recover money from the claimant, and hence that the claimant was under no duty to pay the defendant. Similarly a declaration could be made that a right that the defendant once had has been extinguished.[49] Although such scenarios do not involve a cause of action in the narrow sense described above, they clearly involve the claimant seeking a declaration of a 'right'. The claimant asserts that it has a right in the sense of a privilege or liberty, being a jural relation characterized by the absence rather than the presence of a duty.[50] Similarly, a right in the sense of an immunity or non-liability could also be declared.[51] As Zamir wrote:

Innumerable cases make it absolutely clear that the court may declare any kind of legal relations, including, according to Hohfeld's analysis, duties, powers, liabilities and so on . . . Such a declaration is, in the broad Hohfeldian sense, a declaration of rights: if not the rights of the plaintiff at least those of the defendant.[52]

But where the claimant is not asserting any right in the broad sense, that is, no jural relation, then the declaration must be refused. The claimant is not seeking a declaration of law and the matter is beyond the competence of the courts. A declaration in relation to a government policy statement was refused because it was 'lacking in either intention or capacity to affect legal rights or relationships.'[53]

In the third edition of the leading work on this remedy, *Declaratory Judgments*, Lord Woolf and Jeremy Woolf state that changes in the Civil Procedure Rules[54]

[46] This statement was accepted but qualified in the case of *In re* S [1996] Fam 1. At 22–23, Millett LJ (as he then was) held that there is no requirement that the legal right claimed should be a right which is vested in the parties.

[47] But Woolf (n 27 above) notes at 20 n 66 that a cause of action in a broad sense is necessary for institution of declaratory proceedings.

[48] [1915] 2 KB 536 (CA).

[49] Such a declaration was sought in *Schering Ltd v Stockholms Enskilda Bank* [1946] AC 219 (HL).

[50] W. N. Hohfeld, 'Some Fundamental Legal Conceptions As Applied in Judicial Reasoning' (1913) 23 *Yale LJ* 16, 32.

[51] Woolf (n 27 above), [2.25].

[52] I. Zamir, 'The Declaratory Judgment Revisited' in Lord Lloyd, R. Rideout, S. Guest (eds), *Current Legal Problems 1977 Vol 30* (London: Stevens, 1977) 43, 48–9.

[53] *Johnco Nominees Pty Ltd v Albury-Wodonga (NSW) Corp* [1977] 1 NSWLR 43, 49 (NSWCA) (Street CJ).

[54] CPR Rule 40.20.

have 'made it clear that declarations do not have to declare "rights".'[55] This is correct in so far as it suggests that all jural relations, whether subsisting or future, and not just subsisting rights correlative with duties may be declared. However, any extension of the court's power beyond this is unnecessary and undesirable. It is respectfully submitted that the authors' suggestion that the jurisdiction to grant declarations could extend to purely moral, social, or political issues is unwarranted.

The authors refer to *Re A (Children) (Conjoined Twins: Surgical Separation)*[56] and state that the declaration in that case allowing conjoined twins to be separated where this would cause one to die 'raised issues that were moral and social'.[57] As '[t]he court authorised the operation', the authors suggest, '[i]t can therefore be no longer safely said that the jurisdiction does not extend to purely moral, social or political issues in which no legal or equitable rights arise or public law decisions are involved'.[58]

The decision in fact involved a very clear declaration of a legal 'right', namely, the hospital's 'liberty' (in a Hohfeldian sense) to operate on the twins without fear that it would be breaching duties imposed by the criminal or civil law. The remedy affirmed by the Court of Appeal was 'a declaration that separation surgery could be lawfully carried out'.[59] The court was not asked to declare that it would be morally right or socially acceptable for the hospital to operate.[60] Ward LJ was careful to circumscribe what the court was adjudicating by stating, 'It is, however, important to stress the obvious. This court is a court of law, not of morals'.[61]

Some examples of diverse kinds of substantive *primary* rights that have been replicated in declarations will now be given to illustrate the wide availability of this remedy.

(a) Common law rights

(i) Contractual rights

In *Rajbenback v Mamon*,[62] a landlord and tenant orally agreed that if the tenant vacated the premises before a certain date the landlord would pay him £300. The tenant obtained a declaration 'that in the event of the plaintiff delivering up to the defendant vacant possession of the flat on or before January 1, 1955, he will be entitled to payment from the defendant on January 1 of the sum of £300'.[63]

[55] Woolf (n 27 above), [1.16]. See also v, [2.20], [2.25], [3.007], [3.023], [9.03] contrast [3.134]–[3.136].

[56] [2001] 2 WLR 480 (CA).

[57] Woolf (n 27 above), [1.27].

[58] Ibid [1.27]. However the authors seem to retract from this radical statement on 59 n 87 stating that 'the jurisdiction still does not extend to "moral social or political matters in which no legal or equitable rights arise" *per* Sir Robert Megarry V-C, *Malone v Commissioner of Police* [1979] Ch 344 at 353.'

[59] [2001] 2 WLR 480, 484 (CA).

[60] Nor did the court have to declare that the hospital was under a legal duty to operate.

[61] Ibid 488.

[62] [1955] 1 QB 283.

[63] Ibid 287.

(ii) Property rights usually protected by the law of tort

In *Harrison v Duke of Rutland*[64] the claimant travelled on a public highway over the defendant's land to interfere with the defendant's grouse shooting. The claimant was forcibly ejected and sued for trespass to the person. The defendant counter-claimed for a declaration that the claimant was trespassing. The declaration sought by the defendant was granted. The court in effect replicated the claimant's primary duty not to enter the defendant's land without consent and confirmed that it had been infringed by the claimant.

(b) Equitable rights

Examples of primary equitable rights which are replicated in declarations include liens and certain trusts arising by operation of the law such as some constructive trusts and resulting trusts. Examples of equitable liens which ought to be characterized as primary rights include a seller's lien over land that is conveyed before the price has been paid[65] and a trustee's lien over trust property.[66] An equitable lien is in effect a proprietary right securing a separate right to payment. It can be enforced by demanding that the property be sold. An example of a constructive trust, which ought to be characterized as a set of primary rights, is the trust that arises under a contract for the sale of land. '[T]he vendor of the estate is from the time of his contract, considered as a trustee for the purchasers.'[67] Similarly, a resulting trust which arises, for example, where an express trust fails, may be declared.[68] It is also a set of primary rights as it does not arise from a wrong.

A declaration may also be made of a proprietary right which arose due to proprietary estoppel, that is, an expectation of an interest in land induced by the owner on which the claimant reasonably acted to his or her detriment. In *Crabb v Arun District Council*,[69] the court granted a declaration of such a right arising from estoppel, in this case, a right of way. It was characterized as 'an equitable right possessed by the plaintiff'.[70]

(c) Statutory rights

Declarations can replicate statutory rights. For example, section 96(2) of the Copyright, Designs and Patents Act 1998 (UK) provides that the same relief is available for an infringement of copyright as is available in respect of the infringement of any other property right. This includes declarations.[71]

[64] [1893] 1 QB 142.
[65] *Mackreth v Symmons* (1808) 15 Ves Jr 329; see text to n 33 above.
[66] *Jennings v Mather* [1901] 1 QB 113, 114 (CA).
[67] *Green v Smith* (1738) 1 Atk 572, 573 (Lord Hardwicke).
[68] *Re Vandervell's Trusts (No 2)* [1974] Ch 269 (CA).
[69] [1976] Ch 179 (CA).
[70] Ibid 199 (Scarman LJ).
[71] See text to n 32 above for an example.

4 Enforcement of the remedy

A declaration is traditionally said to be non-enforceable (or non-coercive). This means that it cannot be enforced either against the defendant's assets or by punishment for contempt. Its realization requires an application for an additional enforceable remedy. Forbes J observed in *Webster v Southwark LBC*:

> [W]here a court makes only a declaratory order it is not contempt for the party affected by the order to refuse to abide by it. If he does so refuse no doubt the other party can go back to the court and seek an injunction to enforce the order; but mere refusal of one party to an action to abide by a declaratory order is not, as I understand it, contempt of court.[72]

The defendant may also be liable pay damages for any loss suffered.[73]

However, Forbes J stated that if the defendant refuses to comply with the declaration, the claimant may apply to the court for leave to issue a writ of sequestration.[74] If this is correct then it alters the status of a declaration bringing it within the class of remedies which are enforceable by punishment through sequestration. A declaration ought not to be enforceable by any means. Instead, it should always be replaced by another remedy such as an injunction if the defendant fails to comply so as to put the defendant on notice that he or she will be in contempt and subject to punishment for non-compliance. Otherwise, if the declaration begins to take on the attributes of a injunction, some of its useful advantages may be lost.

[72] [1983] QB 698, 706. [73] Woolf (n 27 above), [1.07], [7.08]–[7.12].
[74] *Webster v Southwark LBC* [1983] QB 698, 709–710.

10

Replicating Secondary Rights: Common Law Remedies

A Introduction

This chapter, and the two that follow, will examine remedies that replicate secondary rights. The focus of this chapter will be the award of damages, a remedy which originated at common law.

As described in Chapter 2, a secondary or remedial right is simply a right which correlates with a duty of a person who has infringed another's right to answer for that infringement. It imposes a sanction or, in Austin's words, an evil in the case of disobedience.[1] For example, a battery infringes the primary right to bodily integrity and generates a secondary right to be paid damages by the tortfeasor. A breach of contract infringes a primary contractual right and generates a secondary right to be paid damages by the contract-breaker.

The need for secondary rights arises because, as we saw in Chapter 7, some primary rights are not replicated in court orders or pronouncements, either because (1) replication would be futile (as with rights which cease to exist on breach) or ineffective as it would not undo something which ought not have been done (as with negative rights); or (2) replication would be inefficient or undesirable as a matter of policy (as with some rights to the performance of services). Secondary rights thus supplant or reinforce infringed primary rights so that the latter may be given at least indirect effect by the courts. They supplant primary rights where the latter cease to exist on infringement; they reinforce primary rights where the latter continue to exist but for some reason replication would not adequately effectuate the primary right in question.

The content of a secondary right does not logically follow from the nature of the primary duty breached. The law could dictate that the sanction for causing personal injury to another is to submit to retaliation in kind or that a pedestrian struck by a negligent driver automatically becomes the owner of the negligent driver's vehicle. The content of a secondary right, that is, what it entitles the

[1] J. Austin, *Lectures on Jurisprudence Vol I* (R. Campbell (ed.) (5th edn., London: John Murray, 1885), 89.

claimant to, is a matter of policy.[2] Generally in the case of wrongs, the policy that has prevailed is that losses should be made good, which in turn dictates that a money award should be made on a compensation measure.[3] However, in the case of some wrongs, a policy of deterrence may give rise to secondary rights to restitution[4] or a policy of punishment may arguably give rise to a secondary right to exemplary damages.[5]

As noted in Chapter 6, these policy choices are made at the institutional level by Parliament or by superior courts. These choices are then enshrined in the law and, in future cases, they may be said to be made 'by the law'. The existence of the secondary right dictates that a judge does not have to arrive at a fresh answer, in each case before him or her, to the difficult policy question that has already been answered by the law, namely, what kind of response is just when a certain kind of primary right is infringed.

B Replication of Secondary Rights

Secondary rights themselves are always capable of being replicated in orders of the court. As Dias writes:

> Secondary duties...can be, and are carried out, for no system will be so futile as to impose them unless they can be carried out. Most secondary duties, which are one form of sanctions, consist of the payment of money. It is therefore the case that apart from the exceptional primary duties mentioned [namely those which are specifically enforceable], only secondary duties are enforced in the sense of their observance being ensured.[6]

It is crucial to note that a remedy which is replicative of a secondary right is taken not to *transform* the claimant's primary right. It is not a 'transformative remedy' as that phrase is used in this work. In making an award of damages for breach of contract, the judge does not make an order that transforms a substantive right, the judge merely makes an order that replicates a secondary right which substitutes for or reinforces the primary right. It should be further observed that a decree of specific performance and an award of damages are given in *direct* response to infringements of different rights. The former redresses the non-performance of a primary right arising from consent and the latter redresses

[2] P. B. H. Birks, 'Equity in the Modern Law: An Exercise in Taxonomy' (1996) 26 *U Western Australia L Rev* 1, 12.

[3] But this was not always the case. 'Prior to the nineteenth century, tort law was as much characterised by deterrence, punishment and consolation as by the aim of financial compensation': M. Tilbury, M. Noone and B. Kercher, *Remedies Commentary and Materials* (3rd edn., North Ryde New South Wales: Law Book Co, 2000), 76.

[4] See p 175 below.

[5] See p 176 below.

[6] R. W. M. Dias, *Jurisprudence* (5th edn., London: Butterworths, 1985), 236.

the non-performance of a secondary right to the payment of damages arising from a wrong.[7]

C Award of Damages

1 Form of the order

An award of damages may be expressed in the following forms:

IT IS ORDERED that the defendant:

1. pay the claimant the sum of £........[8]

IT IS THIS DAY ADJUDGED that the Defendant do pay the Claimant £........ being as to £........ in respect of damages and £........ by way of interest thereon...[9]

IT IS ORDERED that the Defendant do pay to the Claimant the sum of £........ being as to £........ in respect of damages and £........ by way of interest thereon...[10]

Where damages are assessed after a separate hearing, the order provides:

To the Defendant
The claimant obtained judgment against you on................ for an amount to be decided by the court.

[Master][District judge]................ has decided the amount and ordered that you should pay £........ [including interest to date of judgment] and £........ for costs [costs to be assessed].

You must pay to the claimant a total of £........[11]

In the case of awards of damages for personal injuries, since *Jefford v Gee*,[12] the order must specify different categories or 'heads' of damage for the purposes of awarding interest. The following are assessed separately: (a) damages for accrued pecuniary loss such as loss of past earnings (special damages); (b) damages for non-pecuniary loss such as damages for pain and suffering (general damages); and (c) damages for loss of future earnings (future loss). For example, the award made

[7] Thus the two remedies are granted in relation to two separate infringements of two separate rights. See also Chapter 9 p 154.

[8] This is the core provision of Forms such as No 45 Judgment after trial before judge without jury, No 46 Judgment after trial before judge with jury, No 44 Part 24 (Summary) judgment for claimant. Forms No 45 and No 46 are referred to as examples of general forms of a trial judgment: CPR Part 40 PD(B) [14.1.1]. CPR Part 4 PD Table 2 lists these pre-CPR High Court forms as forms which may continue to be used under the new rules: CPR Part 4 PD [1.3].

[9] *Atkin's Court Forms* (2nd edn., 2001 Issue) Vol 17(1) [148]. This is the style employed in the Queens Bench Division.

[10] Ibid [147]. This is the style employed in the Chancery Division.

[11] N34HC Judgment for claimant (after amount decided by court HC) and N34 Judgment for claimant (after amount decided by court CC).

[12] [1970] 2 QB 130 (CA); *George v Pinnock* [1973] 1 WLR 118.

at first instance in *Hunt v Severs*[13] in respect of injuries sustained in a motorcycle accident was £617,004 made up as follows:

General damages for pain and suffering and loss of amenity	90,000
Special damages	90,094
Future loss	412,104
Interest on general damages	6,588
Interest on special damages	18,218
Total	£617,004

Traditionally damages had to be awarded in the form of a lump sum. The court could not require the defendant to make payments over time.[14] Such powers have been conferred by statute.[15]

2 Nature of the remedy

An award of damages is a commonly sought remedy.[16] It gives direct effect to an unliquidated personal right to the payment of money arising from a wrong. This remedy, firmly rooted in the common law, is available as a matter of course where the secondary right which it replicates is proved to exist. Notionally, it is not subject to refusal on 'discretionary' grounds though this does not mean that discretion does not play a significant role in the assessment of damages.[17]

(a) Function of the remedy

An award of damages at common law is always a corrective remedy. This is because the award gives effect to an existing secondary right to payment which has not been satisfied. The claimant can only obtain the remedy after the secondary right has arisen.[18] Damages for an apprehended breach or for future loss that will be caused by a continuing breach are not recoverable at common law.[19] As Lord Millett stated in *Jaggard v Sawyer*, 'Damages at common law are

[13] *Hunt v Severs* [1994] 2 AC 350 (HL) 356; see also *Thompson v Faraonio* [1979] 1 WLR 1157 (PC).

[14] *Fournier v Canadian National Railway Co* [1927] AC 167.

[15] For example, County Courts Act 1984 (UK) s 71 confers a general power on the county court, where any judgment is given or order made for payment of a money sum, to order that the money might be paid 'by such instalments payable at such times as the court may fix'.

[16] In the year 2000, 1,050 claims for breach of contract were issued in the Queens Bench Division of the High Court and 53% of court judgments in that Division related to personal injury claims; approximately 213,788 unliquidated 'money claims' were issued in the county courts: Lord Chancellor's Department *Judicial Statistics England and Wales for the Year 2000* (Norwich: The Stationery Office, 2001), 29, 31, 37–9. However, the number of liquidated claims for an award of money due was much greater: see Chapter 5 n 14.

[17] See Chapter 6 p 89.

[18] However, where there is an anticipatory breach of contract, the claimant can accept the repudiation, bringing the contract to an end, and seek damages: *Hochster v De la Tour* (1853) 2 E & B 678; 118 ER 922.

[19] *Battishill v Reed* (1856) 18 CB 696, 714, 717–718; 139 ER 1544, 1551, 1552–1553; *Mann v CTHC* (1982) 148 CLR 97, 101.

recoverable only in respect of causes of action which are complete at the date of the writ; damages for future or repeated wrongs must be made the subject of fresh proceedings'.[20]

(b) Effect on substantive rights

The judicial remedy is the claimant's new officially restated right to be paid the awarded damages amount. The order of the court replicates and replaces the claimant's secondary right. The judgment generates a new duty on the defendant and extinguishes the old one.[21]

However, the judgment does not extinguish any secondary right which arose from a different cause of action, that is, from an infringement of an entirely different primary right. In *Brunsden v Humphrey*,[22] the defendant's servant negligently collided with the claimant's cab damaging it and injuring the claimant. The claimant obtained an award of damages for damage to his cab and then brought a second action in respect of his personal injuries. Bowen LJ stated:

> the defendant's servant has done one act and one only, the driving of the one vehicle negligently against the other. . .Two separate kinds of injury were in fact inflicted, and two wrongs done. . .One wrong was done as soon as the plaintiff's enjoyment of his property was substantially interfered with. A further wrong arose as soon as the driving also caused injury to the plaintiff's person. Both causes of action, in one sense, may be said to be founded upon one act of the defendant's servant, but they are not on that account identical causes of action[23]

It was held that an award of damages for damage to property did not prevent an action for an award of damages for personal injuries being brought. It can be said that the claimant's secondary right to damages for damage to his cab was merged in the first judgment but not his separate secondary right to damages for personal injury. But, in the case of contract, it is clear that each breach of contract only gives rise to one cause of action.[24] Looking at the jural relationship another way, only one secondary right arises.

An award of damages is given once and for all.[25] In *Fitter v Veal*[26] the claimant obtained an award of damages against the defendant for battery and assault. When

[20] [1995] 1 WLR 269, 284 (CA). In contrast, damages in substitution for an injunction can be awarded under statute for a threatened breach which has not yet occurred: see Chapter 12 p 199 and 13 p 212.

[21] See Chapter 7 p 108; A. W. Scott and W. A. Seavey, *Restatement of the Law of Judgments* (St Paul: American Law Institute Publishers, 1942) 181; *Rysak v Rysak and Bugajaski* [1967] P 179, 184; [1966] 2 All ER 1036.

[22] (1884) 14 QBD 141 (CA); cf *Republic of India v India Steamship Co Ltd* [1993] AC 410 (HL).

[23] Ibid 150–151.

[24] *Conquer v Boot* [1928] 2 KB 336; *Rowntree & Sons Ltd v Allen & Sons Ltd* (1936) 41 Com Cas 90.

[25] *Brunsden v Humphrey* (1884) 14 QBD 141, 147 (CA). However, the assessment of damages can be deferred or postponed in exceptional cases: *Deeny v Gooda Walker Ltd* [1995] 1 WLR 1206, 1214.

[26] (1701) 12 Mod Rep 542; 88 ER 1506; *Todorovic v Waller* (1981) 150 CLR 402 (HCA) 412. For an example in the context of contract see *Conquer v Boot* [1928] 2 KB 336.

it was discovered that the seriousness of his injuries had been underestimated and that he required a further operation on his skull, he sought further damages. The court held that he was not entitled to recover further damages. This finality of the award of damages is a consequence of the extinction of the claimant's secondary right upon the making of such an award.

(c) Advantages of the remedy

The main advantage of an award of damages is that it is easy to obtain. The remedy is not subject to bars that may potentially operate where specific performance or an injunction is sought. But an award of damages may also be more desirable than such remedies for other reasons.

Willing but substituted performance by a third party may be preferable to a grudging compelled performance by the defendant. Beale observes that 'The probable explanation [for business not demanding that specific performance be more widely available] is that obtaining a substitute is usually better than specific performance. It will often be quicker and cheaper, and produce more satisfactory results for two other reasons.'[27] First, it may be important for the claimant purchaser of goods or services that the provider co-operate in relation to the subject matter of the contract. Secondly, it may be desirable for there to be a long-term commercial relationship between the parties. This is especially so in the case of services but it may also apply in the case of contracts for the sale of goods; for example, if complex machinery is purchased pursuant to a specific performance decree, it may be difficult to obtain spare parts from the defendant in the future or additional services such as maintenance.[28]

3 Nature of the substantive right replicated

The law of damages is relatively new.[29] This is because when juries rather than judges awarded damages, the measure was almost entirely left to the discretion of the jury. The jury simply awarded a sum it thought was just without giving reasons or being subject to any significant judicial control. Jury trial has all but disappeared from the civil sphere and with it the remedial discretion enjoyed by juries.[30] The disappearance of jury trials has been put down to a need for greater assessability, uniformity, and predictability in the assessment of damages.[31]

[27] H. Beale, *Remedies for Breach of Contract* (London: Sweet & Maxwell, 1980), 144.
[28] Ibid 144. [29] A. I. Ogus, *The Law of Damages* (London: Butterworths, 1973), 7.
[30] Ibid Chapter 1; F. H. Lawson, *Remedies of English Law* (2nd edn., London: Butterworth & Co, 1980), 54–55; N. Andrews, 'Civil Procedure' in P. B. H. Birks (ed.), *English Private Law Vol II* (Oxford: Oxford University Press, 2000), [19.288-19.290].
[31] *Ward v James* [1966] 1 QB 273, 299 (CA) (Lord Denning).

As Tilbury, Noone and Kercher state:

> the most significant trend of all in the modern law of assessment of damages is that the law has become more technical and to a degree more principled and thus predictable, as the judges have increasingly imposed their views about the assessment of damages over those of juries.[32]

Thus judges have not become 'one-person juries' but rather we have seen an emergence of a sophisticated law of secondary rights. Today it can be said that it is the law of damages that determines the content of the secondary right and hence settles the amount of the award, subject of course to some residual discretion on the part of the judge as the rules are relatively open-textured.

An award of damages replicates an unliquidated personal right to a payment arising out of a breach of primary duty. It restates, liquidates, and replaces the pre-existing secondary right. For example, an award of damages may replicate the right to compensation for negligently caused injury or the right to compensation for loss caused by breach of contract. Rights to damages are shaped by detailed doctrines. For instance, rights to damages for breach of contract or for torts such as trespass or negligence are quantified by reference to detailed rules as to causation, remoteness, and mitigation. On the other hand, some secondary rights are shaped by very few such rules. For example, the right to damages for defamation is quantified by the jury in its largely unfettered discretion.[33]

A number of sub-forms of the award of damages will be distinguished: first, depending on the goal of the secondary right that is replicated in the award, namely compensation, restitution, and punishment; and second, in the case of compensation, depending on the base to which the claimant is to be returned, which informs the expectation and the reliance measures. Some representative cases will be focused upon as illustrations of situations where a particular kind of secondary right was replicated in an award of damages.

As was done in relation to various types of remedies in the previous chapters, examples of awards of damages will be divided according to the content of the replicated right. However, detailed discussions of the content of particular secondary rights will be avoided as far as possible because such matters of substantive law fall outside the scope of the law of remedies. Such matters belong in specialist works on secondary rights.[34] They are touched upon here only in so far as it is necessary to make the point that an award of damages does indeed replicate pre-existing secondary rights in various types of cases and therefore that it belongs in this category.

[32] Tilbury et al (n 3 above), 77.

[33] The process by which juries assess damages in defamation trials does not 'purport to be a scientific, or even pseudo-scientific process. . .The assessment depends upon nothing more than the good sense and sound instincts of jurors as to what is a fair and reasonable award, having regard to all the circumstances of the case': *Carson v John Fairfax & Sons Ltd* (1993) 178 CLR 44, 115 (HCA) (McHugh J).

[34] For example, in relation to the right to compensatory damages the reader is referred to works such as H. McGregor, *McGregor on Damages* (16th edn., London: Sweet & Maxwell, 1997).

(a) Compensation

In most cases secondary rights require the person who breaches a primary duty to make good the claimant's loss by means of a payment of money. Two different approaches to the quantification of the monetary value of loss and hence the determination of the content of such rights are adopted.[35] First, losses which can be estimated or calculated, such as pecuniary loss, are calculated according to particular rules or 'measures' which will be discussed in the next section. Second, losses which are incalculable such as personal injuries (including loss of amenity and pain and suffering) are determined by convention, in particular, the *Guidelines for the Assessment of General Damages in Personal Injury Cases* issued by the Judicial Studies Board.[36] As Sir Thomas Bingham MR stated in *John v MGN Ltd*, 'The conventional compensatory scales in personal injury cases must be taken to represent fair compensation in such cases unless and until those scales are amended by the courts or by Parliament.'[37] Similarly Lord Woolf MR observed in *Heil v Rankin*:

> In the case of pecuniary loss, the courts have progressively been prepared to adopt ever more sophisticated calculations in order to establish the extent of a claimant's loss. . .In the case of non-pecuniary damages, the scale of damages has remained a 'jury question.'. . .In practice, since the 1960s the assessment of damages has been carried out primarily by the judiciary. The assessment requires the judge to make a value judgment. That value judgment has been increasingly constrained by the desire to achieve consistency between the decisions of different judges. Consistency is important, because it assists in achieving justice between one claimant and another and one defendant and another. It also assists to achieve justice by facilitating settlements.[38]

Thus one may conclude that the content of secondary rights to the payment of compensatory damages is chosen by the law. The court merely replicates those rights when an award of damages is made.

(i) **Arising from a breach of contract**[39]

The secondary right most commonly replicated in an award of damages for breach of contract is a right to compensation. As Lord Diplock stated in *Photo Production Ltd v Securicor Transport Ltd*:

> Every failure to perform a primary obligation is a breach of contract. The secondary obligation on the part of the contract breaker to which it gives rise by implication of the

[35] Lawson (n 30 above), 59.

[36] Judicial Studies Board, *Guidelines for the Assessment of General Damages in Personal Injury Cases* (6th edn., Oxford: Oxford University Press, 2002).

[37] [1997] QB 586, 611, 614 (CA).

[38] [2001] QB 272, 294 (CA).

[39] No secondary right to compensation generally arises from a breach of a primary duty to pay money: *London, Chatham and Dover Railway Company v South Eastern Railway* [1893] AC 429 (HL) but contrast *Wadsworth v Lydall* [1981] 1 WLR 598 (CA) where it was held that 'special' damages are recoverable provided that they are not too remote. No secondary right to damages arises where there is a valid liquidated damages clause: *Cellulose Acetate Silk Co Ltd v Widnes Foundry Ltd* [1933] AC 20.

common law is to pay monetary compensation to the other party for the loss sustained by him in consequence of the breach.[40]

The aim of the secondary right to compensation arising from breach of contract is to put the claimant into as good a position as if the contract had been performed. As Parke B stated in *Robinson v Harman*:

> The rule of common law is that where a party sustains a loss by reason of a breach of contract he is, so far as money can do it, to be placed in the same situation, with respect to damages as if the contract had been performed.[41]

The loss suffered by a party to a contract may be characterized in various ways. Hence there are different measures by which compensatory damages may be quantified. These different measures help to determine the content of the secondary right.

(a) Loss of expected enrichment Most commonly, the claimant is entitled to damages which are equivalent to the difference in value between what the claimant actually obtained from the defendant and the market value of the benefit the claimant would have obtained under the contract if the primary contractual duty had not been breached.[42] Where the claimant would have obtained a chance of a gain, the secondary right entitles the claimant to damages in proportion to the likelihood of the chance eventuating.[43] Such a secondary right is concerned with compensating for the loss of the *objective* increase in the claimant's wealth that would have eventuated from the performance of the contract. The right may be said to protect the 'enrichment expectation' interest.[44]

(b) Loss of bargain Less commonly, the claimant is entitled to damages concerned with compensating for the loss of bargain, usually a *subjective* benefit that the claimant expected from the contract.[45] Such a benefit may be aesthetic, altruistic,

[40] [1980] AC 827, 849 (HL). Lord Wilberforce expressly agreed with this analysis at 845.

[41] (1848) 1 Exch 850, 855.

[42] *Koufos v C Czarnikow Ltd, The Herron II* [1969] 1 AC 350 (HL). This right is enshrined in the Sale of Goods Act 1979 (UK). Section 51(3) states that, in the case of non-delivery 'the measure of damages is prima facie to be ascertained by the difference between the contract price and the market or current price of the goods at the time or times when they ought to have been delivered.'

[43] *Chapman v Hicks* [1911] 2 KB 786 (CA).

[44] It is preferable to qualify this expectation interest with 'enrichment' so as to distinguish it from the 'performance' or 'bargain' expectation interest discussed in the next section.

[45] Simplistic economic analysis of contract which focuses only on the maximization of wealth or *objective* benefit breaks down because contracts are made not only with the aim of increasing wealth. Often they are made with the aim of procuring a non-economic (e.g. aesthetic) benefit (e.g. a contract to paint a house black) or with the altruistic aim of conferring a benefit on a third party (e.g. a contract to paint a house belonging to a third party). Where these contracts are not properly performed the innocent party suffers a real 'loss'. Loss is not restricted to a failure to obtain an expected objective increase in wealth: *Ruxley Electronics and Construction Ltd v Forsyth* [1996] AC 344 (HL); *McAlpine (Alfred) Construction Ltd v Panatown Ltd* [2001] 1 AC 518 (HL).

or even eccentric. Sometimes the claimant is entitled to the cost of procuring someone else to confer the benefit that the claimant would have obtained if the primary contractual duty had not been breached (cost of cure)[46] and sometimes the claimant is merely entitled to a sum for loss of pleasure or for mental distress.

An award of damages which replicated a secondary right to damages quantified on the loss of bargain measure was made in *Radford v De Froberville*.[47] The defendant breached her contractual duty to build a wall that would separate her land from the claimant's. The claimant sued for the cost of building the wall. The defendant argued that the claimant was entitled to the difference between the value of his land with and without the wall. This was nil. Oliver J concluded that 'the plaintiff genuinely wants this work done and that he intends to expend any damages awarded on carrying it out. In my judgment, therefore, the damages ought to be measured by the cost of the work, unless there are some other considerations which point to a different measure.'[48]

Another example of an award of damages which may replicate a secondary right to damages on the loss of bargain measure would be an award for the breach of a contract to improve a third party's property.[49]

(c) Reliance loss In certain circumstances, the claimant is entitled to damages for expenses that the claimant incurred in reliance on the contract. 'If the aggrieved party is unable to establish the value of a loss of bargain he may seek compensation in respect of his reliance losses. The object of such an award is to compensate the aggrieved party for expenses incurred and losses suffered in reliance on the contract.'[50]

(ii) Arising from a tort

A breach of a primary duty founded in the law of tort may give rise to a secondary obligation to pay monetary compensation. For example, in relation to wrongful death, Lord Diplock stated in *Cookson v Knowles*[51] that, 'From the juristic standpoint it is that discounted amount [i.e. the discounted value of the benefits which the husband would have provided for the widow in future years] and no more to which the widow *became entitled at the date of her husband's death*.'[52] This makes it

[46] In building cases, reinstatement can be said to be the normal measure of loss: *East Ham Corporation v Bernard Sunley & Sons Ltd* [1966] AC 406, 434–435, 445.

[47] [1977] 1 WLR 1262 applying *Tito v Waddell (No 2)* [1977] Ch 106.

[48] Ibid 1284. In contrast, in *Ruxley Electronics and Construction Ltd v Forsyth* [1996] AC 344 (HL) the claimant was not entitled to the cost of cure because it would have been unreasonable as it was out of all proportion to the benefit to be obtained. Instead, the claimant was entitled to damages for 'loss of amenity' or mental distress.

[49] Such a secondary right would arise on the minority view (Lord Goff and Lord Millett) in *McAlpine (Alfred) Construction Ltd v Panatown Ltd* [2001] 1 AC 518 (HL).

[50] *Surrey CC v Bredero Homes Ltd* [1993] 1 WLR 1361, 1369 (HL) (Steyn LJ); *Anglia Television v Reed* [1972] 1 QB 60 (CA).

[51] [1979] AC 556 (HL).

[52] Ibid 569 (emphasis added); followed in *Thompson v Faraonio* [1979] 1 WLR 1157, 1163 (PC).

clear that the widow's entitlement or secondary right to damages arose at the date of the tort.

The aim of a secondary right to compensation arising from a tort is to put the claimant into as good a position as if the breach of primary duty had not occurred. As Lord Blackburn famously stated in *Livingstone v Rawyards Coal Co*:

> where any injury is to be compensated by damages, in settling the sum of money to be given for reparation of damages you should as nearly as possible get at that sum of money which will put the party who has been injured, or who has suffered, in the same position as he would have been in if he had not sustained the wrong for which he is getting his compensation or reparation.[53]

Secondary rights arising from some wrongs such as deceit are more far reaching than those arising from breach of contract, nuisance, or negligence. As Lord Denning stated in *Doyle v Olby (Ironmongers) Ltd*,[54] 'In contract, the damages are limited to what may reasonably be supposed to have been in contemplation of the parties. In fraud, they are not so limited. The defendant is bound to make reparation for all actual damages directly flowing from the fraudulent inducement.' An award of damages in such a case replicates that far-reaching secondary right. As stressed in Chapter 4, the rules which shape secondary rights are part of the substantive law and not the law of remedies. Such rules in relation to secondary rights to compensation need not be further discussed here.

(b) Restitution

Secondary rights do not necessarily require the person who breaches a primary duty to make good the claimant's loss. A secondary right may require that person to give back or give up a gain made as a result of the breach.[55] It may be a secondary right to restitution rather than compensation.

(i) **Arising from a breach of contract**

The traditional position was that no secondary right to restitution could arise out of a breach of contract.[56] However, an award of restitutionary damages was made under Lord Cairns' Act in lieu of an injunction in *Wrotham Park Estate Co Ltd v Parkside Homes Ltd*.[57] In *Attorney General v Blake* Lord Nicholls stated that, 'In a suitable case damages for breach of contract may be measured by the benefit

[53] *Livingstone v Rawyards Coal Co* (1880) 5 AC 25, 39 (HL); *Todorovic v Waller* (1981) 150 CLR 402, 412 (HCA).

[54] [1969] 2 QB 158, 167 (CA).

[55] The secondary rights in this category have been sub-divided by Edelman into those with the goal of restitution, namely the retransfer of gains wrongfully transferred from the claimant, and those with the goal of disgorgement, namely the stripping of profits in the defendant's hands: J. Edelman, *Gain-Based Damages* (Oxford: Hart, 2002).

[56] *Tito v Waddell (No 2)* [1977] Ch 106, 332 (Sir Robert Megarry V-C).

[57] [1974] 1 WLR 798.

gained by the wrongdoer from the breach. The defendant must make a reasonable payment in respect of the benefit he has gained.'[58]

As the law develops, it may become possible to state with confidence in which situations a secondary right to restitutionary damages for breach of contract will arise.[59] Perhaps it may ultimately be taken to arise in situations similar to those suggested by the Court of Appeal (though not accepted by the House of Lords), namely, where there has been 'skimped performance' being a situation where the defendant did not provide the full extent of the services contracted for but did not cause the claimant any financial loss, or where the defendant has obtained his profit by doing the very thing which he contracted not to do.[60] However, unless and until the law is judicially defined in greater detail in this area, it may be necessary to characterize any awards of restitutionary damages as transformative remedies.

(ii) **Arising from a tort**

Some torts give rise to 'an obligation to make restitution'.[61] A secondary right to restitutionary damages arises from the defendant's unlawful use of the claimant's property.[62] As Lord Nicholls stated:

> It is an established principle concerning the assessment of damages that a person who has wrongfully used another's property without causing the latter any pecuniary loss may still be liable to that other for more than nominal damages. In general, he is liable to pay, as damages, a reasonable sum for the wrongful use he has made of the other's property.[63]

Where another's goods are detained, 'the owner is entitled to a reasonable hire.'[64] Where accommodation is not vacated after a lease is validly terminated, the landlord acquires a right to the payment of restitutionary damages for the occupier's continued use of the premises.[65] These are clearly secondary rights. An award of restitutionary damages simply replicates such rights.

(c) Punishment

Exemplary or punitive damages are a payment of money which is not intended to compensate but to 'punish and deter'[66] and to 'assuage any urge for revenge'.[67]

[58] [2001] 1 AC 268, 283–284 (HL). The orders actually made in this case were an order for an account of profits and a consequential order for payment: Chapter 11 p 187.

[59] See especially J. Edelman, *Gain-Based Damages* (Oxford: Hart, 2002).

[60] *Attorney General v Blake* [1998] Ch 439, 458 (CA).

[61] *United Australia Ltd v Barclays Bank Ltd* [1941] AC 1, 18–19 (PC) (Viscount Simon LC).

[62] *Inverugie Investments Ltd v Hackett* [1995] 1 WLR 713 (PC).

[63] *Stoke-on-Trent City Council v W & J Wass Ltd* [1988] 1 WLR 1406, 1416 (CA).

[64] *Strand Electric and Engineering Co Ltd v Brisford Entertainments Ltd* [1952] 2 QB 246, 253 (CA) (Denning LJ).

[65] *Ministry of Defence v Ashman* [1993] 2 EGLR 102 (CA); *Ministry of Defence v Thompson* [1993] 2 EGLR 107 (CA).

[66] *Rookes v Barnard* [1964] AC 1129, 1221 (HL) (Lord Devlin).

[67] *Lamb v Cotogno* (1987) 164 CLR 1 (HCA).

(i) Arising from a tort

Exemplary damages are available in at least three situations: first, where there was 'oppressive, arbitrary or unconstitutional action by the servants of the government'; second, where 'the defendant's conduct has been calculated by him to make a profit for himself which may well exceed the compensation payable to the plaintiff'; and third, where 'exemplary damages are expressly authorised by statute'.[68]

It is arguable that the conditions for the making of an award of such damages are settled enough that one may say that where they are fulfilled the claimant acquires a secondary right to damages on such a measure. For example, where, as in *Broome v Cassell & Co Ltd*,[69] a publisher knowingly publishes a libellous book and that conduct is calculated to make a profit, it would appear that the claimant acquires a right to exemplary damages, at least in the sense that the question must be left to the jury.[70] However, if all that can be said is that the claimant acquires a right to exemplary damages only when a court order is obtained to that effect then the award of exemplary damages belongs in the class of transformative remedies.[71]

(ii) Arising from a breach of contract

It is generally accepted that an award of exemplary damages is not available for breach of contract in England.[72] But this is a policy choice. In Canada, it is available in this context.[73]

4 Enforcement of the remedy

An award of damages is enforced in the same manner as an award of an agreed sum.[74]

[68] *Rookes v Barnard* [1964] AC 1129, 1226–1227 (HL) (Lord Devlin); *Kuddus v Chief Constable of Leicestershire* [2002] 2 AC 122 (HL); *A v Bottrill* [2002] 3 WLR 1406 (PC).

[69] [1972] AC 1027 (HL).

[70] Where judges rather than juries are to determine the quantum, it seems desirable that they should be guided by rules in the same way that rules guide the quantification of other types of secondary rights to damages.

[71] In *Gray v Motor Accident Commission* (1998) 196 CLR 1, 11 (HCA) Gleeson CJ, McHugh, Gummow, and Hayne JJ stated that it was not helpful to describe exemplary damages as discretionary. Their Honours also asserted that the problem of their availability was not resolved by attempting to analyse it in terms of 'rights' or 'claims' but rather that it should be considered in terms of 'what it is that entitles a plaintiff to an award of exemplary damages or (to put it in the language of discretion) permits or requires the making of an award'.

[72] *Addis v Gramophone Company Ltd* [1909] AC 488 (HL).

[73] *Vorvis v Insurance Corp of British Columbia* [1989] 1 SCR 1085 (SCC); *Whitten v Pilot Insurance Co* (2002) 209 DLR (4th) 257 (SCC).

[74] See Chapter 7 p 112.

11

Replicating Secondary Rights: Equitable Remedies

A Introduction

This chapter deals with a number of equitable remedies which do or may replicate rights arising from wrongs. As will become apparent throughout this chapter, the substantive law in this area is still in a process of development. Therefore, particular emphasis will be placed on determining, where possible, that the awards and orders considered here actually are replicating secondary rights rather than creating rights with an entirely new content; that is, that these remedies ought to be placed in the replicative rather than the transformative category.

B Award of Equitable Compensation

A payment of equitable compensation is a payment of money in substitution for the performance of a primary equitable duty.[1] An equitable duty is a duty that was only recognized by a court of equity, such as a fiduciary duty. Equitable compensation has been referred to as 'equitable damages'.[2] This usage is not yet firmly entrenched but it should be encouraged as the term 'damages' is best applied to any payment of money in substitution for the performance of a primary duty.[3] Its use ought not to be restricted according to the jurisdictional origin of the obligation to make such a payment. However, in order to remain within current

[1] The term 'equitable damages' is sometimes applied only to damages awarded under Lord Cairns' Act and its successors (see p 199 below); this is a confusing usage as, if classified by the provenance of the power to make them, such awards should be labelled 'statutory damages'.

[2] In *Tang Man Sit v Capacious Investments Ltd* [1996] AC 514, 520 (PC), the expression 'damages for breach of trust' was used throughout the reasons for judgment; Tilbury suggests that 'in principle, any general distinctions between [equitable] compensation and damages can only be justified by reference to the discretionary nature of equitable relief': M. J. Tilbury, *Civil Remedies Vol 1 Principles of Civil Remedies* (North Ryde New South Wales: Butterworths, 1990), [3249]. The presence of this residual discretion can be acknowledged by qualifying these damages with the adjective 'equitable'; see also J. Edelman, 'Equitable Torts' (2002) 10 *Torts LJ* 64, 67, 70.

[3] As Edelman demonstrates, there is no necessary connection between damages and compensation: J. Edelman, *Gain-Based Damages* (Oxford: Hart, 2002), Chapter 1.

convention,[4] the phrase 'equitable compensation' will continue to be used in this work.

As we will see in this chapter, the ostensibly new subject of 'equitable compensation' has existed in another guise for a far longer period of time. It has been hidden under the notion of accountability.

1 Form of the order

An award of equitable compensation simply takes the form of an order to pay money. The quantum to be paid may be determined by an account on the basis of wilful default[5] or by an inquiry. As an example, in the case of *Bartlett v Barclays Bank Trust Co Ltd (No 2)*[6] a trustee was required to directly compensate beneficiaries for losses sustained due to unauthorized investments. The relevant parts of the draft minutes of the order are set out in the reasons for judgment. The court ordered:

> [Inquiry no. 2:] An inquiry [as to] what further distributions, if any, of income, in addition to those actually made ought properly to have been made by [companies owned by the trust] during the said period and on what dates to the defendant by way of dividend. . .
>
> [Order no. 1, required the defendant to pay] To each of the plaintiffs a sum equal to the proportion of the further distributions of income which, on inquiry no. 2, it is found ought properly to have been made, corresponding to the proportion of the income of the said trust fund to which such plaintiff was entitled from time to time under the trusts of the said settlement.[7]

It ought to be noted that strictly speaking only the order in the second paragraph ought to be referred to as the award of equitable compensation. The order in the first paragraph merely provided the mechanism for determining the quantum of compensation payable.

2 Nature of the remedy

An award of equitable compensation replicates a secondary right to the payment of compensation arising from an equitable wrong, usually a breach of a negative primary duty. The award may require payment to be made directly to the beneficiaries. As Chambers writes, 'Equitable compensation for breach of trust is the payment of money directly to the beneficiaries to compensate them for the loss they have suffered as a result of the breach'.[8] Alternatively, the award may require

[4] Still firmly entrenched due to decisions such as *Ex parte Adamson* (1878) 8 Ch D 807 (CA) 819. See also *Youyang v Pty Ltd v Minter Ellison Morris Fletcher* (2003) 212 CLR 484 (HCA) [39].

[5] See p 183 below.

[6] [1980] 1 Ch 539.

[7] Ibid 544.

[8] R. Chambers, 'Liability' in P. B. H. Birks and A. Pretto (eds), *Breach of Trust* (Oxford: Hart, 2002), 20; *Target Holdings Ltd v Redferns* [1996] 1 AC 421, 434–435 (HL).

the restoration of money or property to a fund.[9] Though available as an alternative remedy in relation to some breaches of trust and also having a compensatory effect, a common account and consequential order differ from an award of equitable compensation in that they replicate positive primary rights to the performance of the trust, not secondary rights.[10]

Where a common account is available, an award of equitable compensation provides few advantages. It is thus considered to be subsidiary to a common account.[11] However, an award of equitable compensation is the more convenient or practical remedy where the trust is no longer in existence or the distribution of the fund to fully entitled beneficiaries is overdue. In such cases, it may be futile to require the trustee to restore a fund rather than to make a payment of equitable compensation to the beneficiaries directly.[12] In other circumstances, an award of equitable compensation may be the only remedy available; for example, where a loss has been caused by a breach of an equitable duty such as a fiduciary duty or a duty of confidence.[13]

3 Nature of the substantive right replicated

(a) Beneficiary's secondary right to direct payment

An award of equitable compensation replicates a secondary right to compensation arising from a breach of an equitable duty. It is also sometimes referred to as a right to 'restitution'; however, this is a usage of the term in the non-technical sense of 'restoration' or 'compensation'.[14] This usage is confusing and best avoided.

For example, a secondary right to compensation arises immediately on the breach of a trustee's duty not to make unauthorized payments from the trust fund. As Lord Browne-Wilkinson stated in *Target Holdings Ltd v Redferns*:

> A trustee who wrongly pays away trust money, like a trustee who makes an unauthorised investment, commits a breach of trust and comes under an immediate duty to remedy such breach.[15]

Outside the field of trusts, secondary rights to equitable compensation may also arise from breaches of confidence, fiduciary duties such as those owed by a solicitor to his client or a principal to his agent, or other equitable duties such as breaches of covenants running only in equity or equitable leases.

[9] *Bartlett v Barclays Bank Trust Co Ltd (No 2)* [1980] 1 Ch 539, 546.
[10] See Chapter 8 p 145.
[11] Chambers (n 8 above), 21–3; *Target Holdings Ltd v Redferns* [1996] 1 AC 421, 438–439 (HL).
[12] Ibid 434–435; *Bartlett v Barclays Bank Trust Co Ltd (No 2)* [1980] 1 Ch 539.
[13] *Nocton v Lord Ashburton* [1914] AC 932, 952 (HL); *Seager v Copydex Ltd* [1967] 1 WLR 924 (CA).
[14] Tilbury (n 1 above), [3247]–[3248]; Chambers (n 8 above), 13–16.
[15] [1996] 1 AC 421, 437 (HL). See also *Youyang v Pty Ltd v Minter Ellison Morris Fletcher* (2003) 212 CLR 484 (HCA).

Before the final award is given, the content of the secondary right may need to be quantified, particularly where more than just restoration of assets is required. Whereas rights to damages for breach of contract or for torts are shaped by reference to detailed and longstanding rules as to causation, remoteness, and mitigation, the approach in relation to secondary rights arising from breaches of equitable duties is a little different. 'The detailed rules of equity as to causation and the quantification of loss differ, at least ostensibly, from those applicable at common law. But the principles underlying both systems are the same.'[16] Notably, it is said that the rules of remoteness do not apply to equitable compensation.[17] Furthermore, the quantum of a secondary equitable right to compensation is not fixed at the date of the breach.[18] 'The quantum is fixed at the date of judgment at which date, according to the circumstances then pertaining, the compensation is assessed at the figure then necessary to put the trust estate or the beneficiary back into the position it would have been in had there been no breach.'[19]

(b) Beneficiary's secondary right to have the trust fund restored

A secondary right to compensation arising from a breach of trust does not always require the beneficiaries to be paid directly. In most cases, 'the obligation of a defaulting trustee is essentially that of effecting restitution to the trust estate.'[20] Again restitution ought to be read here in the loose sense of restoration to an earlier position.[21] The goal of this secondary duty is actually the making good of a loss irrespective of the defendant's gain, in other words, compensation.

For example, a trustee is under a positive primary duty 'to take such steps as a prudent businessman would have taken to maintain and increase the value of the trust fund'.[22] A failure to receive assets that the trustee ought to have received gives rise to a secondary duty to account on the basis of wilful default[23] and a secondary duty to restore or replenish the fund. As stated previously, the quantum of this particular secondary right to compensation may be determined by the mechanism of an account on the basis of wilful default. An order requiring an account on the basis of wilful default is usually also accompanied by an order for the payment of money, namely, the shortfall attributable to the breach of primary duty. The latter remedy is essentially an award of equitable compensation which replicates the secondary duty to restore the fund.

[16] *Target Holdings Ltd v Redferns* [1996] 1 AC 421, 432 (HL) (Lord Browne-Wilkinson).

[17] *Re Dawson* [1966] 2 NSWR 443. But see S. Elliott and C. Mitchell, 'Remedies for Dishonest Assistance' (2004) 67 *MLR* 16, 29.

[18] However, though common law damages are assessed at the date of the breach, this is not the invariable rule: A. Burrows, *Remedies for Torts and Breach of Contract* (2nd edn., London: Butterworths, 1994), 107–19.

[19] *Re Dawson* [1966] 2 NSWR 443, 437.

[20] *Bartlett v Barclays Bank Trust Co Ltd (No 2)* [1980] 1 Ch 539, 546 (Brightman J).

[21] See n 14 above.

[22] *Nestle v National Westminster Bank Plc* [1993] 1 WLR 1260, 1283 (CA) (Leggatt LJ).

[23] See p 183 below.

Both types of the remedy are subject to the usual equitable bars such as acquiescence and delay.[24]

4 Enforcement of the remedy

An award of equitable compensation, being a money judgment, is enforced in the same manner as an award of damages.

C Orders Giving Effect to Secondary Rights to an Account

In Chapter 10, we examined the order for a common account[25] and found that this order replicates the accounting party's primary duty to render an account. In this section we will consider orders which replicate a secondary duty to render an account, that is, a duty arising from a wrong. There are two cases to discuss: (1) accounts on the basis of wilful default; and (2) accounts of profits.

1 Order for an account on the basis of wilful default

(a) Form of the order

An order directing an account on the basis of wilful default takes the following form:

> AND IT IS ORDERED. . .that the following Inquiry and Accounts be made and taken that is to say:
>
> . . .
>
> An Account of such of the money or funds comprised in the Settlement or from time to time subject to the Trusts thereof as have been possessed or received by the Defendant C.D. or by any person on his behalf or to his order or which might without his wilful neglect or default have been so possessed or received. . .[26]

(b) Nature of the remedy

On a common account, the trustees are only charged with the assets they actually received, that is, only such assets can be added on the receipts side of the account. The trustees are not charged with the assets they should have received if they had not breached their duty to act as prudent trustees ought to. But an order for an account on the basis of wilful default entitles the claimant to a roving inquiry before a master to determine what assets the trustees 'might

[24] *Day v Mead* [1987] 2 NZLR 433, 462 (NZCA); But not all bars that apply to specific performance or injunctions are appropriate for monetary remedies: *Surrey County Council v Bredero Homes Ltd* [1993] 1 WLR 1361, 1370 (CA) (Steyn LJ).

[25] See Chapter 10 p 142ff.

[26] *Atkin's Court Forms* (2nd edn., 2000 Issue) Vol 41 [122]. See also [123] based on *Keech v Sandford* (1726) Set Cas t King 61, 65 ER 223.

have received but for their wilful default or neglect', that is, if they had not breached this primary duty.[27]

Apart from its broader ambit, the other advantage of this remedy over a common account is that it places a heavier burden on the accounting party. As Austin J stated in *Glazier v Australian Men's Health (No 2)*:

> An order for accounts based on wilful default has the effect of casting a much more substantial burden of proof on the accounting party than applies in the case of common accounts. On a falsification, the onus is on the accounting party to justify the account.[28]

That is, if the beneficiary challenges an item entered on the disbursements side of the account, the accounting party must show why it should not be struck out.

(c) Nature of the substantive right replicated

To obtain the remedy, the beneficiary must plead and prove an instance of 'wilful default' being 'an omission by the trustee to do something which, as a prudent trustee, he ought to have done'[29], or more narrowly, a failure to receive assets that he ought to have received.[30] Whereas a common account 'supposes no misconduct', an account on the basis of wilful default is 'entirely grounded on misconduct'.[31] Thus, the trustee's duty to account 'for money he could with reasonable diligence have received'[32] may be said to be a secondary duty arising from this wrong. The secondary right to which it correlates is then replicated in an order for an account on the basis of wilful default.

The court may refuse an order for a roving inquiry in relation to the administration of the *whole* fund where 'the past conduct of the trustees' does not 'give rise to a reasonable prima facie inference that other breaches of trust not yet known to the plaintiff or the court have occurred'.[33]

(d) Consequential remedy (equitable compensation)

Where an order for an account on the basis of wilful default is made, a consequential remedy is also given by the court in the form of an order which replicates the accounting party's secondary duty to restore the fund,[34] that is, to make good any shortfall revealed by the accounting process. This consequential order does not differ from an award of equitable compensation, either in form or substance, and should be characterized as such. The old notion that equity did not 'compensate' and the new notion that 'equitable compensation' is widely

[27] *Re Stevens* [1898] 1 Ch 162, 172 (CA). [28] [2001] NSWSC 6 [42] (Austin J).
[29] *Bartlett v Barclays Bank Trust Co Ltd (No 2)* [1980] 1 Ch 539, 546 (Brightman J).
[30] Chambers (n 8 above), 18–19.
[31] *Partington v Reynolds* (1858) 4 Drew 253, 255–256; 62 ER 98, 99.
[32] *Armitage v Nurse* [1998] Ch 241, 252 (CA) (Millett LJ).
[33] *Re Tebbs* [1976] 1 WLR 924, 930 (Slade J). [34] See p 181 above.

available are reconciled when it is acknowledged that a compensatory response has been concealed behind accounts on the basis of wilful default because the consequential orders to pay have received insufficient attention.[35]

Furthermore such a consequential order could be labelled an award of equitable compensatory 'damages' because it is an order for the payment of money in substitution for the performance of a primary duty.

2 Order for an account of profits

(a) Form of the order

An order for an account of profits may take the following form where shares have been obtained in breach of fiduciary duty:

AND IT IS ORDERED that the following Account and Inquiry be taken and made that is to say:

1. An Account of the profits come to the hands of the Defendants E. F. and G. H. and each of them from the shares
2. An Inquiry as to what sum is proper to be allowed to the Defendants E. F. and G. H. or either of them in respect of their or his work and skill in obtaining the shares and the profits in respect thereof[36]

An order for an account of profits for passing off may provide:

IT IS ORDERED THAT. . .(2). this matter shall be referred to the Master to take an account of those profits made by the business of the Defendants carried on under the name 'L. S. Grunts Chicago Pizza Co.' or any other name including the phrase 'Chicago Pizza' from........ 20........ down to the date when the Defendants ceased to employ such name which are properly attributable to the use by the Defendants of such name in the said business[37]

In the *Blake* case, where an account of profits and a consequential order for payment were awarded for a breach of contract, it was held that the order of the Court of Appeal was to be varied so as to 'declare that the Attorney General is entitled to be paid a sum equal to whatever amount is due and owing to Blake from Jonathan Cape under the publishing agreement of 4 May 1989.'[38]

[35] But now see S. Elliott, 'Compensation Claims Against Trustees' (DPhil Thesis Oxford University 2002); S. Elliott and C. Mitchell, 'Remedies for Dishonest Assistance' (2004) 67 *MLR* 16.

[36] *Atkin's Court Forms* (2nd edn., 2000 Issue) Vol 41 [125]. This example is based on *Boardman v Phipps* [1967] 2 AC 46 (HL).

[37] *Atkin's Court Forms* (2nd edn., 2001 Issue) Vol 37 [467] based on the order made by the trial judge in *My Kinda Town v Soll* [1983] RPC 15.

[38] *Attorney General v Blake* [2001] 1 AC 268, 290 (HL).

(b) *Nature of the remedy*

An account of profits is a mechanism 'to determine as accurately as possible the true measure of the profit or benefit obtained'[39] in breach of a primary duty.[40] It allows the amount of profits earned in breach of duty to be ascertained and distinguished from profits derived from sources other than the breach of duty. The claimant is not entitled to the latter.[41] The accounting need not be a complicated process. As Lord Nicholls stated in *Attorney General v Blake*:

> These formal steps may be capable of being short-circuited. Despite the niceties and formalities once associated with taking an account, the amount payable under an account of profits need not be any more elaborately or precisely calculated than damages.[42]

Where an order for an account of profits is made, the court usually also makes an order which replicates the accounting party's secondary duty to pay the profits to the person to whom the duty to account is owed or into the fund which the accounting party is charged with administering.[43] It will be argued below that this consequential remedy should be characterized as a separate remedy under its own label.

(c) *Nature of substantive right replicated*

An order for an account of profits replicates a secondary duty of the accountable party to render an account of profits. As Chambers states in respect of trustees who are one class of accountable parties, 'the trustees have a primary duty to account for their management of trust assets and also have a secondary duty to provide information about activities that conflict with their duty of loyal service to the trust.'[44] Such a secondary right arises not only in the case of wrongs committed by trustees but also from other equitable wrongs and, possibly, from breaches of contract.

(i) **Arising from an equitable wrong**

A secondary right to an account of profits may arise from the breach of certain primary duties originating in equity. Such duties include a duty of confidence,[45] a director's fiduciary duty not to make an unauthorized profit from his position,[46] a trustee's duty not to profit from the trust,[47] and duties correlating with intellectual property rights.

[39] *Warman International Ltd v Dwyer* (1995) 182 CLR 544, 558 (HCA).
[40] An inquiry could be characterized as a similar mechanism to determine the measure or quantum of compensation to which a person is entitled.
[41] *Vyse v Foster* (1872) LR 8 Ch App 309, 333–334 (CA).
[42] [2001] 1 AC 268, 288 (HL).
[43] See p 182 above.
[44] Chambers (n 8 above), 27.
[45] *Attorney General v Guardian Newspapers Ltd (No 2)* [1990] 1 AC 109 (HL).
[46] *Regal (Hastings) Ltd v Gulliver* (1942) [1967] 2 AC 134n (HL).
[47] *Boardman v Phipps* [1967] 2 AC 46 (HL).

An order for an account of profits in relation to recognized equitable wrongs is given almost as a matter of course.[48] Of course, having originated in equity, the remedy is subject to the usual equitable bars such as unclean hands, acquiescence, and delay. Thus the court will refuse the order where the claimant stands by while the defendant takes risks and expends effort to make profits.[49]

(ii) Arising from a breach of contract

The watershed case of *Attorney General v Blake*[50] concerned a former spy who stood to profit by writing a book which disclosed information in breach of a contractual undertaking to the Crown not to do so. The House of Lords held that the Crown was entitled to an account of profits. Lord Nicholls stated that an account of profits would be available for breach of contract in 'exceptional' cases where 'the plaintiff had a legitimate interest in preventing the defendant's profit making activity' and where other remedies were inadequate.[51]

But can one sensibly speak of a secondary right to an account of profits post-*Blake*? Lord Nicholls cautioned:

> No fixed rules can be prescribed. The court will have regard to all the circumstances, including the subject matter of the contract, the purpose of the contractual provision which has been breached, the circumstances in which the breach occurred, the consequences of the breach and the circumstances in which relief is being sought. A useful general guide, although not exhaustive, is whether the plaintiff had a legitimate interest in preventing the defendant's profit-making activity and, hence, in depriving him of his profit.
>
> It would be difficult, and unwise, to attempt to be more specific.[52]

Though such language may seem incompatible with the existence of a 'right' to an account of profits and a consequential remedy, it is submitted that the discretion reserved by Lord Nicholls is a rule-building discretion which will narrow over time rather than a rule-failure discretion which will always be exercised afresh.[53] This is made clear by Lord Steyn:

> But since I recognise that it would be wrong to create a remedy simply to cover this case, it is right that I should explain the specific considerations which lead me to conclude that it is right on a principled basis to develop the law in a way which covers this case and other cases sharing materially similar features.[54]

Thus, it seems that where events materially similar to those in the *Blake* case occur, a secondary right to an account of profits and a consequent secondary right to restitutionary damages do arise. Just what events are 'materially similar' is a question of substantive law. The substantive law will be incrementally

[48] *Attorney General v Blake* [2001] 1 AC 268 (HL) 287.
[49] *Re Jarvis* [1958] 2 All ER 336, 341–342.
[50] [2001] 1 AC 268 (HL). See also *Experience Hendrix LLC v PPX Enterprises Inc* [2003] EWCA 323 (CA).
[51] Ibid 286.
[52] Ibid 286.
[53] Chapter 6 p 87.
[54] Ibid 291.

refined in subsequent cases according to the ordinary processes of judicial development. Lord Nicholls, remarks are a guide to that future development. They should be read as meaning that in the *Blake* case itself it was premature to prescribe specific rules and not as denying that such rules will evolve through precedent.

(d) Consequential remedy (equitable restitution)

A consequential order granted with an order for an account of profits for passing off may provide:

> Further the Defendants shall pay to the Claimant the said profits together with such interest thereon as the Master shall think fit.[55]

In the *Blake* case, Lord Nicholls referred to the consequential remedy when he stated that 'The Crown is entitled, on the taking of the account, to a money judgment which can then be enforced by attachment of the debt in the usual way.'[56]

In *Regal (Hastings) Ltd v Gulliver*[57] the court repeatedly referred to the respondents' liability to account but it did not actually order an account of profits. The respondents were not ordered to actually render an account. The court held that it was proper to 'enter judgment as against each of these four respondents for a sum of £1,402 1s. 8d. with interest. . .'. It is unhelpful and confusing to insist on calling such an order for payment 'an account of profits' when no account is to be rendered. The consequential order for the payment of money must be characterized as a separate remedy and given a different label. The two remedies are entirely different as they replicate entirely different rights. They could be granted in two separate documents and at different times.

This consequential order may be characterized as an award of equitable restitution, in opposition to an award of equitable compensation. This consequential order gives effect to a secondary right to restitution[58] which arises from a breach of duty,[59] such as the duty not to profit from one's fiduciary position.

Furthermore, such an order could be labelled an award of equitable restitutionary 'damages' because it is an order for the payment of money in substitution for the performance of a primary duty. This is suggested despite the decision in

[55] *Atkin's Court Forms* (2nd edn., 2001 Issue) Vol 37 [467]. Obviously the duty created by this utterance is entirely different from the duty to account created by the utterance that is reproduced in the text to n 55.

[56] [2001] 1 AC 268, 288 (HL).

[57] (1942) [1967] 2 AC 134n, 152 (HL).

[58] More accurately 'disgorgement' according to Edelman (n 3 above), 72.

[59] An account of profits is merely a mechanism for quantifying this secondary right to restitution just as an account on the basis of wilful default is merely a mechanism for quantifying a secondary right to compensation: see p 183 above.

the case of *Watson v Holliday*.[60] There the question arose whether an account of profits was a 'demand in the nature of unliquidated damages arising otherwise than by reason of contract' so as to be excluded from proof in a bankruptcy by section 31 of the Bankruptcy Act 1869 (UK). The account of profits was held not to be 'damages' for historical reasons.[61] However, if we view the order for an account of profits as providing a quantification mechanism then the secondary right to the payment that is to be quantified should be characterized as a right to 'damages'. It is no different, apart from its goal, from a secondary right to the payment of compensation at common law which is called a right to damages and also often requires quantification by the court.

3 Enforcement of the remedies

Both an order for an account on the basis of wilful default and an order for an account of profits are enforced in the same way as an order for a common account.[62] As stated above, the consequential remedy is enforced in the same way as an award of damages.

D Mandatory Injunction to Undo or Prevent a Wrong

1 Form of the order

A mandatory injunction to undo a wrong, also known as a restorative injunction, forbade the defendant from permitting the continuance of a wrongful state of things. The court would state: 'Do not permit the continuance of any wall to the injury of the plaintiff's right of light' thereby requiring a defendant to pull down an existing wall.[63] But there has been a stylistic change and such a mandatory injunction is now put in the form of a direct order to do the required act.[64]

The form of a mandatory injunction to undo or prevent a wrong is governed by the same rules as a mandatory injunction which replicates a primary right. It has the same advantages and the same effect on substantive rights.[65] Material which relates to all injunctions need not be repeated here.

An example of a mandatory restorative injunction provides:

[IT IS ORDERED or IT IS THIS DAY ADJUDGED] that the Defendant do remove from the Claimant's land mentioned in paragraph 3 of the Particulars of Claim so much

[60] (1882) 20 ChD 780, this point was not dealt with on appeal 50 LJ Ch 543 (CA). See also *Attorney General v Blake* [2001] 1 AC 268, 284–286 (HL) where Lord Nicholls preferred 'to avoid the unhappy expression "restitutionary damages".'

[61] P. B. H. Birks, *Restitution — The Future* (Leichhardt NSW: Federation Press, 1992), 18.

[62] See Chapter 8 p 146.

[63] F. W. Maitland, *Equity: A Course of Lectures* (Cambridge: Cambridge University Press, 1936), 320–1.

[64] *Jackson v Normanby Brick Co* [1899] 1 Ch 438 (CA).

[65] See Chapter 8 p 125.

of the wall and fences and steps and staircases therein mentioned as stand on or over the Claimant's said land including the verandah but excluding the main walls forming the north-western corner of........ Cottage therein referred to BUT the operation of this Order is suspended until after........ 20........[66]

An order for delivery up for destruction or destruction on oath is an order which is very closely related to a mandatory injunction to prevent a wrong. It may provide:

IT IS ORDERED. . .(2) that the Defendant deliver up to the Claimant or destroy upon oath all synthetic trundlehumpers in the Defendant's possession custody or power which infringe the Patent[67]

2 Nature of the remedy

A mandatory injunction *to undo* a wrong functions as a corrective remedy. By definition, this type of mandatory injunction cannot be obtained before the wrong has occurred because there is nothing to undo. For instance, a mandatory injunction for pipes to be removed could not be obtained before they are laid. The proper course would be to seek a prohibitory injunction to prevent the defendant from breaching his primary duty not to lay the pipes.

However, the courts also grant a second type of mandatory injunction, a mandatory injunction *to prevent* a wrong, not just by requiring the defendant to forebear from acting but by requiring the defendant to act to remove a danger that may cause an infringement of the claimant's right. In the leading case of *Redland Bricks Ltd v Morris*, the defendant was ordered to carry out works to prevent a landslide that would affect the claimant's land.[68] Lawson draws a useful distinction:

[O]ne should distinguish between: (a) mandatory injunctions which order the removal or destruction of something already done, and which therefore are destructive in character; and (b) mandatory injunctions which order precautionary measures to be taken.[69]

The former are granted to undo a wrong; the latter to prevent one.

Precautionary measures can also include the destruction of goods so as to prevent the possibility of a future infringement of intellectual property rights. In *Mergenthaler v Linotype Co v Intertype Co Ltd* Russell J stated:

[S]o long as there is still what I might call infringing stock in the possession of the infringer, he may be subject to too serious and grave a temptation and may therefore

[66] *Atkin's Court Forms* (2nd edn., 2001 Issue) Vol 17(1) [208]. See also [209] and *Kennard v Cory Brothers & Co* [1922] 2 Ch 1, 15 (CA).

[67] *Atkin's Court Forms* (2nd edn., 2001 Issue) Vol 29(1) [127]; see also Vol 12(2) [474].

[68] [1970] AC 652 (HL).

[69] F. H. Lawson, *Remedies of English Law* (2nd edn., London: Butterworth & Co, 1980), 202.

be tempted to commit a breach of the injunction which he would otherwise not commit. Accordingly, in order to assist the plaintiff and as a relief ancillary to the injunction he has obtained, the Court may in its discretion make an order for destruction or delivery up of infringing articles.[70]

As Burrows points out, it is the use of the infringing goods that is the claimant's main concern, not their mere existence.[71]

A mandatory injunction may be suspended. But the courts appear to be becoming more cautious in granting suspensions.[72]

The courts have power to grant interlocutory mandatory injunctions.[73]

3 Nature of the substantive right replicated

As stressed in Chapter 8, the courts have repeatedly held that an injunction gives effect to rights.[74] But does a mandatory restorative injunction replicate a secondary right? It has been held that 'Every one of this class of cases must depend on its own peculiar circumstances',[75] though the grant of such a remedy was later taken to require no more care and caution than the grant of a prohibitory injunction.[76] However, Lord Upjohn stated in *Redland Bricks Ltd v Morris*[77] that 'The grant of a mandatory injunction is, of course, entirely discretionary and unlike a negative injunction can never be "as of course." '[78]

This can be taken to mean that the claimant has no substantive right that the defendant do the positive acts to undo or prevent a wrong until the court creates such a right by making a court order. This was the view taken in the controversial case of *Law Debenture Trust Corporation v Ural Caspian Oil Corporation Ltd*.[79] The claimant owned shares in four Russian companies, the first to fourth defendants, whose only substantial assets were rights to compensation for assets that they had lost as a result of the Revolution of 1917. The claimant sold its shares to L. L undertook by contract to procure that the Russian companies pursue the compensation claims and pay any compensation received to the claimants. L also contracted not to sell the shares without requiring the purchaser to give the same undertaking. L sold the shares to the fifth defendant but, in flagrant breach of contract, did not obtain the required undertaking from the purchaser. The fifth defendant then sold the shares to the sixth defendant. The fifth and sixth defendants had knowledge of L's breach of contract as they were under common control. The trial judge found that the claimant had a cause of action against the sixth defendant.

[70] (1926) 43 RPC 381, 382.
[71] Burrows (n 18 above), 459.
[72] See Chapter 8 p 124.
[73] *London & Manchester Assurance v O & H Construction* [1989] 29 EG 65.
[74] See Chapter 8 p 127.
[75] *Isenberg v East India House Estate Co* (1863) 46 ER 637, 641.
[76] *Smith v Smith* (1875) LR 20 Eq 500, 504 (Jessel MR).
[77] [1970] AC 652 (HL).
[78] Ibid 665.
[79] [1995] Ch 152 (CA).

The court of appeal disagreed. It held that there was a cause of action against the fifth defendant based on its breach of its duty not to interfere with the contractual relations between L and the claimant and a restorative mandatory injunction may have been available to order a retransfer of shares by the fifth defendant to L. But Sir Thomas Bingham and Beldam LJ held that the fifth defendant was not under a duty to retransfer the shares until the injunction was actually granted.[80] Saville LJ took the same view:

In the present case the suggested legal right [that the sixth defendant procured the breach of] is the secondary right to obtain an order against [the fifth defendant] for the return of the shares. [The sixth defendant's counsel] submitted that until such an order was actually obtained, it was not unlawful for [the fifth defendant] to dispose of the shares, so that in truth at the material time there was no violation of the plaintiff's legal rights. . .The plaintiff has to assert that it had the right, from the time of the original tort, to an injunction requiring [the fifth defendant] to transfer back the shares. An injunction is a discretionary remedy. As to this the plaintiff submits that on the pleaded facts the court would have exercised its discretion in its favour. Thus it asserts the existence of a legal right and obligation predating the grant of such an injunction. . .It seems to me that the right asserted by the plaintiff only arises when the court makes the order in question.[81]

If this decision is correct then mandatory restorative injunctions to undo transfers in breach of contract are transformative remedies. The claimant has no right to a retransfer against the person who procured the breach and the contract-breaker. The duty to retransfer depends entirely on an exercise of the court's discretion[82] and upon the claimant's good fortune in discovering the breach and getting to the court in time. The creation of such a duty would be a gift from the court.

However, not all mandatory restorative injunctions are transformative. The authorities support the view that a mandatory restorative injunction to remove an encroaching structure gives effect to a substantive right to its removal. In *London & Manchester Assurance v O & H Construction*[83] Harman J stated:

I cannot see that any court could ever say that a trespass by the building of a structure on a neighbour's land, in circumstances where the neighbour has in no way encouraged but has at all times protested against the building, where the neighbour would have had great difficulty in establishing the boundary after the works had been started, and where the neighbour had behaved in an entirely reasonable way, should not be rectified by removal of the structure. In my judgment, no court could conceivably refuse to that neighbour the right to possession of his own land and the right to removal of structures wrongly placed on it. As it seems to me, there is not a question of discretion; it is a question of right; and in my view there is no question of arguable case and balance of convenience so far as concerns the trespass.

[80] [1995] Ch 152 (CA), 166, 170. [81] Ibid 172–173.

[82] This suggests it is a rule-failure discretion to be exercised afresh from case to case.

[83] [1989] 29 EG 65, 67.

Similarly in *Harrow London Borough Council v Donohue*,[84] the claimant council sought a mandatory injunction for the defendant to remove part of a garage that was built on its land. At first instance, the trial judge approached the matter as one of discretion and awarded damages. Waite LJ, with whom Hirst LJ and Sir Stephen Brown P agreed, reversed his decision stating:

> Was there really any discretion at all? If a defendant acts in total breach of the plaintiff's proprietary rights, by dispossessing him altogether through the erection of building works which have the effect of excluding him totally from the land to which he has title, does the court have any real choice in the matter? Is it not rather the plaintiff who has the option; either of accepting the building works as an accretion to his title. . .or, alternatively, of coming to court and insisting as of right upon either an order for possession of the encroached land or an order for demolition of the encroaching building works? If the plaintiff makes the latter choice, does the court have any discretionary power beyond the right perhaps to make a choice as between those last two remedies?. . .[T]he plaintiffs do indeed have an option. . .[If they take their remedy at court] they are entitled as of right to one or other of two remedies that is to say an order for possession, or to a mandatory order for the taking down of the offending building. The court may well retain a limited discretion, according to the circumstances of each particular case, in making a choice between those two remedies. . .[T]he case appears to me to be plainly one where the grant of a mandatory injunction was inevitable. . .[85]

It seems clear that the courts, at least in the case of trespassing structures, are here recognizing a substantive right to the performance of acts to undo the wrong. It is a secondary right arising from a breach of the primary duty not to interfere with the claimant's possession. It is submitted that it is desirable as a matter of policy for such a right to exist. But it must be emphasized that the recognition of such a substantive right does not oblige the court to replicate it in every case. Warrington LJ stated in *Kennard v Cory Brothers & Co*,[86] where a mandatory restorative injunction was given to undo the effects of a tort:

> There is a difference, which I think has been ignored, if I may say so with respect, by [counsel for the defendant], between imposing or recognizing by judgment an obligation to repair and enforcing it by a mandatory injunction, and the Court will have to consider, whenever the plaintiffs come for a mandatory injunction, the terms in which that injunction is asked for and whether it is one which can properly be granted.[87]

Clearly, it is open to the court to recognize a substantive right without replicating it in the particular case. It can take this course where a recognized bar to the remedy is found to operate. It routinely does so in the case of decrees of specific performance when it recognizes a contractual right but declines to grant the decree in the particular circumstances due to the operation of one of the usual bars.

[84] [1995] 1 EGLR 257 (CA). [85] Ibid 259. [86] [1922] 2 Ch 1 (CA).
[87] Ibid 18, see also 12 and 16.

Similarly, there a number of factors, or bars, that the court takes into account before granting a mandatory injunction to undo or prevent a wrong. The remedy may be refused because of the state of completion of the infringing works.[88] But this bar may not be applicable where the defendant was given a notice of objection but nonetheless persisted with the work or, *a fortiori*, increased his efforts so to 'steal a march' on the claimant and the court.[89] The court may refuse the remedy on the basis of hardship where the infringement is not unreasonable and the detriment to the defendant is out of proportion to the benefit to the claimant.[90] Mandatory restorative injunctions are also subject to the usual equitable bars such as unclean hands, acquiescence, and delay,[91] or the difficulty of supervision.

(a) Arising from a breach of contract

A mandatory injunction may be granted to undo the effects of a breach of contract. Though in earlier cases there was palpably less emphasis on discretion,[92] the courts have come to lay great stress on the discretion involved in the grant of such a remedy.[93] In *Wakeham v Wood*,[94] the defendant, in flagrant disregard of the claimant's rights under a restrictive covenant, constructed a building blocking the claimant's view. The Court of Appeal held that an order requiring demolition ought to have been made. Watkins LJ stated:

> It must of course be acknowledged that in the vast majority of cases of breaches of restrictive covenants it will be inevitable, almost inevitable that the court will exercise its discretion so as to grant the mandatory injunction sought but that result will nevertheless have been achieved by the exercise of discretion.[95]

It is submitted that this discretion should be construed as no more than the residual discretion inherent in open-textured rules — rules which are subject to

[88] *Durrell v Pritchard* (1865) 1 Ch App 244.

[89] *Daniel v Ferguson* [1981] 2 Ch 27 (CA); *Von Joel v Hornsey* [1895] 2 Ch 774 (CA).

[90] *Redland Bricks Ltd v Morris* [1970] AC 652, 665 (HL). Lawson suggests that this bar only applies to mandatory injunctions to prevent a wrong, not to undo a wrong: Lawson (n 69 above), 202.

[91] *Senior v Pawson* (1866) LR 3 Eq 330; *Shaw v Applegate* [1977] 1 WLR 970 (CA).

[92] *Goodson v Richardson* (1874) 9 Ch App 221 (CA); *Morris v Grant* (1875) 24 WR 55; In *Lord Manners v Johnson* (1875) 1 Ch D 673 Hall V-C granted a mandatory injunction to remove bow windows built in breach of covenant, stating at 681, 'I see no reason why the Court should not exercise its jurisdiction by a mandatory injunction as to the bow windows. I cannot listen to suggestions of hardship and loss of value, and so forth.' In *Achilli v Tovell* [1927] 2 Ch 243 Austbury J held, at 247–248, 'In my opinion I have no jurisdiction or discretion to force the plaintiff Achilli against her will to accept damages in lieu of an injunction. On the authorities she is plainly entitled to a mandatory order if she asks for it. . .I have no jurisdiction or discretion to refuse a mandatory order. There must therefore be a mandatory order to pull down so much of this wall as materially restricts or interferes with the access of light and air enjoyed by these windows before the recent raising.' But in *Sharp v Harrison* [1922] 1 Ch 502, Austbury J had refused a mandatory injunction for the breach of a restrictive covenant by the construction of a window because the defendant had given certain undertakings as to the use of the window.

[93] *Shepherd Homes Ltd v Sandham* [1971] Ch 340, 351.

[94] (1982) 43 P & CR 40 (CA).

[95] Ibid 46.

further refinement in subsequent cases. Nonetheless, it is difficult to say that a secondary duty to undo the effects of the breach of contract arises from a breach, except perhaps in the case of a breach of a restrictive convenant where the circumstances are not distinguishable from a decided case. But in most cases, mandatory injunctions for breaches of contract are still transformative remedies. The rights which are created do not replicate any prior substantive rights.

(b) Arising from a tort

As has already been argued, a secondary duty to undo the effects of a trespass to land may arise. In such a case, a mandatory injunction merely replicates that secondary right. Since the injunction is an equitable remedy, there is some residual discretion at play based on the usual equitable bars and the power to award damages in lieu.[96]

However, in the case of other torts it seems that at present the remedy is transformative. As the *Ural Caspian* case decided, a breach of the primary duty not to interfere with contractual relations does not generate a secondary right to a retransfer of property. The court may, exercising a remedial discretion, create such a remedy; for example, by ordering that land transferred to a tortfeasor in breach of contract be retransferred to the contract-breaker to undo the tort of interference with contractual relations (and the breach of contract).[97]

(c) Arising from an equitable wrong

A mandatory injunction ordering delivery up or destruction of documents containing confidential information may be obtained.[98] This is a mandatory injunction to undo a wrong. It may be arguable that a secondary right to the delivery up arises when the equitable wrong of breach of confidence occurs but that its replication involves a degree of residual discretion similar to that involved in the grant of a mandatory injunction to under the effects of a trespass to land.

(d) Arising from an infringement of an intellectual property right

Where there is an actual or apprehended infringement of intellectual property rights, a mandatory injunction may be given which orders the delivery up for destruction, destruction on oath or forfeiture of goods[99] or the means of making such goods[100] or the alteration of the infringing features of such goods.[101] Such a

[96] *Kelsen v Imperial Tobacco Co Ltd* [1957] 2 QB 334, 346.

[97] *Esso Petroleum Co Ltd v Kingswood Motors (Addlestone) Ltd* [1974] QB 142.

[98] *Alperton Rubber Co v Manning* (1917) 86 LJ Ch 377; *Ansell Rubber Co Pty Ltd v Allied Rubber Industries Pty Ltd* [1972] RPC 811.

[99] See authorities in Burrows (n 18 above), 458–9 and Copyright, Designs and Patents Act 1988 (UK) ss 99, 114, 230 and 231.

[100] *Rosedale Associated Manufacturers Ltd v Airfix Products Ltd* [1956] RPC 306.

[101] *Slazenger & Sons v Feltham & Co* (1889) 6 RPC 531.

remedy may in the future be found to replicate secondary rights arising from infringements of intellectual property rights, such as copyright, patents, trade-marks, or registered designs. However, at this stage of the law's development, it may be more accurate to characterize a mandatory injunction ordering such delivery up or alteration as a remedy which creates an entirely new right when it is given, that is, as a transformative remedy.

4 Enforcement of the remedy

A mandatory injunction to undo a wrong is enforceable in the same manner as any other mandatory injunction.[102]

[102] See Chapter 8 p 133 above.

12

Replicating Secondary Rights: Statutory Remedies

A Introduction

Statutory remedies which replicate primary rights were examined in Chapter 9. This chapter deals with three statutory (or statute-based) remedies which replicate secondary rights: orders for the recovery of the value of goods, awards of damages in lieu of specific relief, and declarations of secondary rights.

B Order for the Recovery of the Value of Goods (or the Goods Themselves)

As stated in Chapter 9, where there has been a wrongful interference with goods, the court has power to make an order for the delivery up of goods, an order in alternative form for the recovery of the goods or their value or an order for the damages representing the value of the goods.[1] In Chapter 9 we examined the first order and the second in so far as it replicates the primary right to possession of the goods. The second order in so far as it replicates the secondary right to the payment of the value of the goods and the third order will be examined here.

1 Form of the order

As stated in Chapter 9, the core provision of an order in alternative form states:

District judge [master] .... ordered
that you return the goods to the claimant or that you pay £................, their value, to reach the claimant by................

And also that you pay (£................ damage) and £................ for costs to reach the claimant by........[2]

[1] Torts (Interference with Goods) Act 1977 (UK) s 3. See Chapter 9 p 153.

[2] Based on Form N32 Judgment for return of goods: CPR Part 4 PD Table 1.

An order for damages representing the value of the goods takes the same form as an award of damages.[3]

2 Nature of the remedy

The advantages of these remedies, in so far as they help to realize the claimant's right to the value of the goods, are similar to the advantages of awards of damages. Where the goods are available in the market, the claimant may prefer to have their value and to purchase a replacement rather than recovering the used goods from the defendant. An important feature of an order in alternative form or an order for damages for wrongful interference with goods is that the claimant has a priority in the defendant's insolvency because the order does not, without satisfaction, vest property in the goods in the defendant. The claimant retains ownership of the goods until the order is satisfied.[4]

3 Nature of the substantive right replicated

The remedies replicate the secondary right to payment of the value of the goods that arises at the time of the wrongful interference of goods, that is, at the time that the tort of conversion, trespass, or negligence is committed by the defendant. As Lord Templeman stated in *BBMB Finance (Hong Kong) Ltd v Eda Holdings Ltd*:

> The general rule is that a plaintiff whose property is irreversibly converted has vested in him a right to damages for conversion measured by the value of the property at the date of conversion.[5]

This secondary right to damages vests on the occurrence of the conversion.[6] For instance, 'the general position in relation to the conversion of a cheque is that the conversion gives the person entitled to the cheque a right to damages measured by the face value of the cheque.'[7] An award of damages in such a case replicates that secondary right.

4 Enforcement of the remedy

The remedy is enforced in the same way as an award of an agreed sum. However, in the case of an order in the alternative, the claimant may also apply for a writ of specific delivery to recover the goods themselves.[8]

[3] See Chapter 10 p 167; *Atkin's Court Forms* (2nd edn., 2000 Issue) Vol 39 [468].

[4] Torts (Interference with Goods) Act 1977 (UK) s 5(1). The legislation did not alter the position that had evolved at common law in relation to detinue and trover: *Brinsmead v Harrison* (1871) LR 6 CP 584 affirmed (1872) LR 7 CP 547; *Ellis v John Stenning & Son Ltd* [1932] 2 Ch 81 (CA); *General and Finance Facilities Ltd v Cook Cars (Romford) Ltd* [1963] 1 WLR 644 (CA).

[5] [1990] 1 WLR 409, 412 (PC).

[6] *Solloway v McLaughlin* [1938] AC 247, 257–258 (PC).

[7] *International Factors v Rodriguez* [1971] QB 351, 358 (CA).

[8] *General and Finance Facilities Ltd v Cook Cars (Romford) Ltd* [1963] 1 WLR 644 (CA); see Chapter 9 p 157.

C Award of Damages 'in Addition to' Specific Relief under Section 50 of the Supreme Court Act

1 Form of the order

An award of damages under section 50 of the Supreme Court Act 1981 (UK) takes the same form as an award of damages made at common law.[9]

2 Nature of the remedy

The High Court has statutory power to 'award damages in addition to, or in substitution for, an injunction or specific performance'.[10] This should be treated as conferring power to award two types of remedies: (a) damages 'in addition to' specific relief—such an award is a replicative remedy, at least in so far as it effectuates a common law right to damages; and (b) damages 'in substitution for' specific relief—such an award appears to be a transformative remedy.

When common law and equity were administered in different courts, a claimant seeking (1) a decree of specific performance or an injunction *and* (2) damages was forced to engage in two sets of litigation. He or she would have to seek replication of his primary right in a court of equity and replication of his or her secondary right to damages in a court of common law. Lord Cairns' Act was enacted to provide a mechanism for replicating the common law secondary right to damages by a court of equity.[11] It allowed the court to award damages 'in addition to' specific relief. As Lord Sumner stated in *Leeds Industrial Co-operative Society Ltd v Slack*:

> [I]ts object was to save the litigant from being harassed by the necessity for applying to two Courts for complete relief in respect of one wrong and from being "turned over," as the phrase was, by equity to law, if the case was not one for an injunction, or was a case for damages as well.[12]

The judicature reforms of the late nineteenth century alleviated most of this inconvenience and Lord Cairns' Act was repealed.[13]

However, the courts held that despite its repeal the jurisdiction it created survived and the relevant provision was re-enacted in the Supreme Court Act

[9] *Atkin's Court Forms* (2nd edn., 2001 Issue) Vol 17(1) [150–151]; see Chapter 10 p 167 above.

[10] Supreme Court Act 1981 (UK) s 50; the power was originally conferred by the Chancery Amendment Act 1858 (UK) s 2 which was also known as Lord Cairns' Act.

[11] Although the Act has been repealed, it is still in common to refer to an award of damages in lieu of or in addition to specific performance or an injunction as an award of damages under Lord Cairns' Act. Their alternative characterization as an award of 'equitable damages' is not adopted here as it implies that the remedy differs from common law damages. In many cases, the remedy itself is the same whether given in the court's common law jurisdiction or under the statutory power traceable to Lord Cairns' Act.

[12] [1924] AC 851, 870–871 (HL).

[13] Statute Law Revision and Civil Procedure Act 1883 (UK); Statute Law Revision Act 1898 (UK).

1981 (UK).[14] Why was the jurisdiction preserved? Lord Cairns' Act was construed as doing more than providing procedural advantages, it had also been held to expand the court's jurisdiction by allowing damages to be given where they would not be available at common law.[15]

As Lord Millett stated in *Jaggard v Sawyer*: 'Damages *in substitution for* an injunction. . .relate to the future, not the past, they inevitably extend beyond the damages to which the plaintiff may be entitled at law.'[16] The Act allowed equitable damages to be given where no common law secondary right to damages had yet arisen, that is, where a future breach of primary duty was threatened or where the continuance of an existing breach was anticipated. That is, it allowed the court to award damages 'in substitution for' specific relief. Such an award of damages for an anticipated breach seems to be a transformative remedy as the claimant does not appear to have a right to the payment of damages in lieu until the court exercises its discretion under the Act.[17] It is further discussed in Chapter 13.[18]

Furthermore, an award of damages under the Act can also be made where an obligation enforceable only in equity, such as a duty not to misuse confidential information, is breached.[19] Whether this is a replicative or transformative remedy depends on whether it can be said that a right to the payment of damages arises in such circumstances prior to a court order being made. An attempt to answer this question will not be made in this overview.

3 Nature of the substantive right replicated

An award of damages under section 50 of the Supreme Court Act 1981 (UK) for a past breach, that is 'in addition to' specific relief, may replicate the secondary common law right to compensatory damages. It may replicate the same right that an award of common law damages would have replicated. The content of that right would be determined by the same rules whether it was replicated in a common law award of damages or an award made under the statute.[20] Here equity follows the law.

An award of damages under the statute in relation to a past breach of a common law duty should be available as a matter of course because the claimant should not be in a worse position for seeking specific performance or an injunction than if no such remedy had been claimed, that is, if the claimant had only sought replication of his or her secondary right to damages at law.

[14] *Leeds Industrial Co-operative Society Ltd v Slack* [1924] AC 851, 862–863 (HL).

[15] Ibid 856, 865. The statutory jurisdiction also saved a premature claim for damages for breach of contract: *Oakacre Ltd v Claire Cleaners (Holdings) Ltd* [1982] 1 Ch 197.

[16] [1995] 1 WLR 269, 284 (CA) (emphasis added).

[17] *Jaggard v Sawyer* [1995] 1 WLR 269, 288 (CA) (Lord Millett) reproduced in Chapter 6 text to n 42.

[18] See Chapter 13 p 212.

[19] A. Tettenborn, *An Introduction to the Law of Obligations* (London: Butterworths, 1994), 225.

[20] *Johnson v Agnew* [1980] AC 367, 400 (HL).

4 Enforcement of the remedy

This remedy, being a money judgment, is enforced in the same way as other awards of damages.

D Declaration of a Secondary Right

1 Form of the order

The leading case of *Boardman v Phipps* provides an example of a declaration of a secondary right:

IT IS DECLARED that the Defendants E. F. and G. H. hold [5/18] of the [21,500] Ordinary Shares of £[1] each in........ Ltd mentioned in the Particulars of Claim as constructive trustees for the Claimant[21]

2 Nature of the remedy

The nature of a declaration has already been discussed in Chapter 9. It is unnecessary to reproduce that material here.

3 Nature of the substantive right replicated

Some representative examples of secondary rights which may be replicated in declarations will now be briefly discussed.

(a) Arising from a breach of contract

In *Louis Dreyfus & Cie v Parnaso Cia Naviera SA*[22] Lord Diplock granted a declaration that the defendant had breached a contract and that the damages amounted to particular sum. Such a declaration simply replicates the claimant's secondary right to the payment of damages that arose from the breach of contract. However, it does not actually order the payment of such damages.

(b) Arising from an equitable wrong

A declaration of a constructive trust often replicates secondary proprietary rights; that is, rights *in rem* arising from a breach of duty.[23] For example, in *Boardman v Phipps*[24] the defendants profited from knowledge and information obtained

[21] *Atkin's Court Forms* (2nd edn., 2000 Issue) Vol 41 [125]; *Boardman v Phipps* [1967] 2 AC 46 (HL).

[22] [1959] 1 QB 498 reversed on an unrelated point [1960] 2 QB 49 (CA). For the declarations made at first instance see [1959] 1 Lloyd's Rep 125.

[23] Secondary proprietary rights are further discussed in A. Pretto, 'Primary Rights and Rights *in Rem*' in P. B. H. Birks and A. Pretto (eds), *Themes in Comparative Law in Honour of Bernard Rudden* (Oxford: Oxford University Press, 2002), 76–7.

[24] [1967] 2 AC 46 (HL).

because of their fiduciary positions and in breach of the duty to avoid conflicts of interest. The shares which they acquired in breach of duty were held by them on constructive trust for the claimants.[25] The declaration of constructive trust which was made did no more than replicate this secondary proprietary right.[26]

Similarly in *Attorney General for Hong Kong v Reid*[27] a defendant agent who had taken bribes in breach of his fiduciary duties and used them to purchase land was found to hold the bribes and consequently the land on trust for his principal. 'As soon as the bribe was received, whether in cash or in kind, the false fiduciary held the bribe on a constructive trust for the person injured.'[28] A declaration of constructive trust in this case simply replicated the secondary right that the principal had acquired because of the wrong.

In cases such as these, the constructive trust is not being created by the court order. The remedy which is being granted is not transformative but is clearly replicative.

4 Enforcement of the remedy

A declaration is non-enforceable without further applications to court.[29] But where, for example, a constructive trust is declared, a consequential remedy is usually given at the same time, such as a mandatory injunction requiring the defendant to convey the trust property to the claimant.

[25] [1967] AC 46 117, (HL).
[26] See text to n 21 above.
[27] [1994] 1 AC 324 (PC).
[28] Ibid 331 (Lord Templeman).
[29] But see Chapter 9 p 164.

13

Transformative Remedies

A Introduction

As was demonstrated in the previous chapters, replicative remedies simply restate prior substantive rights. They do not require the defendant to do anything that the defendant was not required to do already. Nor do they release the defendant from doing something that the defendant was required to do. All other remedies are transformative. They transform or modify the legal relations between the claimant and defendant which existed before trial. A transformative remedy is a legal relation that significantly differs from any legal relation that existed before the court order was made.

This chapter will identify a number of transformative remedies. The remedies will be divided according to whether they originated in statute, equity, or common law. However, the other criterion which was used to distinguish between replicative remedies, namely, whether they replicate a primary or secondary right, will not be used here because asking whether a transformative remedy transforms a primary or secondary right does not provide us with meaningful categories. Instead, a distinction between constitutive and immediately enforceable remedies, suggested by Lawson's work, will be referred to throughout the discussions as it is particularly helpful in this area. The nature of the discretion involved in the grant of transformative remedies will also be briefly discussed.

The examples of transformative remedies that will be set out here are intended to be merely illustrative. They do not purport to be a comprehensive list of all transformative remedies.

1 Distinction between constitutive and immediately enforceable remedies

Transformative remedies can be divided into constitutive and enforceable[1] (or 'coercive') remedies.[2] Lawson wrote that a 'constitutive remedy':

> creates a legal situation which did not formerly exist, and automatically changes the relative legal positions of the parties. It is therefore self-executing, it neither need nor can be executed. A familiar example is a decree of divorce, which automatically cancels the marriage.[3]

Thus constitutive remedies are non-enforceable without further court proceedings. They are akin to declarations in this regard. Like declarations they can lead to further orders if ignored by the defendant.[4]

Following Zamir,[5] Lawson sub-divided constitutive remedies into investitive and divestitive remedies.[6] Investitive remedies are 'new' duties (and correlative rights) or powers. They are 'new' in that they do not reflect existing duties or powers. An example of an investitive remedy is a vesting order which vests property in a particular person. Divestitive remedies destroy existing duties (and correlative rights) or powers. An example of a divestitive remedy is a decree of divorce. It must be noted that most remedies can be said to be investitive or divestitive only from one party's perspective. From the perspective of another party they may have the opposite effect. As Nourse J observed in *Re Polly Peck (No 2)*[7] in relation to investitive remedies that would comprise new proprietary rights, 'You cannot grant a proprietary right to A, who has not had one beforehand, without taking some proprietary right away from B.' Thus, the remedy would be investitive from A's perspective and, at the same time, divestitive from B's perspective.

By way of contrast to constitutive remedies, there are a number of transformative remedies that are enforceable in that they require the defendant to do or abstain

[1] 'Enforceable remedies' refers to remedies which are capable of enforcement (whether by direct recourse to the defendant's assets or by punishment for contempt) upon the defendant's contravention without a prior application to court. Of course punishment for contempt requires a court application but this is taken to be a means of enforcing a remedy. They are to be contrasted with purely declaratory or non-enforceable remedies (however, as noted in Chapter 9 p 164, this distinction may be breaking down). See Chapter 5 n 135 for an explanation of why the term 'coercive' has not been preferred here.

[2] A similar distinction between enforceable and non-enforceable remedies can also be applied to replicative remedies. Each of the boxes set out in figure 5.1 on p 84 could be further sub-divided on this basis.

[3] F. H. Lawson, *Remedies of English Law* (2nd edn., London: Butterworth & Co, 1980), 13.

[4] That is, they are self-executing in so far as the alter the legal relations between the parties but any newly established duties may require further proceedings if they are not performed by the defendant. For example, if a contract, as varied by a constitutive remedy, is not performed, the claimant will have to bring further proceedings for its breach to obtain an enforceable remedy.

[5] I. Zamir, *The Declaratory Judgment* (London: Stevens, 1962), 1.

[6] Lawson (n 3 above), 239.

[7] [1998] 3 All ER 812, 831 (CA).

from doing something and the claimant may execute them or seek enforcement of them upon non-compliance without a prior court application. They may be executed or enforced in same manner as any similar enforceable replicative remedy. Lawson discusses some such remedies under the heading 'Discretionary Monetary Awards' characterizing them as 'remedies of a genuinely discretionary character, where the judge is directed to make a choice as to the amount of money, if any, he is to award to a claimant.'[8] As will be seen, Lawson's focus was too narrow: not all remedies of this nature are monetary. Enforceable transformative remedies often require the defendant to do acts other than make payments of money.

2 Example of statutory power to grant transformative remedies

To further illustrate the definitions and distinction drawn in the previous section, we can refer to section 87 of the Trade Practices Act 1974 (Cth).[9] This Australian enactment goes further than any United Kingdom statute in conferring jurisdiction to grant transformative remedies in commercial situations. Subsection (1) states that where there is a contravention of Parts IV, IVA, IVB, or V of the Act,[10] the court may:

> make such order or orders as it thinks appropriate against the person who engaged in the conduct or a person who was involved in the contravention (including all or any of the orders mentioned in subsection (2) of this section) if the Court considers that the order or orders concerned will compensate the first-mentioned person in whole or in part for the loss or damage or will prevent or reduce the loss or damage.

Subsection (2) enumerates the types of orders that may be made:

> (a) an order declaring the whole or any part of a contract made between the person who suffered, or is likely to suffer, the loss or damage and the person who engaged in the conduct or a person who was involved in the contravention constituted by the conduct, or of a collateral arrangement relating to such a contract, to be void and, if the Court thinks fit, to have been void *ab initio* or at all times on and after such date before the date on which the order is made as is specified in the order;
> (b) an order varying such a contract or arrangement in such manner as is specified in the order and, if the Court thinks fit, declaring the contract or arrangement to have had effect as so varied on and after such date before the date on which the order is made as is so specified;
> (ba) an order refusing to enforce any or all of the provisions of such a contract;
> (c) an order directing the person who engaged in the conduct or a person who was involved in the contravention constituted by the conduct to refund money or return property to the person who suffered the loss or damage;

[8] Lawson (n 3 above), 161.

[9] Equivalent sections include: Fair Trading Act 1987 (NSW) s 72; Fair Trading Act 1999 (Vic) s 158; Fair Trading Act 1989 (Qld) s 100; Fair Trading Act 1987 (WA) s 77; Fair Trading Act 1987 (SA) s 85; Fair Trading Act 1990 (Tas) s 41. The Contracts Review Act 1980 (NSW) ss 7–8 or the Fair Trading Act 1986 (NZ) s 43 could also serve as excellent examples in this context.

[10] Part IV proscribes restrictive trade practices; Part IVA proscribes unconscionable conduct; Part IVB deals with industry codes; and Part V deals with consumer protection.

(d) an order directing the person who engaged in the conduct or a person who was involved in the contravention constituted by the conduct to pay to the person who suffered the loss or damage the amount of the loss or damage;
(e) an order directing the person who engaged in the conduct or a person who was involved in the contravention constituted by the conduct, at his or her own expense, to repair, or provide parts for, goods that had been supplied by the person who engaged in the conduct to the person who suffered, or is likely to suffer, the loss or damage;
(f) an order directing the person who engaged in the conduct or a person who was involved in the contravention constituted by the conduct, at his or her own expense, to supply specified services to the person who suffered, or is likely to suffer, the loss or damage; and
(g) an order, in relation to an instrument creating or transferring an interest in land, directing the person who engaged in the conduct or a person who was involved in the contravention constituted by the conduct to execute an instrument that:

(i) varies, or has the effect of varying, the first-mentioned instrument; or
(ii) terminates or otherwise affects, or has the effect of terminating or otherwise affecting, the operation or effect of the first-mentioned instrument.

A remedy given under this section must be transformative as it cannot be said to replicate any prior substantive right that existed between the parties before the section 87 order was made. Substantive rights to the acts listed in paragraphs (c) to (g) above cannot be said to exist before an order is made because the defendant's duties depend on an exercise of the court's remedial discretion.[11] The defendant is not under a duty to do any of the acts referred to in paragraphs (c) to (g) unless and until the defendant is ordered to do so by the court.

Orders made under paragraphs (a) and (b) are constitutive remedies. They automatically change the relative legal positions of the parties. Those made under paragraph (a) are divestitive as they extinguish existing duties and powers. Those made under paragraph (b) may be divestitive or investitive as they may extinguish existing duties and powers or create entirely new duties and powers. Refusal of enforcement under paragraph (ba) is equivalent to a denial of a remedy. It operates in the same way as bars to equitable replicative remedies.[12] The court does not deny the existence of the substantive right but refuses to replicate it in an order. Orders made under paragraphs (c) to (g) are enforceable transformative remedies. They create a new duty on the defendant to do an act which the substantive law did not require the defendant to perform.

3 Discretion and transformative remedies

Many statutory transformative remedies involve fairly strong discretion. It is may not be possible, upon being presented with a set of facts, to identify rules allowing one to conclude with a great degree of certainty whether the remedy will be withheld or granted, and sometimes what content it will have if granted, that is,

[11] See Chapter 6 p 97ff. [12] See Chapter 6 p 91ff.

what the court in the exercise of its remedial discretion will require of the defendant. However, some transformative remedies, in particular some constitutive remedies, can be said to be available as a matter of course. Their grant does not involve a significant degree of discretion. They must be given by the court if the legislative requirements laid down for their grant are satisfied. For example, where the statutory requirements have been satisfied,[13] a judge cannot refuse a decree of divorce because he does not think that the parties should be divorced at the particular time. Of course, the statutory requirements may include fairly open-textured bars,[14] just as sometimes replicative remedies which are available as a matter of course are subject to bars.[15]

Constitutive remedies available as a matter of course are necessary where the concern for certainty overrides other considerations. The law could provide that upon five years' separation a marriage is automatically dissolved. But this would be obviously undesirable, particularly from the perspective of third parties. Therefore, a solemn judicial utterance that the marriage has irretrievably broken down and is over is required for it to be over in the eyes of the law.

With the above observations in mind, it would be wrong to assume that that the distinction between replicative and transformative remedies is coextensive with the distinction between remedies which do and those which do not result from the exercise of remedial discretion. Remedies which involve remedial discretion are merely a sub-set of transformative remedies.

Some representative examples of transformative remedies available under English law will now be considered, starting with various statutory transformative remedies. After a general discussion of the jurisdiction to grant various such remedies, particular examples of the form taken by orders made pursuant to the relevant powers will be given.

B Statutory Transformative Remedies

1 Constitutive remedies

(a) Jurisdiction to grant the remedy

The jurisdiction to grant constitutive remedies is generally conferred by Acts of Parliament. Such remedies are very common in family law. They include a decree of divorce which dissolves a marriage from the date that the decree is made,[16] a decree of the nullity of a marriage which annuls a voidable marriage

[13] Set out in the Matrimonial Causes Act 1973 (UK) s 1.

[14] For example, Matrimonial Causes Act 1973 (UK) s 13(1) sets out bars to a decree of nullity of a voidable marriage. There are no such bars to a decree of nullity of a void marriage.

[15] For example, specific performance of a contract for the sale of land.

[16] Matrimonial Causes Act 1973 (UK) s 1. The Family Law Act 1996 (UK), if brought into force, will substantially replace the Matrimonial Causes Act. Decrees of divorce will become known as divorce orders, s 2.

from the time that it is made absolute,[17] and an adoption order which gives parental responsibility for a child to the adopters and extinguishes prior parental responsibility.[18] An order varying an ante-nuptial or post-nuptial settlement under section 24(1)(c) or (d) of the Matrimonial Causes Act 1973 (UK) made upon the dissolution of a marriage may also take the form of a constitutive remedy.[19]

Constitutive remedies are also common in the law of trusts. The jurisdiction to alter beneficial interests under the Variation of Trusts Act 1958 (UK) provides a good example of a power to grant such a remedy. In *Re Holt's Settlement*[20] it was expressly decided that it is the order of the court that effects the variation, so that it is not necessary to direct trustees to execute further documents. Similar constitutive remedies also include orders for the removal of trustees and the appointment of new trustees,[21] vesting orders which create and extinguish rights in property,[22] and the variation of trusts to expand the powers of trustees.[23]

Further examples of statutory constitutive remedies include grants of probate and letters of administration[24] which confer a particular status and orders for the dissolution of a partnership[25] which prospectively extinguish the powers and duties of partners. The court also has a statutory power to make an order modifying the effect of the public policy forfeiture rule which provides that a person who has unlawfully killed another is precluded from acquiring any interest in property as a consequence of the killing.[26] Such an order is a constitutive remedy. New property rights are created in the court's discretion to replace rights extinguished because of the homicide.

(b) Form of the 'order'

The core provision of a decree nisi for divorce provides:

> On........ 20........, THE [DISTRICT] JUDGE HELD that [*reason for decree*] AND THAT the marriage solemnised on........ 19/20........, at [ ] between A. B. Petitioner and C.B. Respondent, has broken down irretrievably and decreed that the said marriage be dissolved unless sufficient cause be shown to the Court within six weeks from the making of this Decree why such Decree should not be made Absolute.[27]

[17] Matrimonial Causes Act 1973 (UK) s 16.

[18] Adoption Act 1976 (UK) ss 12, 39(2).

[19] However, the orders made under this section may also be enforceable transformative orders. For example in *Brooks v Brooks* [1996] AC 375 (HL) the order directed that a variation be made to a husband's pension scheme to provide two pensions for the wife. It did not purport to directly vary the settlement. But the wording of s 21(1)(c) and (d) empowers the court to directly vary settlements without needing to order that steps be taken to vary the documents.

[20] [1969] 1 Ch 100, 115 (Megarry J); For the form of a variation order see *Atkin's Court Forms* (2nd edn., 2000 Issue) Vol 41 [216].

[21] Trustee Act 1925 (UK) s 41.

[22] Ibid s 44; Law of Property Act 1925 (UK) s 9.

[23] Trustee Act 1925 (UK) s 57; *Steel v Wellcome Custodian Trustees Ltd* [1988] 1 WLR 167.

[24] Supreme Court Act 1981 (UK) s 113; Administration of Estates Act 1925 (UK) s 21.

[25] Partnership Act 1890 (UK) s 35.

[26] Forfeiture Act 1982 (UK) ss 1–2; *Dunbar v Plant* [1998] Ch 412 (CA).

[27] *Atkin's Court Forms* (2nd edn., 2001 Issue) Vol 16(2) [467].

The relevant part of a certificate of making a decree nisi absolute provides:

[*Decree for divorce:*] It is hereby certified that the decree was on .... 20 .... made final and absolute and that the said marriage was thereby dissolved.[28]

or:

[*Decree for nullity — voidable marriage:*] [I]t is hereby certified that the said decree was on .... 20 .... made final and absolute and that the said petitioner was free from that date and is free from all bond of marriage with the said respondent.[29]

An adoption order creates a new legal relationship between the adopters and the child, stating:

IT IS ORDERED that the applicant(s) do adopt the child[30]

An order for the removal of a trustee is a divestitive remedy. It relevantly provides:

IT IS ORDERED (1) that the Defendant C. D. be removed from office as a Trustee of the Will of X. Y. deceased[31]

An order for the appointment of trustees is an investitive remedy. It relevantly provides:

THE COURT HEREBY APPOINTS the Claimant A. B. and the Defendant C. D. new trustees of the [Settlement] in place of R. S. the last surviving trustee thereof now deceased.[32]

It is also usually accompanied by a vesting order, which may provide:

IT IS ORDERED that the [interests in] land now subject to the trusts of a [Settlement] made .... 20 .... between .... and .... particulars of which are set forth in the Schedule hereto do vest in P. Q. [and *or* jointly with] N. O. . . .such [interests in] land to be held by them upon the trusts of the said [Settlement][33]

Section 57 of the Trusts Act 1925 (UK) allows the court to vary a trust, for example, by conferring a power to buy a house as a residence for a beneficiary. Such an order may relevantly provide:

THE COURT being of opinion that the transactions hereinafter mentioned are expedient but cannot be effected without the assistance of the Court by reason of the absence of any power for that purpose vested in the Claimant as Trustee of the [Settlement] by the Settlement or by law HEREBY CONFERS upon the Claimant the Trustee of the Settlement the power to purchase out of the funds subject to the trusts of the Settlement a freehold house and land which they consider a proper investment at a price not exceeding the amount of a valuation of such house and land or the sum of £100,000 whichever shall be the smaller amount.[34]

28 Ibid [495].

29 Ibid [496].

30 *Atkin's Court Forms* (2nd. edn., 1997 Issue) Vol 21(2) Form 246.

31 *Atkin's Court Forms* (2nd edn., 2000 Issue) Vol 41 [124].

32 Ibid [134].

33 Ibid [137]. See also [262]–[274].

34 Ibid [207].

An order for the dissolution of a partnership provides:

IT IS DECLARED AND ADJUDGED that the partnership mentioned in the claimant's particulars between the claimant and [defendant] [was dissolved as from the date of this judgment *or* the day of........, 20........;] (*or as the case may be*).[35]

2 Enforceable transformative remedies

(a) Jurisdiction to grant the remedy

Enforceable transformative remedies are common in family law. The Matrimonial Causes Act 1973 (UK) provides that on the grant of a decree of divorce, a decree of nullity of marriage or a decree of judicial separation or at any time thereafter spouses and children can obtain various financial provision and property adjustment orders. These include orders for unsecured and secured periodical or lump sum payments or the transfer or settlement of property.[36] The court, in making such orders must have regard to all the circumstances of the case.[37] The court may also make maintenance orders on the application of either party to the marriage.[38] All these remedies are transformative. In *Sugden v Sugden* Lord Denning stated that 'In [the Divorce Court] there is no right to maintenance, or to costs, or to a secured provision, or the like, until the court makes an order directing it.'[39]

Enforceable transformative remedies may also be obtained under the Domestic Proceedings and Magistrates' Courts Act 1978 (UK) and the Children Act 1989 (UK). Section 8 of the latter Act empowers the court to make orders of this nature in relation to the upbringing of children including residence orders, contact orders, prohibited steps orders, and specific issue orders.

Family provision and property adjustment remedies are granted in the exercise of a high degree of discretion. However, such a wide discretion has attracted strong criticism:

[E]xperience led to growing professional disquiet at a number of cases in which the costs incurred equalled or exceeded the sums in dispute. At the same time many academic commentators criticised the absence of any predictability, let alone certainty, of outcome. Litigants seeking advice from solicitors often received no better answer than that all would depend on the judge before whom the case might be listed. If that was the state of the law how were sensible litigants to plan for the future or to settle their responsibilities by compromise?

. . .

[35] Form N303 Order for dissolution of partnership: CPR Part 4 PD Table 3.

[36] Matrimonial Causes Act 1973 (UK) ss 23–24.

[37] Ibid s 25(1); see *White v White* [2001] 1 AC 596, 606 (HL) 'The judge has regard to all the facts of the case and to the overall requirements of fairness.' Section 25(2) provides a list of particular matters that the court must have regard to.

[38] Ibid s 27; see *Atkin's Court Forms* (2nd edn., 1997 Issue) Vol 21(1) Form 55.

[39] [1957] P 120, 135 (CA).

A review of the decided cases over the last 30 years demonstrates that the judges have felt it necessary to supplement the statutory provision in order to inject some mechanism or yardstick to provide some stepping stone towards a reasonably fair and ascertainable outcome.[40]

The need for guidance and like cases to be decided alike led to the adoption of a 'one-third rule'[41] and a 'yardstick of reasonable requirements' of the wife.[42] However, demands for equality between spouses later caused the House of Lords to prohibit the use of such rules, though the establishment of 'presumption of equal division' was denied.[43] In *Cowan v Cowan* Thorpe LJ reviewed the authorities and found that 'the only yardstick is a subjective judicial perception of fairness after a careful appraisal of the section 25 criteria.'[44] The court recognized that this was a difficult task and called for more guidance from the legislature.[45] Although in *Lambert v Lambert*[46] the Court of Appeal expressly denied a presumption of equality as it was bound to do by the legislation, the judicial policy in situations where there is a surplus of assets over the spouses' needs may be moving in this direction. Within this area there is a clear tension between the legislative requirement to retain remedial discretion and a judicial tendency towards the development of rules.

The Inheritance (Provision for Family and Dependants) Act 1975 (UK) provides that certain dependants can obtain an order for reasonable financial provision to be made for them out of the estate of a deceased person.[47] The remedy given under this Act[48] has taken the form of a right to the entire estate,[49] a lump sum payment,[50] a share in the income of the estate,[51] an additional annuity,[52] or the purchase and occupation of a house.[53]

Enforceable transformative remedies are not limited to the family and succession law spheres. The Company Law Act 1985 (UK) allows the court to make an order where a company's affairs have been conducted in a manner which is unfairly prejudicial to the interest of its members. Section 461 states that the court may 'make such order as it thinks fit for giving relief in respect of the matters complained of'.

The Law Reform (Frustrated Contracts) Act 1943 (UK) provides that, where a contract is discharged due to frustration, a party is discharged from making payments and has a right to recover payments already made provided that a court may 'if it considers it just to do so having regard to all the circumstances

[40] *Cowan v Cowan* [2002] Fam 97, 110, and 112 (CA) (Thorpe LJ).
[41] *Wachtel v Wachtel* [1973] Fam 72, 94 (CA).
[42] *Duxbury v Duxbury* [1992] Fam 62n (CA).
[43] *White v White* [2001] 1 AC 596, 605 (HL) (Lord Nicholls).
[44] *Cowan v Cowan* [2002] Fam 97, 119 (CA) (Thorpe LJ).
[45] Ibid 115–116, 119, 131.
[46] [2003] Fam 103 (CA).
[47] Section 1. See S. M. Cretney, 'Succession — Discretion or Whim, Freedom of Choice or Caprice?' (1986) 6 *OJLS* 299.
[48] Ibid s 2.
[49] See text to n 65 below.
[50] *Atkin's Court Forms* (2nd edn., 2001 Issue) Vol 29(1) [431].
[51] Ibid [432].
[52] Ibid [433].
[53] Ibid [434].

of the case' allow a party who has incurred expenses to recover the expenses or require a party who has obtained benefits to pay for the benefits.[54]

The court has jurisdiction to make orders giving relief from forfeiture which reinstate a terminated lease. It has power to grant relief against forfeiture of a lease as it thinks fit.[55] Such an order is constitutive, as Lord Hobhouse observed in *On Demand Plc v Michael Gerson Plc*: 'It is true that there has been no relief against forfeiture until a court has made an order granting that relief and that the contractual or proprietary rights do not consequentially revive until the relief has been granted.'[56] The discretion may be characterized as quite narrow as it is a choice only as to whether the order ought to be made, not as to its content. There is generally no need for the court to determine the content of the newly created rights because the formerly existing substantive rights are simply reinstated.[57] Thus it is not a remedial discretion as described in Chapter 6.

As noted in Chapter 12, an award of damages for *future* breaches 'in substitution for' specific relief under section 50 of the Supreme Court Act 1981 (UK) appears to be a transformative remedy.[58] Lord Sumner in *Leeds Industrial Co-operative Society Ltd v Slack* called it a 'novel power' and its use has sometimes been controversial because 'until a wrong has been actually committed, to award a sum of money in substitution for an injunction is to fix the price at which a Court will license an intending tortfeasor to commit a wrong, to which the victim of it refuses consent.'[59] For instance, an award of equitable damages 'in substitution for' an injunction may be given where there is a threatened or apprehended tort, such as an obstruction of ancient lights[60] or a nuisance caused by the erosion of a hillside.[61] The factors which guide the court's discretion were enumerated in *Shelfer v City of London Electric Lighting Co*.[62]

[54] Law Reform (Frustrated Contracts) Act 1943 (UK) s 1(2), (3).

[55] In the case of non-payment of rent, jurisdiction is conferred by Supreme Court Act 1981 (UK) s 38; in the case of other breaches, jurisdiction is conferred by of the Law of Property Act 1925 (UK) s 146; in the case of situations not covered by legislation, it is an equity jurisdiction: *Shiloh Spinners Ltd v Harding* [1973] AC 691, 725 (HL).

[56] [2002] 2 WLR 919, 923 (HL) (Lord Hobhouse).

[57] Though where this is impossible, as in *On Demand Plc v Michael Gerson Plc* because the leased property had been sold, relief may still be given in relation to the sale proceeds that represent the property. 'Instead, orders which the court would otherwise have made are replaced by orders for payment out of the money (if in court) or declarations of entitlement to give a good receipt for the money (if in an escrow account)': Ibid 929 (Lord Millett). At 930 Lord Millett indicated that these orders gave effect to rights.

[58] However, in relation to *past* breaches, an award of damages 'in addition to' specific relief under the Act is a replicative remedy. As we have seen in Chapter 12, it replicates the same secondary right to the payment of damages that an award of common law damages would have replicated.

[59] [1924] AC 851, 867–868 (HL). Compare *Jaggard v Sawyer* [1995] 1 WLR 269, 285–286 (CA) where Millett LJ stated 'it is not the award of damages which has the practical effect of licensing the defendant to commit the wrong, but the refusal of injunctive relief.'

[60] *Leeds Industrial Co-operative Society Ltd v Slack* [1924] AC 851 (HL).

[61] *Hooper v Rogers* [1975] Ch 43 (CA).

[62] [1895] 1 Ch 287, 322–323 (CA). Reproduced in Chapter 8 p 129.

(b) Form of the Order

Orders under the Matrimonial Causes Act 1973 (UK) may provide:

IT IS ORDERED THAT:

1. the Respondent do pay to the Applicant as from [decree absolute *or*........ 20........ (*a date after decree absolute*)] periodical payments for herself during their joint lives or until such date as she shall re-marry or until the [*fixed date e.g.* 31 March 2008] or further order at the rate of £........ per annum payable [monthly *or* weekly][63]

or:

IT IS ORDERED THAT:

1. the Respondent do within [14] days of decree absolute transfer all his estate and interest in the property known as........ into the joint names of himself and the Applicant subject only to the existing mortgage to the........ Building Society[64]

An example of an order for family provision from a deceased's estate provides:

The court is of the opinion that the disposition of the estate of B. B. deceased effected by his will is not such as to make reasonable financial provision for the Claimant

IT IS ORDERED pursuant to the provisions of Section 2(1) of the Inheritance (Provision for Family and Dependants) Act 1975 that the whole of the net estate of the Testator [less a sum of £........] be awarded to the Claimant[65]

An order for relief from forfeiture of a lease is an investitive remedy as it recreates rights which a lessee has lost. It relevantly provides:

IT IS ORDERED that upon the Defendant complying with the following conditions: [*list of conditions*]

The Defendant be relieved from forfeiture and that he holds the premises referred to in the Particulars of Claim according to the lease therein referred to without any new lease and that all further proceedings in this action be stayed.[66]

An award of damages for *future* breaches 'in substitution for' specific relief made in *Senior v Pawson* provided:

Declare that the Defendants, having caused damage and injury to the Plaintiff by the obstruction occasioned by their buildings, and having interfered with the access of air and light to the ancient windows of the Plaintiff's house, called the *Mulberry Tavern*, at

[63] *Atkin's Court Forms* (2nd edn., 2001 Issue) Vol 16(2) [307].

[64] Ibid [308]. Whereas this order is an enforceable remedy, the order which follows it in the model form is a constitutive remedy. It states: '2. the Applicant and the Respondent shall thereafter hold the property upon a trust of land for themselves as beneficial tenants in common upon the following terms: [*terms of trust set out including terms that the wife be entitled to reside in the property until the children are of age, etc*].' This is another example of multiple remedies being given in one document.

[65] *Atkin's Court Forms* (2nd edn., 2001 Issue) Vol 29(1) [430].

[66] *Atkin's Court Forms* (2nd edn., 1999 Issue) Vol 24(2) Form 171.

Sheffield, an inquiry ought to be made what amount of compensation should be paid to the Plaintiff in respect of that damage and injury. Let inquiry be made accordingly what proper sum should be paid to the Plaintiff in compensation, such sum to be certified by the Chief Clerk, and to be paid to the Plaintiff within one month from the date of his certificate.[67]

C Equitable Transformative Remedies

1 Constitutive remedies

(a) *Jurisdiction to grant the remedy*

A longstanding constitutive remedy available in the court's equitable jurisdiction is an order for foreclosure which extinguishes a mortgagor's equity of redemption and correlatively confers absolute ownership on the mortgagee.[68] As with the discretion to grant relief against forfeiture, the court's discretion in relation to this remedy may be characterized as narrow, namely, only as to whether the order ought to be made, not as to what content it should have. It is not a remedial discretion to determine the content of newly conferred rights.

Another constitutive remedy available in the court's equitable jurisdiction is an order granting relief against forfeiture, in situations to which the statutory powers to do so do not extend.[69] Recission by decree would also belong in this category.[70]

In the area of trusts, constitutive remedies made in the court's inherent jurisdiction include Benjamin orders authorizing the distribution of a trust estate where one or more beneficiaries cannot be found.[71] They also include orders for the guidance of trustees.[72] Such a remedy is useful where the trustees are unsure whether to take a particular step or not. 'The trustees. . .may always deliberately surrender to the court an exercise of their discretion in particular existing circumstances, and the court will then make what it considers to be the appropriate exercise of the discretion.'[73] The court's order will confer upon the trustees an immunity from suit in relation to the consequences of taking the court authorized step.

An order imposing a 'remedial constructive trust' would belong in the category of constitutive remedies. In *Re Polly Peck (No 2)*[74] Nourse LJ stated: 'In referring to a remedial constructive trust, I mean an order of the court granting by way of remedy, a proprietary right to someone who, beforehand, had no proprietary

[67] (1866) LR 3 Eq 330, 336.
[68] *Twentieth Century Banking Corp Ltd v Wilkinson* [1977] Ch 99.
[69] *Shiloh Spinners Ltd v Harding* [1973] AC 691, 725 (HL).
[70] Chapter 8 p 149.
[71] *Re Benjamin* [1902] 1 Ch 723.
[72] *Chapman v Chapman* (1954) AC 429, 446 (HL); CPR Part 64 PD.
[73] *Atkin's Court Forms* (2nd edn., 2000 Issue) Vol 41 [24].
[74] [1998] 3 All ER 812, 830 (CA); P. B. H. Birks, 'The end of the remedial constructive trust?' (1998) 12(4) *Trust Law International* 202.

right.'[75] In *Fortex Group Ltd v MacIntosh*, the New Zealand Court of Appeal lucidly described how this trust differs in this respect from an institutional constructive trust:

An institutional constructive trust is one which arises by operation of the principles of equity and whose existence the Court simply recognizes in a declaratory way. A remedial constructive trust is one which is imposed by the Court as a remedy in circumstances where, before the order of the Court, no trust of any kind existed.

The difference between the two types of constructive trust, institutional and remedial, is that an institutional constructive trust arises upon the happening of the events which bring it into being. Its existence is not dependent on any order of the Court. Such an order simply recognizes that it came into being at an earlier time and provides for its implementation in whatever way is appropriate. A remedial constructive trust depends for its very existence on the order of the Court; such order being creative rather than simply confirmatory.[76]

This passage elegantly illustrates the difference between replicative and transformative remedies. The former arises from an order which replicates substantive rights, such as the secondary rights that comprise the institutional constructive trust.[77] The latter arises from an order which creates entirely new rights, such as the rights that would comprise a remedial constructive trust.

The second characteristic of this remedy, not explicitly referred to in the above quotations, is that it involves a high degree of discretion.[78] Nourse LJ also identified this in *Re Polly Peck (No 2)* stating that 'we must recognise that the remedial constructive trust gives the court a discretion to vary property rights.'[79] It involves 'remedial discretion' as described in Chapter 6.[80] These two characteristics — that it is transformative and that its availability involves remedial discretion — led the English Court of Appeal to reject the notion that such a remedy could be granted under English law.[81] Nourse LJ stated that, 'It is not that you need an Act of

[75] In the earlier House of Lords case of *Westdeutsche Landesbank Girozentrale v Islington LBC* [1996] AC 669, 714–715 (HL) Lord Browne-Wilkinson stated: 'A remedial constructive trust, as I understand it, is. . .a judicial remedy giving rise to an enforceable obligation: the extent to which it operates retrospectively to the prejudice of third parties lies in the discretion of the court.' It is submitted that the 'enforceable obligation' would be given effect in an ancillary order such as an order to transfer the subject matter of the trust to the claimant. The order creating the trust itself would be a constitutive remedy.

[76] [1998] 3 NZLR 171, 172 (NZCA). See also D. Wright, *The Remedial Constructive Trust* (Sydney: Butterworths, 1998), 103.

[77] See Chapter 12 p 186 for a discussion of this replicative remedy.

[78] Birks (n 74 above), 204. But some argue that a remedial constructive trust need not involve a high degree of discretion; that over time it could evolve into a transformative remedy which is not based on remedial discretion: *Muschinski v Dodds* (1985) 160 CLR 583, 623 (HCA).

[79] [1998] 3 All ER 812, 831 CA.

[80] See Chapter 6 p 97ff.

[81] However, there have been signs that the law of Australia and New Zealand may move in a different direction: *Muschinski v Dodds* (1985) 160 CLR 583 (HCA); *Giumelli v Giumelli* (1999) 161 ALR 473 (HCA); *Fortex Group Ltd v MacIntosh* [1998] 3 NZLR 171 (NZCA). It has already done so in Canada: *LAC Minerals Ltd v International Corona Resources Ltd* (1989) 61 DLR (4th) 14 (SCC). Wright (n 76 above) argues in favour of the development of the remedial constructive trust.

Parliament to prohibit a variation of property rights. You need an Act of Parliament to permit it: see the Variation of Trusts Act 1958 and the Matrimonial Causes Act 1973'. Birks has forcefully argued that the rejection of the remedial constructive trust is correct as matter of law and policy.[82] Others have taken a different view.[83] This normative debate is an endeavour different from that engaged in throughout this work. The purpose of this book is primarily analytical. The analysis presented here provides a toolkit of concepts, terms, and ideas which can be used to better construct and assess arguments in that debate. Although the normative issues relating to the legitimacy of transformative remedies based on remedial discretion are extremely important, they have no part in this particular project.

(b) *Form of the order*

An order for foreclosure on the defendant's mortgage is a divestitive remedy from the defendant's perspective as it extinguishes the defendant's rights. It provides:

> IT IS ORDERED that the defendant do stand absolutely debarred and foreclosed of and from all right, title, interest, and equity of redemption of, in and to the property comprised in the said mortgage, the particulars of which property are set forth in the schedule hereto[84]

An order giving directions to trustees as to how they may exercise their discretion may provide:

> AND THE COURT being of the opinion that this Order is for the benefit of the child defendant C. D. and of all persons who may hereafter become beneficially interested under the trusts of the [Settlement]. . .HEREBY AUTHORISES the Claimants as trustees of the [Settlement] to sell the said property either in one or more lots and whether by public auction or private treaty as they shall think fit[85]

2 Enforceable transformative remedies

Enforceable transformative remedies originating in equity may include some remedies that have already been touched upon in previous chapters. Remedies that may or do, at this stage of their development, fall into this category appear to include remedies given in relation to estoppel[86] and some mandatory injunctions to undo or prevent a wrong.[87]

Where a remedy is granted in circumstances where it was not previously available or the conditions for its grant are not judicially expounded with sufficient clarity for one to be able to make the assertion that substantive rights will arise in similar

[82] P. B. H. Birks, 'Three Kinds of Objection to Discretionary Remedialism' (2000) 29 *U Western Australia L Rev* 1; P. B. H. Birks, 'Rights, Wrongs and Remedies' (2000) 20 *OJLS* 1.

[83] For example, D. Wright, *The Remedial Constructive Trust* (Sydney: Butterworths, 1998).

[84] Form N309 Order for foreclosure absolute: CPR Part 4 PD Table 3. This order is accompanied by an order for delivery up of possession: 'that the defendant do forthwith deliver up possession to the claimant of the property comprised in the said schedule.'

[85] Ibid [188]. [86] Chapter 8 p 132. [87] Chapter 11 p 191.

situations due to the availability of the remedy in such situations then the remedy belongs in the transformative category. However, this status may change. Due to the development of the law surrounding it, its availability may in time come to be seen as giving rise to substantive rights in which case it will move to the replicative category.[88]

D Common Law Transformative Remedies

It is difficult to unequivocally point to examples of transformative remedies, whether constitutive or enforceable, which originated in common law courts. At this stage of their development, some may argue that an award of restitutionary damages[89] or an award of exemplary damages[90] belong in this category. However, it is open to argument that the law in this area has developed or is developing to the extent that it is possible to say that, if a particular set of conditions is satisfied, a claimant has a substantive right to the payment of restitutionary or exemplary damages. If this is or becomes the case then these remedies must be placed in the replicative category.

E Enforcement of Transformative Remedies

1 Constitutive remedies

As was already stressed, a constitutive remedy is always non-enforceable (or 'non-coercive'). It cannot be enforced upon non-compliance. However, further orders may be made if the legal relations that are established require protection or enforcement. For example, a foreclosure order is often accompanied by a possession order.[91]

2 Enforceable transformative remedies

Generally orders for the payment of money are enforced in the same manner as an award of an agreed sum[92] and orders requiring the doing of other acts are enforced in the same manner as injunctions.[93] However, certain orders in the family law sphere are bolstered by special enforcement provisions. For example, a maintenance order made under the Domestic Proceedings and Magistrates' Courts Act 1978 (UK) may be enforced by attachment of earnings, distress, a fine, or by committal to prison.[94] A residence order determining with whom a child is to live made under section 8 of the Children's Act 1989 may be enforced under section 63(3) of the Magistrates' Courts Act 1980 (UK) as if it were an order requiring the production of the child to the claimant,[95] that is, by fine or committal to prison.

[88] Chapter 4 p 58. [89] Chapter 10 p 176. [90] Chapter 10 p 177.
[91] See n 84 above. [92] Chapter 7 p 112. [93] Chapter 8 p 133.
[94] Magistrates' Courts Act 1980 (UK) ss 59B, 76. [95] Children Act 1989 (UK) s 14.

14
Conclusion

True to its title, this book was concerned with the classification of remedies in private law. In the first part, it considered why remedies constitute a separate category of rights alongside substantive rights. In the second part, it demonstrated how the category of remedies could be further sub-divided. Thus remedies were 'reclassified' in two senses: externally vis-à-vis other legal concepts and internally vis-à-vis each other.

At the outset it was necessary to identify and differentiate the most stable use of 'remedy'. Chapter 2 examined the multifarious usages of the term 'remedy'. The chapter illustrated its instability and the need for the work presented in this book. To emphasize the extent of the problem, Chapter 3 considered how five leading writers on remedies used the term, what they considered the law of remedies to cover, and how they structured their expositions of it. This investigation assisted in the selection of the stable core meaning of remedy. It also showed that texts on remedies are to a significant extent, perhaps without knowing it, really about substantive rights, duplicating the work of texts on contract, tort, and restitution (or, more accurately, unjust enrichment). That which has been treated as the law of remedies for the last thirty years or more has been no more than a conglomerate of different themes loosely bound together by the notion of a response to a grievance.

In Chapter 4, remedies were defined as the rights arising from certain kinds of judicial commands and statements. Remedies were thus distinguished from all rights existing before a matter comes before a court, that is, from substantive rights. In particular, it was emphasized that secondary or remedial rights belong within the realm of substantive law. It was argued that we should separate substantive rights from the orders which effectuate them. The two are clearly different. Both should not be called 'remedies'. They ought not be treated together in works on 'remedies' as if they were parts of the very same subject matter. In particular, it is incongruous to treat rights arising from wrongs alongside rights arising from judicial commands as part of a single field of law.[1] Although there is no opposition between right and remedy, there is a sharp distinction to be drawn between substantive rights and remedies as described

[1] When studied side by side, they ought to be studied under a title such as 'Remedial Rights and Remedies', which would constantly remind the reader of what this book demonstrates, namely that they are entirely different concepts.

here. Whereas the line between substance and remedy has often been drawn at the point of the breach of a primary duty, here it was argued that the line ought to be drawn at the point of the making of a court order.

An investigation of the concept of a remedy and the adoption of a stable meaning have the primary benefit of clarifying thinking and communication. The points Corbin makes are particularly relevant in relation to this part:

> No word in any language has a 'true meaning', or an 'objective' meaning, a 'legal' meaning, which everyone is required to adopt at his peril, in his conversation, in his letters, his contracts, his statutes or his constitutions. There is peril, however, in this common multiple usage of important words; it very frequently, especially when it occurs in a contract, a court opinion or a statute, causes misunderstanding, litigation, conflict, and inconsistent decisions. . .One whose own mind is cloudy and confused is certain to convey only cloudy and confused thoughts to others, but the identification of a specific word that will convey an exact thought and no other is an almost necessary process in the clarification of one's own mind.[2]

The next part of this book involved an examination of the structure of the law of remedies in light of the definition of a remedy developed in the first part. This part provided a taxonomy of this area of law, one which allows us to better appreciate how remedies relate to the primary and secondary rights that they effectuate, what impact jurisdictional origin has on the grant of remedies, and how particular remedies are related and how they differ. The importance of a logically consistent taxonomy for legal reasoning and hence the stability, transparency and future development of the common law is clear.[3] Taxonomy may be implicit rather than explicit, but it is unavoidable.[4] Unfortunately, its most basic principles are too often neglected.

Chapter 5 dealt with the abstract principles applicable to the taxonomy of remedies and, negatively, with problems and errors to be avoided. It demonstrated that 'specific enforcement', 'perfection', 'coercion', and 'declaration' categories should not be placed alongside the goal-based categories of compensation, restitution, and punishment. They potentially cut across the goal-based categories, just like categories based on author and content have the potential to cut across each other if concurrently used to order a set of books. This is because remedies which specifically enforce or declare substantive rights can have a goal of compensation, restitution, or punishment.

Chapter 6 examined the role that discretion plays in the area of remedies. It drew a distinction between discretion to refuse a replicative remedy and remedial discretion to fashion the content of a remedy *de novo*. It distinguished remedial

[2] W. N. Hohfeld, *Fundamental Legal Conceptions* (A. Corbin (ed.), New Haven: Yale University Press, 1964), viii (Foreword).

[3] P. B. H. Birks, 'Equity in the Modern Law: An Exercise in Taxonomy' (1996) 26 *U Western Australia L Rev* 1.

[4] E. Bant, 'Book Review of *An Introduction to Property Law in Australia* by Robert Chambers' (2002) 26 *MULR* 211, 221–2.

discretion from the judicial development of the law. This chapter also explained why remedies in the proposed taxonomy were not sub-divided according to whether they are 'discretionary' or 'non-discretionary' but rather along jurisdictional lines. This was because a jurisdictional division better accords with the availability of certain bars to replication.

The second half applied the above analyses to particular remedies. It showed how they fit within the proposed framework. Chapters 7, 8, and 9 examined remedies which merely restate or 'replicate' primary rights. Chapters 10, 11, and 12 dealt with remedies which replicate rights arising from wrongs, in other words, secondary rights. These chapters showed that the development of private law is such that we can speak of a distinct law of secondary rights — or, more descriptively, of 'remedial rights' — hitherto subsumed in works on 'remedies' which define their subject matter too broadly or leave it undefined.

At the outset, it was stressed that this was a work which could only hope to set out the structure rather than the pith of the law of remedies. Nor was it appropriate for it to set out the substantive law of primary or secondary rights in any significant detail. It simply provided an overview which showed that the significant majority of remedies could be seen to be judicial restatements of primary or secondary rights. Particular aspects of the application of the proposed framework, such as whether particular remedies do or do not replicate prior rights, are sometimes open to debate. Similarly, whether a replicated right is primary or secondary is also at times debatable. But these are predominantly questions of substantive law. When they are answered, the categorization of the corresponding remedies becomes an easy task.

It was observed that even when works on remedies define some remedies in terms of court orders, they do not provide any examples of court orders. All of the works reviewed in Chapter 3 equated specific performance and injunctions with court orders but failed to provide examples of such orders. This book filled that lacuna. The form that a court order takes sometimes provides the best formulation of what the court found the substantive rights of the parties to have been.[5] Of course this is true in relation to some but not all orders. Orders for the payment of money are not, of themselves, particularly instructive as to the nature of the underlying rights to which they give effect.

Chapter 13 dealt with remedies that are radically different from those which merely replicate substantive rights. It enumerated a number of 'transformative' remedies, that is, remedies the content of which is created afresh from case to case and which bear little resemblance to prior rights. It noted that nearly all of these were based on statute and that not all involved remedial discretion.

The distinction between replicative and transformative remedies formed the *summa divisio* of the new taxonomy. This distinction is simply another and, it is

[5] Consequently, it is regrettable that court orders are not reproduced in modern law reports as they were in some older reports.

suggested, clearer way of looking at aspects of the 'institutional/remedial'[6] or the 'monism/dualism' distinctions. In relation to the latter, Hammond J stated:

> Essentially, English legal theory and practice on remedies is monistic. That is, right and remedy are perceived to be congruent. But in the United States, and increasingly in Canada and New Zealand, our courts proceed on a dualistic basis. The Court first enquires as to the obligation the Court is asked to uphold; it then (and only then) makes a context-specific evaluation of that remedy which will best support and advance that obligation.[7]

Supporters of dualism assert that 'remedies' for wrongs or liability should be chosen in the court's discretion from a 'basket of remedies' based on what is the most appropriate remedy in the circumstances.[8] If we equate monism with a preference for replicative remedies and dualism with a preference for transformative remedies based on remedial discretion, we can say that Chapters 7 to 12 demonstrated just how strongly monistic English law is. Dualism is presented as being evolutionary. Yet, when we better understand the manner in which nearly all non-statutory remedies presently function, the new paradigm appears revolutionary. It threatens to fracture the direct correlation between substantive rights and replicative remedies which has developed over centuries of legal thought. This should not be allowed occur without a most careful consideration of all that it implies.

Terminology which contrasts 'institutional' and 'remedial' or 'monism' and 'dualism' compounds confusion, for these words serve only to conceal the questions at issue. By comparison the contrast between the order which replicates the right brought into court and the order which transforms that right exposes these questions and facilitates their discussion. It assists in the analysis of arguments that have been advanced in this area. For example, it casts serious doubt on the assertion that 'the assumption that a dualist analysis would effect a radical change in the present law is unfounded',[9] discredits the notion that discretion to refuse an equitable remedy is of a similar type to remedial discretion to fashion a remedy that transforms the parties' substantive rights,[10] and refutes the suggestion that since the courts make laws which have the effect of redistributing property rights, it follows that the courts may award property rights as a redistributive remedy on a case-by-case basis.[11]

[6] R. Pound, 'The Progress of the Law' (1920) 33 *Harvard L Rev* 420, 420–1; D. W. M. Waters, *The Constructive Trust* (London: Athlone Press, 1964), 9–19; P. O'Connor, 'Happy Partners or Strange Bedfellows: The Blending of Remedial and Institutional Features in the Evolving Constructive Trust' (1996) 20 *Melbourne Uni L Rev* 735.

[7] *Brown v Pourau* [1995] 1 NZLR 252, 268. See also M. Tilbury, 'Remedies and the Classification of Obligations' in A. Robertson (ed.), *Law of Obligations: Connections and Boundaries* (London: Cavendish, 2004).

[8] Chapter 6 n 60. Birks dubbed this doctrine 'discretionary remedialism': P. B. H. Birks, 'Three Kinds of Objection to Discretionary Remedialism' (2000) 29 *U Western Australia L Rev* 1.

[9] Tilbury (n 7 above), 24. [10] Chapter 6 p 97. [11] Chapter 6 p 99.

Thus this was not an attempt at neatness for neatness sake. It was more than a semantic exercise about the meanings of a word. Remedies are the basis of the system of civil justice. The way we view remedies has crucial consequences for the manner in which remedies function. This in turn directly impacts on the structure of private law and the settlement of disputes through adjudication.

Our concept of what a judicial remedy is, and knowledge of how remedies function, determine the role that the judge should play in the settlement of disputes. At the core of the distinction between replication and transformation based on remedial discretion (or monism and dualism) is a difference between two models of a system of adjudication: one focused on substantive rights which the courts may or may not have a narrow discretion in replicating and one focused on remedies which the courts have a broader and stronger discretion to create *de novo*. The concept of a remedy and the taxonomy presented here serve to crystallize an important issue at the heart of private law adjudication: should judges merely replicate substantive rights as closely as possible or should they creatively 'fashion' a remedy, that is, create rights with new content in and for the particular case? This is a fundamental question about our system of adjudication and the Rule of Law. This book did not purport to answer it. A stable concept and a consistent taxonomy do not remove the need for policy, if not political, decisions of this nature. But they do cast a bright light on what is at stake and will assist in the making of and the discussion of the relevant decisions.

But adjudication policy aside, this paradigm has the potential to affect the way in which legal problems are approached in private law. The orthodox approach to legal problems appears to be as follows:

1. Is the defendant liable? (Or, is there an infringement of the claimant's rights?)
2. What are the remedies?[12]

Question 1 is concerned with primary rights such as rights under contracts or rights protected by the law of tort. It asks whether a cause of action has arisen. Question 2 deals with whether remedies such as specific performance, damages, or declarations can be obtained; and if damages can be obtained, how they are to be calculated. Answering this second question involves discussing *both* the law relating to secondary rights and the law governing the grant of various court orders. The orthodox approach draws the line between substance and remedy at the point of an infringement of a right.

The approach in light of this work would be slightly but significantly different:

1. What primary *and secondary* rights govern the relationship between the parties?
2. What remedies are available to replicate or transform those substantive rights?

[12] Derived from *Remedies (Inns of Court School of Law) 2003/2004* (Oxford: Oxford University Press, 2003), 1.

This approach places greater emphasis on substantive rights, particularly secondary rights. It draws the line between substance and remedy at the point of the making of a court order. Question 1 is concerned entirely with the law of substantive rights. It draws on the primary/secondary distinction which, as we saw in Chapter 2, appears to be firmly entrenched in English law. Question 2 is concerned entirely with the law of remedies as defined as presented here.[13]

Remedies are a *sine qua non* of the legal system. They are the beginning and end of private law: 'beginning' because the existence of substantive rights is inferred from their availability and 'end' because they are what every trial is geared towards. Unfortunately, the current law of remedies is a hotchpotch. This was an attempt to introduce order. It proffered a new way of looking at the existing law of substantive rights and remedies. It set out a hypothesis, not a *fait accompli*. It is hoped that its insights will promote development and that its shortfalls will promote discussion. A rigorous separation of remedies from substantive rights has radical implications for the future of both subjects.

[13] An answer to Question 2 would also require knowledge of which remedies can be awarded in combination and which are mutually exclusive: S. Watterson, 'Alternative and Cumulative Remedies: What is the Difference?' [2003] 11 *RLR* 7. These matters are important to the law of remedies but their consideration would require a diversion from the argument developed here.

Bibliography

Andoh, B. and Marsh, S., *Civil Remedies* (Aldershot: Dartmouth 1997).

Andrews, N., *Principles of Civil Procedure* (London: Sweet & Maxwell 1994).

——, 'Civil Procedure' in P. B. H. Birks (ed.), *English Private Law Vol II* (Oxford: Oxford University Press, 2000).

Aristotle, *Politics* Book III Chapter XI.

——, Parts of Animals *De partibus animalium* (A. L. Peck (trans), Cambridge Massachusetts: Harvard University Press, 1961).

Atiyah, P., 'From Principles to Pragmatism: Changes in the Function of the Judicial Process and the Law' (1979–1980) 65 *Iowa L Rev* 1249.

——, *Introduction to the Law of Contract* (5th edn., Oxford: Clarendon Press, 1995).

Atkin's Encyclopaedia of Court Forms in Civil Proceedings (2nd edn., London: Butterworths).

Austin, J., *Lectures on Jurisprudence Vol II* (R. Campbell (ed.) 5th edn., London: John Murray, 1885).

Bant, E., 'Book Review of *An Introduction to Property Law in Australia* by Robert Chambers' (2002) 26 *MULR* 211.

Barak, A., *Judicial Discretion* (New Haven: Yale University Press, 1989).

Barker, K., 'Rescuing Remedialism in Unjust Enrichment Law: Why Remedies are Right' [1998] *CLJ* 301.

Beale, H., *Remedies for Breach of Contract* (London: Sweet & Maxwell, 1980).

Beatson, J., *The Use and Abuse of Unjust Enrichment* (Oxford: Clarendon Press, 1991).

——, *Anson's Law of Contract* (27th edn., Oxford: Oxford University Press, 1998).

Bentham, J., *Comment on the Commentaries* (C. W. Everett (ed.) Oxford: Clarendon Press, 1928).

Birks, P. B. H., *Introduction to the Law of Restitution* (Revised edn., Oxford: Clarendon Press, 1989).

——, *Restitution—The Future* (Leichhardt NSW: Federation Press, 1992).

——, 'Proprietary Rights as Remedies' in P. B. H. Birks (ed.), *The Frontiers of Liability Vol 2* (Oxford: Oxford University Press, 1994).

——, 'Equity in the Modern Law: An Exercise in Taxonomy' (1996) 26 *U Western Australia L Rev* 1.

——, 'Definition and Division: A Meditation on *Institutes* 3.13' in P. B. H. Birks (ed.), *The Classification of Obligations* (Oxford: Oxford University Press, 1997).

——, 'The end of the remedial constructive trust?' (1998) 12(4) *Trust Law International* 202.

——, 'The Law of Restitution at the End of an Epoch' (1999) 28 *U Western Australia L Rev* 1.

——, 'Introduction' in P. B. H. Birks (ed.), *English Private Law Vol 1* (Oxford: Oxford University Press, 2000).

—— and Mitchell, C., 'Unjust Enrichment' in P. B. H. Birks (ed.) *English Private Law Vol II* (Oxford: Oxford University Press, 2000).

Birks, P. B. H., 'Three Kinds of Objection to Discretionary Remedialism' (2000) 29 *U Western Australia L Rev* 1.
——, 'Rights, Wrongs and Remedies' (2000) 20 *OJLS* 1.
——, 'Personal Property: Proprietary Rights and Remedies' [2000] 11 *KCLJ* 1.
——, and Pretto, A., 'Introduction' in P. B. H. Birks and A. Pretto (eds), *Breach of Trust* (Oxford: Hart, 2002)
——, 'Review of Proprietary Remedies in Context: A Study in the Judicial Redistribution of Property Rights' (2003) 119 *LQR* 156.
——, *Unjust Enrichment* (Oxford: Oxford University Press, 2003).
Blackstone, W., *Commentaries on the Laws of England Vol III* (16th edn., London: T. Cadell & J. Butterworth, 1825).
Burrows, A., *The Law of Restitution* (London: Butterworths, 1993).
——, *Remedies for Torts and Breach of Contract* (2nd edn., London: Butterworths, 1994).
——, 'Judicial Remedies' in P. B. H. Birks (ed.), *English Private Law Vol II* (Oxford: Oxford University Press, 2000).
——, 'We Do This at Common Law But That in Equity' (2002) 22 *OJLS* 1.
——, *Hochelaga Lecture 2001: Fusing Common Law and Equity: Remedies Restitution and Reform* (Hong Kong: Sweet & Maxwell Asia, 2002).
Cane, P., *Tort Law and Economic Interests* (2nd edn., Oxford: Clarendon Press, 1996).
Chambers, R., 'Liability' in P. B. H. Birks and A. Pretto (eds), *Breach of Trust* (Oxford: Hart, 2002).
Cooke, R., 'Remoteness of Damage and Judicial Discretion' [1978] *CLJ* 288.
Corbin, A., 'Rights and Duties' (1922–24) *Yale LJ* 501.
Covell, W. and Lupton, K., *Principles of Remedies* (Sydney: Butterworths, 1995).
Cretney, S. M., 'Succession — Discretion or Whim, Freedom of Choice or Caprice?' (1986) 6 *OJLS* 299.
Davis, K. C., *Discretionary Justice: A Preliminary Inquiry* (Louisiana: Louisiana State University Press, 1969).
Dias, R. W. M., *Jurisprudence* (5th edn., London: Butterworths, 1985).
Derham, S. R., *The Law of Set-Off* (3rd edn., Oxford: Oxford University Press, 2003).
Dickson, B., 'The Contribution of Lord Diplock to the Law of Contract' (1989) 9 *OJLS* 441.
Dobbs, D., *Law of Remedies Damages-Equity-Restitution Practitioner Treatise Series Vol 1* (2nd edn., St Paul Minnesota: West Publishing Co, 1993).
Dworkin, R., *Taking Rights Seriously* (London: Duckworth, 1977).
Edelman, J., 'Remedial Certainty or Remedial Discretion in Estoppel after Giumelli' (1999) 15 *JCL* 159.
——, *Gain-Based Damages* (Oxford: Hart, 2002).
——, 'Equitable Torts' (2002) 10 *Torts LJ* 64.
Edwards, R. and Stockwell, N., *Trusts and Equity* (5th edn., Harlow: Longman, 2002).
Elias, G., *Explaining Constructive Trusts* (Oxford: Clarendon Press, 1990).
Elliott, S., 'Compensation Claims Against Trustees' (DPhil Thesis Oxford University 2002).
—— and Mitchell, C., 'Remedies for Dishonest Assistance' (2004) 67 *MLR* 16.
Envis, G., *Enforcing Money Judgments* (London: Butterworths, 1995).
Evans, S., 'Defending Discretionary Remedialism' [2001] 23 *Sydney LRev* 463.

Finn, P., 'Equitable Doctrine and Discretion in Remedies' in W. R. Cornish, R. C. Nolan, J. O'Sullivan and Virgo, G. (eds) *Restitution: Past, Present and Future* (Oxford: Hart, 1998).
Frank, J., *Law and the Modern Mind* (2nd edn., London: Stevens, 1963).
Friedman, D., 'Rights and Remedies' (1997) *LQR* 424.
Fry, E., *A Treatise on the Specific Performance of Contracts* (3rd edn., London: Stevens, 1892).
Gardner, S., 'Equity, Estate Contracts and the Judicature Acts: *Walsh v Lonsdale* Revisited' (1987) 7 *OJLS* 60.
——, 'The Element of Discretion' in P. B. H. Birks, 'Proprietary Rights as Remedies' in P. B. H. Birks (ed.), *The Frontiers of Liability Vol 2* (Oxford: Oxford University Press, 1994).
——, 'The Remedial Discretion in Proprietary Estoppel' (1999) 115 *LQR* 438.
Gerwitz, P., 'Remedies and Resistance' (1983) 92 *Yale LJ* 585.
Goff, R. and Jones, G., *The Law of Restitution* (5th edn., London: Sweet & Maxwell, 1998).
Goode, R., 'Property and Unjust Enrichment' in A. Burrows (ed.), *Essays on the Law of Restitution* (Oxford: Clarendon Press, 1991).
—— and Worthington, S., 'Commercial Law: Confining the Remedial Boundaries' in D. Hayton (ed.), *Law's Futures: British Legal Developments in the 21st Century* (Oxford: Hart, 2000).
Grantham, R. B. and Rickett, C. E. F., 'Property Rights as a Legally Significant Event' [2003] *CLJ* 717.
Gummow, W., 'Equity: Too Successful?' (2003) 77 *Australian LJ* 30.
Hammond, G., 'Rethinking Remedies: The Changing Conception of the Relationship between Legal and Equitable Remedies' in J. Berryman (ed.), *Remedies: Issues and Perspectives* (Ontario: Carswell 1991).
——, 'The Place of Damages in the Scheme of Remedies' in P. Finn (ed.), *Essays on Damages* (North Ryde New South Wales: Law Book Co, 1992).
Harpum, C. et al, *Megarry and Wade—The Law of Real Property* (6th edn., London: Sweet & Maxwell, 2000).
Harris, D., Campbell, D., Halson, R., *Remedies in Contract and Tort* (2nd edn., London: Butterworths, 2002).
Harris, J. W., *Property and Justice* (Oxford: Clarendon Press, 1996).
Hart, H. L. A., *The Concept of Law* (2nd edn., Oxford: Clarendon Press, 1994).
Hawkins, K., 'Using Legal Discretion' in K. Hawkins (ed.), *The Uses of Discretion* (Oxford: Clarendon Press, 1992).
Hohfeld, W. N., 'Some Fundamental Legal Conceptions As Applied in Judicial Reasoning' (1913) 23 *Yale LJ* 16.
——, 'The Relations between Equity and Law' (1913) 11 *Michigan LRev* 537.
——, *Fundamental Legal Conceptions* (A. Corbin (ed.), New Haven: Yale University Press, 1964).
Holmes, O. W., 'The Path of the Law', (1897) 10 *Harv L Rev* 457.
Honoré, T., 'Ownership' in A. G. Guest (ed.), *Oxford Essays in Jurisprudence* (Oxford: Oxford University Press, 1961).
Ingpen, A. R. (et al), *Seton's Forms of Judgments and Orders in the High Court of Justice and Court of Appeal: Having Special Reference to the Chancery Division* (7th edn., London: Stevens, 1912).

Inns of Court School of Law *Remedies 2003/2004* (Oxford: Oxford University Press, 2003).
Jacob, J., *Fabric of English Civil Justice* (London: Stevens, 1987).
——, 'General Report' in J. Jacob and U. Jacobsson (eds), *Trends in the Enforcement of Non-money Judgments and Orders* (Deventer: Kluwer 1988).
Jensen, D., 'The Rights and Wrongs of Discretionary Remedialism' [2003] *Singapore J of Legal Studies* 178.
Jones, G., and Goodhart, W., *Specific Performance* (London: Butterworths, 1986).
Judicial Studies Board *Guidelines for the Assessment of General Damages in Personal Injury Cases* (6th edn., Oxford: Oxford University Press, 2002).
Kercher, B. and Noone, M., *Remedies* (2nd edn., Sydney: Law Book Co, 1990).
——, 'Legal History and the Study of Legal Remedies' (2001) 39 *Brandeis L Rev* 619.
Kerr, W. W., *On the Law and Practice of Injunctions* (3rd edn., London: Maxwell, 1888).
Kocourek, A., *Jural Relations* (2nd edn., Indianapolis: Bobbs-Merrill, 1928).
Law Commission, *Shareholder Remedies* Report No 246 (London: The Stationery Office, 1997).
Law Commission, *Aggravated, Exemplary and Restitutionary Damages* Report No 247 (London: The Stationery Office, 1997).
Lawson, F. H., *Remedies of English Law* (London: Butterworth & Co, 1972).
——, *Remedies of English Law* (2nd edn., London: Butterworth & Co, 1980).
Laycock, D., 'The Triumph of Equity' (1993) 56(3) *Law and Contemporary Problems* 53.
Lord Chancellor's Department *Judicial Statistics England and Wales for the Year 2000* (Norwich: The Stationery Office, 2001).
Loughlan, P., 'No Right to a Remedy? An Analysis of Judicial Discretion in the Imposition of Equitable Remedies' (1989) 17 *Melbourne ULRev* 131.
Maitland, F. W., *Equity: A Course of Lectures* (Cambridge: Cambridge University Press, 1936).
——, *The Forms of Action at Common Law* (Cambridge: Cambridge University Press, 1936).
Mason, A., 'Legislative and Judicial Law Making: Can We Locate an Identifiable Boundary?' (2003) 24 *Adelaide L Rev* 15.
McCracken, S., *The Banker's Remedy of Set-Off* (London: Butterworths, 1998).
McGhee, J., *Snell's Equity* (30th edn., London: Sweet & Maxwell, 2000).
McGregor, H., *McGregor on Damages* (16th edn., London: Sweet & Maxwell, 1997).
McGuire, B. et al, *Tolley's Claims to the Possession of Land* (Croydon: Tolly, 2001).
Meagher, R. P., Gummow, W. M. C. and Lehane, J. R. F., *Equity: Doctrines and Remedies* (3rd edn., Sydney: Butterworths, 1992).
——, Heydon, J. D. and Leeming, M. J., *Meagher, Gummow and Lehane's Equity: Doctrines and Remedies* (4th edn., Sydney: Butterworths, 2002).
Miller, C. J., *Contempt of Court* (3rd edn., Oxford: Oxford University Press, 2000).
Lord Millett, 'Equity's Place in the Law of Commerce' (1998) 114 *LQR* 214.
Noyes, C. R., *The Institution of Property* (New York: Longmans, Green & Co, 1936).
O'Connor, P., 'Happy Partners or Strange Bedfellows: The Blending of Remedial and Institutional Features in the Evolving Constructive Trust' (1996) 20 *Melbourne Uni L Rev* 735.

O'Sullivan, D., 'The Evolving Structure of Equitable Rescission with Particular Reference to Rescission for Fraud and Breach of Fiduciary Duty' (DPhil Thesis Oxford University 2001).

Ogus, A. I., *The Law of Damages* (London: Butterworths, 1973).

Penner, J. E., *The Idea of Property* (Oxford: Oxford University Press, 1997).

Pomeroy, J. N., *Remedies and Remedial Rights by the Civil Action* (Boston: Little, Brown and Co, 1876).

Pound, R., 'The Progress of the Law' (1920) 33 *Harvard L Rev* 420.

Pretto, A., 'Primary Rights and Rights *in Rem*' in P. B. H. Birks and A. Pretto (eds), *Themes in Comparative Law in Honour of Bernard Rudden* (Oxford: Oxford University Press, 2002).

Re, E. D. and Re, J. R., *Cases and Materials on Remedies* (4th edn., New York: Foundation Press, 1996).

Lord Reid, 'The Judge as Law Maker' (1972) 12 *Journal of the Society of Public Teachers of Law* 22.

Rogers, W. V. H., *Winfield & Jolowicz on Tort* (15th edn., London: Sweet & Maxwell, 1998).

Rotherham, C., *Proprietary Remedies in Context: A Study in the Judicial Redistribution of Property Rights* (Oxford: Hart, 2002).

Rudden, B., 'Correspondence' (1990) 10 *OJLS* 288.

——, 'Some Thoughts on Monetary Obligations' (unpublished manuscript, 19 May 1997).

Samuel, G., *Law of Obligations and Legal Remedies* (2nd edn., London: Cavendish, 2001).

——, *English Private Law: Old and New Thinking in the Taxonomy Debate* (2004) 24 *OJLS* 335.

Schneider, C. E., in Hawkins, K. (ed.), *The Uses of Discretion* (Oxford: Clarendon Press, 1992).

Scott, A. W. and Seavey W. A., *Restatement of the Law of Judgments* (St Paul: American Law Institute Publishers, 1942).

Sheridan, L. A., *Injunctions and Similar Orders* (Chichester: Barry Rose, 1999).

Simpson, J. and Weiner, E. (eds), *Oxford English Dictionary* (2nd edn., Oxford: Clarendon Press, 1989).

Spence, M., *Protecting Reliance: The Emergent Doctrine of Equitable Estoppel* (Oxford: Hart, 1999).

Spry, I. C. F., *The Principles of Equitable Remedies: Specific Performance, Injunctions, Rectification and Equitable Damages* (6th edn., Pyrmont New South Wales: Law Book Co, 2001).

Stephen, L., (ed.), *Dictionary of National Biography Vol V* (London: Smith, Elder & Co, 1886).

Sunderland, E. R., 'A Modern Evolution in Remedial Rights—The Declaratory Judgment' (1917) 16 *Michigan LR* 69.

Swadling, W., 'Opening the Numerous Clausus' (2000) 116 *LQR* 354.

Tettenborn, A., *An Introduction to the Law of Obligations* (London: Butterworths, 1984).

——, 'Remedies: A Neglected Contribution' [1999] *Denning LJ* 41.

——, *Law of Restitution in England and Ireland* (3rd edn., London: Cavendish, 2002).

Thayer, J. B., *Preliminary Treatise on Evidence at the Common Law* (London: Sweet & Maxwell, 1898).
Thompson, B., 'Injunction Negotiations: An Economic, Moral and Legal Analysis' (1975) 27 *Stan LR* 1563.
Tilbury, M. J., *Civil Remedies Vol 1 Principles of Civil Remedies* (North Ryde New South Wales: Butterworths, 1990).
——, *Civil Remedies Vol II Remedies in Particular Contexts* (Sydney: Butterworths, 1993).
——, 'Remedies and the Classification of Obligations' in A. Robertson (ed.), *Law of Obligations: Connections and Boundaries* (London: Cavendish, 2004).
——, Noone, M. and Kercher, B., *Remedies Commentary and Materials* (2nd edn., North Ryde New South Wales: Law Book Co, 1993).
——, Noone, and M. Kercher, B., *Remedies: Commentary and Materials* (3rd edn., Sydney: Law Book Co, 2000).
Treitel, G. H., *Remedies for Breach of Contract* (Oxford: Clarendon Press, 1988).
——, *The Law of Contract* (10th edn., London: Sweet & Maxwell, 1999).
Tudge, C., *The Variety of Life* (Oxford: Oxford University Press, 2000).
Virgo, G., *The Principles of the Law of Restitution* (Oxford: Clarendon Press, 1999).
Waddams, S. M., 'Remedies as a Legal Subject' (1983) 3 *OJLS* 113.
——, 'Judicial Discretion' [2000] *Oxford U Commonwealth LJ* 59.
——, *Dimensions of Private Law* (Cambridge: Cambridge University Press, 2003).
Walker, D. M., *The Law of Civil Remedies in Scotland* (Edinburgh: W. Green & Son, 1974).
——, *The Oxford Companion to Law* (Oxford: Clarendon Press, 1980).
——, *Principles of Scottish Law: Volume IV* (4th edn., Oxford: Clarendon Press, 1989).
Waters, D. W. M., *The Constructive Trust* (London: Athlone Press, 1964).
——, 'Liability and Remedy: An Adjustable Relationship' (2001) *Saskatchewan L Rev* 429.
Watterson, S., 'Alternative and Cumulative Remedies: What is the Difference?' [2003] 11 *RLR* 7.
Lord Woolf and Woolf, J., *The Declaratory Judgment* (London: Sweet & Maxwell, 2002).
Wright, D., *The Remedial Constructive Trust* (Sydney: Butterworths, 1998).
——, 'Wrong and Remedy: A Sticky Relationship' [2001] *Singapore J of Legal Studies* 300.
Wróblewski, J. (R. Bankowski and N. MacCormick (eds)), *The Judicial Application of Law* (Dordrecht: Kluwer Academic Publishers, 1992).
Zamir, I., 'The Declaratory Judgment Revisited' in Lord Lloyd, R. Rideout, S. Guest (eds), *Current Legal Problems 1977* Vol 30 (London: Stevens & Sons, 1977).

Index